**INTERORGANIZATION
THEORY**

INTERORGANIZATION THEORY

Edited by

[ANANT R. NEGANDHI]

Center for Business and Economic Research
Kent State University

The Comparative Administration Research Institute

Distributed by The Kent State University Press

First printing

Published by the Comparative Administration
Research Institute in cooperation with the Center
for Business and Economic Research of Kent State University, Kent
Ohio 44242

Photosetting by Thomson Press (India) Limited, New Delhi

Preface

During the past decade or so, the impact of external environments on organizational functioning has become the concern of many organization theorists. This relatively new but vital area of interest caught our attention from the very inception of the Comparative Administration Research Institute (CARI) in 1968. Ever since this institute was formed at Kent State University, the interorganization focus has been reflected at our annual conferences. More particularly, our annual conferences for the past five years have been organized around this very topic. This volume examines some of the leading conceptual schemes and research studies in interorganization theory presented at these gatherings.

The main purpose of initiating the CARI conferences was to enable scholars of differing viewpoints and orientations to freely discuss the various conceptual problems encountered in studying the functioning of complex social organizations. Particularly, we have endeavored to critically evaluate the utility of alternative models and conceptual schemes in undertaking field research in this area. We have made serious attempts, both during the conferences and afterwards, to generate dialogue among numerous scholars from leading universities here in the United States and abroad. Thus far, some 250 scholars have visited our campus to participate in these endeavors.

All but three of the papers in this book were presented at annual CARI conferences held between 1970 and 1973. This volume is the second in our series. The first, *Modern Organizational Theory*, was published in 1973 by the Kent State University Press.

These conferences were made possible through the efforts of many, though space permits us to mention only a few. They include Professors Raymond Adamek, Raghbir Basi, John Doutt, Donald Domm, Arlyn Melcher, Joseph Schwitter, Lee Spray, Andrew Van de Ven, and Eugene Wenninger, all of Kent State University. Many friends from other institutions also contributed untiring support to our efforts. And while space limitations again prohibit listing each of our supporters, we are nevertheless grateful to them all.

In our efforts to successfully organize these intellectual gatherings, we were more than fortunate in securing unqualified cooperation from all of the scholars who presented their studies. We were likewise most fortunate in eliciting the true spirit of cooperation from participants and commentators who came from great distances at their own expense to be a part of our pursuits. The names of the authors and commentators appear in this volume and we are most appreciative of their contributions.

Like any major undertaking, the success of our conferences has been due in great measure to the contributions made by several people behind-the-scenes. This includes Dr. Gail E. Mullin, Dean of the Graduate School of Business Administration; Dr. John K. Ryans, Jr., Associate Dean; and Dr. Gerald Ridinger, then director of the Bureau of Management Development. It is their dedication to academic excellence which enables us to stage this drama of intellectual dialogue year after year. Through their work and cooperation, the annual CARI conference is now in its eighth year.

Much credit for the smooth functioning of these meetings can also be attributed to the dedicated efforts of Mrs. Mary Uzzle, Mrs. Pauline Hagat, and a number of graduate students. Mrs. Barbara Fisher contributed greatly in turning rough drafts into readable pages. We extend our warmest thanks for their efforts.

Personally, this volume represents a kind of "signing off" on my part. The publication of this book completes and wraps up some of the loose ends of projects I undertook between 1969 and 1973. During all of these years, I seem to have vented my frustrations on my family, and they were always there to lend a helping hand. This volume is thus jointly dedicated to the institution, CARI, which enriched my understanding of the functioning of complex organizations, and to my family, who let me do so.

Beechwood Island   A.R.N.
January, 1975

to
CARI
and
Amin, Pia, and Erny

CONTRIBUTORS

Raymond J. Adamek
Kent State University
Howard Aldrich
Cornell University
Ann F. Burgunder
Legal Aid Society of New ·York
John P. Clark
University of Minnesota
Dennis C. Emmett
Kent State University
Jerald Hage
University of Wisconsin
Richard H. Hall
University of Minnesota
Richard Koenig, Jr.
Kent State University
Bebe F. Lavin
Kent State University
Mark Lefton
*Case Western Reserve
University*
Sol Levine
Boston University

Jay W. Lorsch
Harvard University
Anant R. Negandhi
Kent State University
J. Wayne Newton
*Virginia Commonwealth
University*
Bernard C. Reimann
University of Pennsylvania
Stephen M. Rose
*State University of New York
at Stony Brook*
Andrew H. Van de Ven
Kent State University
George J. Vlasak
The Johns Hopkins University
Roland L. Warren
Brandies University
Paul E. White
The Johns Hopkins University
Gerald Zeitz
*State University of New York
at Stony Brook*

COMMENTATORS

Raymond J. Adamek
Kent State University
Michael R. Ferrari
Bowling Green University
Malcolm MacNair
North Carolina University
Arlyn J. Melcher
Kent State University

Winston Oberg
Michigan State University
Richard N. Osborn
*Southern Illinois University at
Carbondale*
Richard Viola
Temple University

Contents

1

Interorganization Theory: Introduction and Overview

ANANT R. NEGANDHI

Although interdependency among different social units has been intuitively recognized for some time, incorporating this seemingly factual phenomenon into theoretical and conceptual schemes is of recent vintage. Heretofore, organization theorists have been too preoccupied with the elements in a given organization and how these elements affect its structure, behavior patterns, and effectiveness.

During the past two decades or so, two separate but interrelated concerns among the social scientists seem to have stimulated a need to develop some understanding about interorganizational relationships. The first is that social units are an integral part of the social system itself, and as such, the individual unit can be examined only in relation to the other units in a total system (Durkheim, 1947). Although Durkheim recognized this concept long ago, it has only been in recent years that interorganization theorists have begun to incorporate this concept in their studies. The second concern is that social organizations are embedded in their environments and, accordingly, a comprehensive understanding of individual organizational functioning will require not only knowledge concerning its internal apparatus (technology, size, location, etc.), but also, and perhaps more importantly, some knowledge of the variety of energy transfers (inputs) between the organizations and their external environments.

Physical and biological scientists, in their quest to understand interdependence and interconnectedness among living and nonliving units, have long preceded their colleagues in the social sciences and accordingly have developed a conceptual apparatus to reflect these concerns in terms of the systems theory. Lately, the spillover of these developments has provided social scientists with a new perspective for studying the functioning of complex organizations. This new perspective, particularly among organization theorists, is referred to in the literature as the open-systems approach (Von Bertalanffy, 1950).

An open system (in contrast to a closed system), by its very name requires the consideration of how the external environment influences the internal properties of an organization. However, to understand the open-systems perspective, one needs to examine the overall systems and the general systems concepts.

A system is defined as "a regularly interacting or interdependent group of items forming a unified whole" which "is in or tends to be in equilibrium" (Webster, 1967: 895). Alternately, it is defined as a "set of objects together with relationships between the objects and their attributes."

The interdependence and interlinking of various subsystems seem to be the two most important attributes of a system. These attributes thus force one to think in terms of *multiple causation* in contrast to the common habit of thinking in single causal terms.

The general systems approach, conceived at still a higher level of abstraction, visualizes the study of all living organisms within a singular framework with a view to testing hypotheses at cross-levels of living systems. This includes the cell, organ, organism, group, organization, society, and supernational systems (Miller, 1955).

The key attributes of general systems are: subsystems or different components in a given system; holism; open systems; input-transformation-output phenomenon; system boundaries; negative entropy; steady state; dynamic equilibrium; feedback mechanism; cybernetics; hierarchy; internal elaboration; multiple goal-seeking; and equifinality (Kast and Rosenzweig, 1972).

Thus, interorganization theorists seem to rely in part on a broad conceptualization at the general systems level. Their overall aim, as it would seem, is to examine the impact of the external environment and/or the other social units on the internal functioning of a parent organization.

This brings up another vital question that should be considered before we proceed. Just exactly what is interorganization theory, and how does it differ from organization theory? In other words, what are, if any, the salient differentiating features of interorganizational theory?

To explore this question, perhaps it may be necessary to begin at the beginning and ask, what is a theory? As Homans (1966) has stated:

> A theory is nothing--It is not a theory unless it is an explanation. . . . A theory of phenomenon consists of propositions, each stating a relationship between properties of nature. . . . Not until one has properties, and propositions stating relations between them and the propositions form a deductive system--not until one has all three--does one have a theory (p. 38).

Judging from the existing literature on interorganizational studies, it is evident that the current state of knowledge in this area falls short of satisfying all of the above requirements for a theory. Indeed, many scholars would even question whether the present study of the organization theory area itself is sufficiently developed to "qualify" as theory. This so-called "interorganization theory" can more realistically be described as an approach or a perspective rather than a theory.

Nonetheless, attempts have been made to differentiate between *inter*organizational analysis and *intra*organizational analysis. Litwak and Hylton (1962), for example, have argued that the two can be differentiated on the basis of notions and assumptions about conflict and authority. These authors suggest that *inter*organizational analysis assumes the conflict between organizations as given, and hence they directed their investigations toward the forms of social interaction necessary under such conditions. In constrast, *intra*organizational analysis assumes that the conflicting values lead to a breakdown in the organizational structure and thus attempts are made to establish harmonious relationships between different units and/or personnel. Further, *inter*organizational analysis stresses the examination of social interaction under conditions of unstructured authority. *Intra*organizational analysis, on the other hand, places emphasis on formal authority in studying behavior patterns in a given organization (Litwak and Hylton, 1962: 398).

In terms of an open-systems perspective, it is evident that interorganizational analysis is not only different in its orientation, but it also differs in its basic assumptions about conflict and authority. These differences at two levels of the analysis, coupled with a growing interdependence among social units and the individual organization's resultant awareness of its openness to the external environment, thus make it increasingly important to develop interorganization theory to its fullest potential.

This volume represents one such effort. All but three[1] of the papers were first presented at yearly conferences on complex organizations, sponsored by the Comparative Administration Research Institute at Kent State University.

---

[1]The two papers by Negandhi and Reimann provide some additional data on interorganizational relationships in the industrial context of a developing country. The majority of the papers on interorganizational relationships, included in this volume and published elsewhere, deal with the nonprofit, nonindustrial sectors. The inclusion of the Negandhi-Reimann papers thus enables us to provide a little broader perspective on the area. Although these papers were not presented at any of the CARI conferences, they were based on the studies undertaken under the auspices of CARI. They previously appeared in *Human Relations* and the *Academy of Management Journal*.

The paper by Adamek and Lavin has not been previously published. However, it has been included in this volume to provide the reader with an alternate hypothesis to the concept of exchange relationships among organizations suggested by White, Levine, and Vlasak in Chapter 14.

ORGANIZATION OF THE BOOK AND AN OVERVIEW

The Organization of this volume generally follows the stages of development in interorganizational studies, namely:

A. The examination of the impact of external environmental factors on the internal properties of an organization. Here, the conceptualization is to understand the characteristics of the environment itself (i.e., stable-unstable, placid-turbulent, etc.), and then to explore the impact of differing characteristics on the functioning, structure, and behavior of a given organization (Emery and Trist, 1965; Lawrence and Lorsch, 1969; Burns and Stalker, 1961; Thompson, 1967; Khandwalla, 1972; Duncan, 1972, etc.).

B. The examination of group interaction among different social units. Attempts are made here to identify the appropriate sets of organizations which interact frequently, and then to explore the implications of their interaction processes. The concepts, such as organization-set theory and task environments, have been developed to examine relationships between and among organizations (Thompson, 1967; Dill, 1958; Evan, 1966; Hall and Clark, 1974; etc.).

C. The examination of interorganizational relationships at the social systems level. Here, the conceptualization is to conceive all social units as a part of the total social system and attempt to explore the relationships among different organizations in this light. The concept of the interorganization field (Warren, Rose, and Bergunder, 1974; Warren, *et al.*, 1973) was developed to undertake an analysis at this level.

We have attempted to provide two or more studies at each of these three levels.

Part I

Preceding the three-level discussion explained above, this first section attempts to provide both an overview of the interorganization theory literature and some conceptual underpinnings to develop interorganization theory. Three papers are included in this section.

The first paper, by Van de Ven and his colleagues, reviews the developments in interorganizational analysis. Their review is organized with respect to the three different levels of conceptualization mentioned above: organization-environment interaction; a collection of interacting organizations, groups, or persons; and analysis of interaction processes at the social systems level. Their overall conclusions seem to be that the analysis of interorganizational relationships at the social systems level offers a unique device to incorporate conceptualizations at two other levels. However, at the same time they warn us that considerable work is needed to achieve this objective.

In the main, Zeitz argues the same point in the second paper. But in so doing, he attempts to identify some of the reasons why interorganizational theorists have thus far not attempted to analyze interorganizational interactions at the societal level. The reasons for this failure to utilize "field" level analysis, according to Zeitz, are the present substantive assumption that organizational units are functionally autonomous, and practical concerns of governments and businesses to achieve coordination between diverse organizational units. Like Van de Ven and his colleagues, Zeitz argues that efforts to study interorganizational interaction processes at the societal ("field") level would enrich theoretical developments in organization theory, as well as in community and societal theory.

In the third paper in this section, Aldrich argues that conflict between and among organizations has not received enough attention. He feels that an open-systems perspective which underscores organization-environment interaction would provide a meaningful avenue for studying conflict among different social units. Specifically, he seeks to understand conflict by examining the nature of interdependence among the organizations themselves, and the nature of organization-environment interaction. In so doing, he provides seven dimensions of the organizational environment, and four dimensions of interorganizational relations.

The seven organizational-environment dimensions are: stability/instability; homogeneity/heterogeneity; concentration/dispersion; environmental capacity in terms of rich/lean; domain consensus/dissensus; environmental turbulence/placidness; and mutability/immutability.

The four dimensions in interorganizational relationships are: the nature of formalization; intensity of involvement; the nature of reciprocity; and the nature of standardization of transactions between and among organizations.

Based on these dimensions, Aldrich attempts to test the following two hypotheses, utilizing preliminary data from his manpower training system study:[2]

---

[2]For further analysis of data, see Howard Aldrich, "An Interorganizational Dependency Perspective on Relations between the Employment Service and its Organization-Set." Paper presented at the Management of Organization Design Conference, University of Pittsburgh, Pittsburgh, Pa., Oct. 24–26, 1974.

1. ENVIRONMENTAL STABILITY LEADS TO THE DEVEL-
   OPMENT OF FORMALIZED RELATIONS WITH OTHER
   ORGANIZATIONS BECAUSE IT INCREASES THE OPPOR-
   TUNITIES FOR AND THE PREDICTABILITY OF CONT-
   ACT BETWEEN SPECIFIC ORGANIZATIONS.

2. ENVIRONMENTAL HETEROGENEITY AND INSTA-
   BILITY JOINTLY LEAD ORGANIZATIONS TO ADOPT
   DIFFERENT STRATEGIES.

Part II

The two papers included in this section attempt to identify the attributes
or characteristics of environments by examining the impact of external
environments on the internal functioning of organizations. In the first
paper, Lorsch provides an extension and further refinements of the now
famous Lawrence and Lorsch (1967) contingency theory of organizations.

In the main, the contingency theory postulates that there must be a
fit between internal organizational characteristics and external environmental requirements if an organization is to perform effectively in dealing
with its environment. Their overall conclusions seem to indicate that the
formality of a unit structure is related to the relative certainty of that unit's
environment. Organizational units operating in dynamic environments
seem to be decentralized, while those facing more stable environments tend
to be centralized. These authors further proposed that decentralization
under stable environmental conditions and centralization under dynamic
conditions may actually be dysfunctional. They also explored the proposition
that the total organization must achieve the pattern of integration required
by the total environment in spite of the differentiation among its units
(Lawrence and Lorsch, 1967, 1969).

In this volume, Lorsch carries the argument further by raising the
following questions:

> Why is it that the fit between a functional unit's organizational
> characteristics and its part of the environment, which creates the
> necessity of differentiation, is related to effective performance?
> Does this match of a unit organization and environment simply
> meet the information-processing requirements, or does this
> consistency also affect an organization's members in such a way
> as to motivate them toward more effective performance?

To examine these questions, Lorsch tests the following hypotheses:

1. INDIVIDUALS WHO FEEL COMPETENT WORKING IN

HIGHLY UNCERTAIN ENVIRONMENTS AND IN AN
ORGANIZATION WITH LOW FORMALITY WOULD
NEED TO HAVE GREATER INTEGRATIVE COMPLEXITY
THAN THOSE WHO FEEL COMPETENT WORKING ON
MORE CERTAIN TASKS IN A MORE HIGHLY FORMAL-
IZED ORGANIZATION.

2. PERSONS WHO DEVELOP FEELINGS OF COMPETENCE
   BY WORKING IN DIFFERENT ORGANIZATION-
   ENVIRONMENT SETTINGS MIGHT ALSO VARY IN
   THEIR TOLERANCE FOR AMBIGUITY.

3. PERSONS FEELING COMPETENT IN DIFFERENT
   ORGANIZATIONAL SETTINGS MIGHT ALSO VARY
   IN THEIR CUSTOMARY WAYS OF RELATING TO
   AUTHORITY.

4. DIFFERENT ORGANIZATION-ENVIRONMENT SET-
   TINGS FIT PEOPLE WHO HAVE DIFFERENT ATTITUDES
   ABOUT WORKING WITH OTHERS.

The hypothesized relationships which Lorsch explores are shown in
Figure 1.

Figure 1
HYPOTHESIZED RELATIONSHIPS

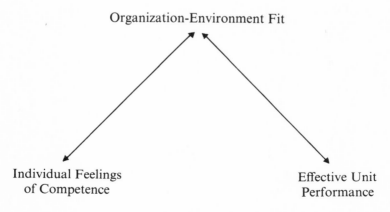

Organization-Environment Fit

Individual Feelings
of Competence

Effective Unit
Performance

In the second paper in this section, Negandhi and Reimann attempt
to test the validity of a contingency theory in the altogether different sociocultural and environmental settings of a developing country. Based on

data from 30 industrial firms in India, their findings indicate some support for the contingency theory advanced by Lawrence and Lorsch (1967, 1969). However, the authors argue that decentralization under stable conditions is not necessarily dysfunctional. Their results simply show that dynamic conditions (i.e., a competitive market) make decentralization *more important* in achieving higher organizational effectiveness than do stable, non-competitive conditions.

Part III

In analyzing interorganizational relationships, the second level of conceptualization is attempted at the group level. The focus at this level is to examine the interaction process between the groups of either units or people. Two of the most articulated concepts developed at this level are the organization-set concept and the task environment.

Utilizing the "role-set" concept developed by Merton (1957), Evan (1966) proposed the concept of the "organization-set" to examine inter-organizational relationships. Analogous to the role-set concept, the organization-set "takes as the unit of analysis organization or a class of organizations and traces its interactions with the network of organizations in its environment, i.e., with elements of its organization-set" (Evan, 1966: 219).

To analyze these interactions, Evan proposed seven dimensions of organization-sets. These are input vs. output organization-sets; comparative vs. normative reference organizations; size of organization-set; concentration of input organization resources; overlap in membership; overlap in goals and values; and boundary personnel.

The other concept frequently used to analyze interorganizational relationships at the group level is the task environment. As Thompson (1967 : 27–28) has remarked, "the notion of environment turns out to be a residual one; it refers to 'everything else.'" To undertake a meaningful analysis of organization-environment interaction, many other researchers, including Dill (1958) and Thorelli (1967), have advanced the notion of the task environment. Dill (1958:409), for example, has defined task environment as "that part of the total environment of management which is potentially relevant to goal settings and goal attainment." Similarly, Thorelli (1967:66) has defined it as "that part of the total setting with which the organization is transacting and in which it is competing." The following factors have been identified as relevant task agents: customers, suppliers, employees, competitors, distributors, governmental agencies, stockholders, and regulatory groups.

Three papers in this section examine the utility of these two concepts—the organization-set and the task environment—in analyzing interorganizational relationships.

In the first paper, Hall and Clark indicate the difficulty encountered in deciding what is inside and what is outside the boundary of the focal organization, and what constitutes the organization-set for a given organization. They say that, "no matter how careful a researcher may be, some subjective decisions have to be made about which organizations to include and which to exclude. ... It is a selective thing. ... Different sets of organizations are selected for different purposes. It (always) remains a distortion of reality" (Hall and Clark, Chapter 9).

In their study of problem youth, they first conducted unstructured interviews with various public agencies dealing with youth; and second, turned to structured interviews and a questionnaire to determine the relevant organization-set. The information gathered through the questionnaire was then utilized to draw "orgio-grams" reflecting the relevant organization-set for the problem youth agencies. This method of determining an organization-set places more emphasis on the views and opinions of the relevant agency and thus "releases" a researcher to make subjective decisions about what to include and what to exclude in studying the interorganizational interaction within the organization-set. Although the method itself cannot be labled as "objective," and in many ways it substitutes the "subjective judgment" of a researcher with the "subjective opinion" of the focal organizational members, it represents perhaps a move in the right direction. The authors also discuss some preliminary findings of their study and test certain hypotheses concerning interorganizational relationships.

In the second paper, Lefton utilizes one component of the task agents or environments, namely clients, in examining interorganizational relationships. He explores the impact of the client's characteristics on organization structure, client-organization relationships, and interorganizational collaboration. In earlier work, Rosengren and Lefton (1968) developed two constructs, *laterality* and *longitudinality*, to examine the above relationships. Laterality refers to an interest in the client's biographical space, while longitudinality represents a time dimension centering on the organization's interest in its clients.

Building on this earlier scheme, Lefton introduces another construct in this volume which he labels *laterality II.* It is defined as "the extent to which an organization is responsive to the reaction or reaction-potential of its clients in determining formal procedures in the delivery of service." He discusses the utility of this construct in examining interorganizational collaboration and proposes the following hypothesis:

THE ORGANIZATIONS CHARACTERIZED BY GREATER DEGREES OF LATERAL AND LONGITUDINAL INTEREST IN THEIR CLIENTS WILL MANIFEST GREATER READINESS FOR INTERORGANIZATIONAL COLLABORATION.

In the last paper in this section, Negandhi and Reimann argue that the key decision-makers' perception of their task agents may have a greater influence on organization structure than the nature of the task environment per se. Analyzing data from a cross-cultural study (Negandhi and Prasad, 1971; Negandhi, 1974), they show the impact of the managers' attitudes and perceptions on the degree of decentralization in decision making. The study also explores the relationships between decentralization and organizational effectiveness.

Part IV

The four papers included in this last section elaborate on the necessity for examining interorganizational relationships in a social systems context. The basic notion here is to conceive all interacting social units in a collective sense, and emphasis shifts from examining interorganizational relationships *between* organizations to *among* organizations. Such concepts as "inter-organizational collectivity" (Van de Ven, Emmett, and Koenig, this volume), and "interorganizational field" (Warren, et al., this volume) have been used to identify this specific focus in examining interorganizational relationships. For example, Van de Ven and his colleagues defined interorganizational collectivity as "a particular social action system" where the participant organizations' orientation is to achieve collective goals and objectives. Warren and his colleagues define the interorganizational field as "the properties of an aggregate of interacting organizations as distinguished from the properties of the individual organizations themselves." They further note that "the interorganizational field (is) an institutionalized thought structure characterized by a high degree of consensus and by a process of competitive mutual adjustment at the margins where issues arise (Warren, et al., this volume).

In the first paper in this section, Warren and his colleagues elaborate on this concept. Based on the earlier typology provided by Warren (1967) concerning the nature of interorganizational relationships that may exist among different types of social units (e.g., unitary, federative, etc.), this paper reports preliminary findings of a study of community decision organizations which includes public school administration offices, health and welfare planning councils, community action agencies, mental health planning units, urban renewal agencies, and model city organizations.

The independent variables in this study are leadership style, input-output constituency configuration, organizational decision-making context, ratio of planning activities to program activities, and the nature of resolving internal contradictions. The dependent variables are responsiveness, innovation, and the dimensions of cooperation/contest.

The authors attempt to test the following hypotheses at four different levels: intraorganizational, organizational position, specific organizational interaction, and interorganizational field.

1. ORGANIZATIONS WITH CHARISMATIC LEADERS WILL BE MOST INNOVATIVE, WITH COLLEGIAL, LESS, AND WITH BUREAUCRATIC, STILL LESS.

2. UNITARY ORGANIZATIONS WILL PRODUCE MORE INNOVATIONS THAN WILL FEDERATIVE ORGANI- ZATIONS.

3. THE HIGHER THE RATIO OF REGULAR PROGRAM TO PLANNING, THE LOWER THE INNOVATION.

4. POSITIVE ASSOCIATIONS EXIST BETWEEN PERCEN- TAGE OF PROGRAM ACTIVITIES AND A UNITARY FORM OF ORGANIZATION, BETWEEN PERCENTAGE OF PROGRAM ACTIVITIES AND LEADERSHIP STYLE, AND BETWEEN LEADERSHIP STYLE AND ORGANIZA- TIONAL STRUCTURE.

5. INNOVATION IS INVERSELY RELATED TO DEPEN- DENCE OF THE COMMUNITY DECISION ORGANIZA- TIONS (CDOs) OR LOCAL COMMUNITY ORGANIZA- TIONS FOR INPUT RESOURCES.

6. THE UNITARY ORGANIZATION TAKES LESS INITIA- TIVE IN COOPERATION THAN DOES THE FEDERATIVE ORGANIZATION.

7. ORGANIZATIONS WITH CHARISMATIC LEADERS WILL TAKE THE LEAST INITIATIVE TOWARD CO- OPERATION, WHILE THOSE WITH COLLEGIAL LEADERS WILL TAKE THE MOST.

8. A DIRECT RELATIONSHIP EXISTS BETWEEN OR- GANIZATIONAL INNOVATION AND INTEROGANIZA- TIONAL CONTEXT.

In the second paper, White, Levine, and Vlasak further elaborate on their earlier conceptualization of exchange theory in understanding inter- organizational relationships (Levine and White, 1961). Like Warren and his colleagues, these authors focus on the social systems level and thus emphasize the examination of interorganizational relationships *among* rather than *between* organizations.

The authors argue that like profit-making organizations, nonprofit health organizations can utilize the market exchange concept in a somewhat modified form to effect a transfer of resources and integration among different organizations. They define exchange as "any voluntary activity between two organizations which has consequences, actual or anticipated, for the realization of their respective goals or objectives."

To utilize the exchange concept for health organizations, they have advanced the concept of *primitive barter*, in which "the needs of both parties are ... met simultaneously without benefits of intervention of a middle-man or a common currency."

White, Levine, and Vlasak argue that there are several advantages in using the exchange concept to examine the interorganizational relationships among nonprofit health organizations. According to them, it focuses attention on the factors determining the need for resources and special services required by the community. It also facilitates a researcher in conceiving "exchange" among organizations as dependent variables, and open-systems variables as independent variables.

The third paper in this section, by Adamek and Lavin, takes issue with the White, Levine, and Vlasak hypothesis concerning the relationship between scarcity and exchange among organizations. Utilizing the data from 321 health and welfare agencies in 60 Ohio communities, the authors test the alternate hypothesis which indicates that the relative abundance of resources, and not scarcity, is likely to create exchange relationships among organizations.

In the fourth paper, Hage further elaborates on how interorganizational relationships can be examined at the social systems level. Based on his study of mental retardation agencies, he examines the networks of organizations and the relationships *among* them. This approach differs from his earlier conceptual scheme (Aiken and Hage, 1968), which mainly dealt with predicting the impact of the internal organization structure on the development of a joint program. The conceptual scheme he outlines in this volume examines how the external strategies create a network of interdependence among organizations. He argues that, "the concept of network is broader than the unit-set (Evan, 1966) which takes a single focal organization, but, like the unit-set, includes the competitors as well as the integrators." Thus, his "unit of analysis is an aggregate of organizations whose boundaries are defined relative to some input-throughput-output process." He further elaborates that the "network ... is more than a confederation and less than a federalism ... (it) is somewhere between an elitist and pluralist structure." Furthermore, Hage advances the concept of a coalition and examines how this concept could be useful in creating interdependencies among organizations which, in turn, would provide better services to the community.

CRITICAL EVALUATION

As mentioned earlier, all of the papers included in this volume (except the two by Negandhi and Reimann and the Adamek and Lavin paper) were presented at annual conferences organized by the Comparative Administration Research Institute at Kent State University. In these conferences, we were interested in a critical examination and appraisal of alternative models and conceptual schemes used in undertaking interorganizational studies. We were likewise concerned with identifying the problems encountered in using various conceptual schemes for field studies. To achieve these objectives, we made serious attempts to generate a scholarly dialogue among the participants and speakers. A number of scholars were invited to these conferences from leading universities in the United States and abroad.

This dialogue, as well as the critical evaluation of various schemes, is presented in Chapters 5, 8, 12, and 17. All of the authors were invited to respond to the critical comments. Some of them chose to do so and their responses are included at the end of these chapters.

In the last chapter, instead of summarizing what has been said before, we have attempted to identify additional issues in developing a comprehensive interorganizational theory.

REFERENCES

Aiken, Michael, and Jerald Hage. "Organizational Interdependence and Intra-
1968   Organizational Structure." *American Sociological Review*, 3:912–30.

Aldrich, Howard. "An Interorganizational Dependency Perspective on Relations
1974   between the Employment Service and its Organization-Set." Paper presented
        at the Management of Organization Design Conference. Pittsburgh: University of Pittsburgh, October 24–26.

Bertalanffy, L. Von   "The Theory of Open Systems in Physics and Biology." *Science*,
1950   3:23–29.

Burns, T., and G. M. Stalker. *The Management of Innovation*. London: Tavistock.
1961

Dill, William R. "Environment as an Influence on Managerial Autonomy." *Adminis-*
1958   *trative Science Quarterly*, 2:409–43.

Duncan, Robert B. "Characteristics of Organizational Environments and Perceived
1972   Environmental Uncertainty." *Administrative Science Quarterly*, 17:313–27.

Durkheim, Emile (trans. by George Simpson). *Division of Labor in Society*. Glencoe,
1947   Ill.: The Free Press.

Emery, F. E., and E. L. Trist. "The Causal Texture of Organizational Environments."
1965   *Human Relations*, 18:21–32.

Evan, William M.   "The Organization-Set: Toward a Theory of Interorganizational
   1966   Relations." In James Thompson (ed.), *Approaches to Organizational Design*.
             Pittsburgh: University of Pittsburgh Press.
Hall, Richard H., and John P. Clark.   "Problems in the Study of Interorganizational
   1974   Relationships." *Organization and Administrative Sciences*, 5, 1:45–66.
Homans, George C.   "Bringing Men Back In." *American Sociological Review*, 20
   1966   (1964). Reprinted in A. H. Rubenstein and C. J. Haberstroh (eds.), *Irwin-
             Dorsey Series in Behavioral Sciences in Business* (rev. ed.):38. Homewood,
             Ill.: Irwin-Dorsey.
Kast, Fremont E., and James E. Rosenzweig.   "General Systems Theory: Applications
   1972   for Organization and Management." *Academy of Management Journal*,
             15:463.
Khandwalla, P. N.   "Environment and Its Impact on the Organization." *International
   1972   Studies of Management and Organization*, 2:297–313.
Lawrence, Paul R., and Jay W. Lorsch.   *Organization and Environment*. Homewood,
   1969   Ill.: Richard D. Irwin, Inc.
_____.   *Organization and Environment: Managing Differentiation and Integration*.
   1967   Cambridge, Mass.: Division of Research, Harvard Business School, Harvard
             University.
Levine, Sol, and Paul White.   "Exchange as a Conceptual Framework for the Study
   1961   of Interorganizational Relationships." *Administrative Science Quarterly*,
             5:583–601.
Litwak, Eugene, and Lydia F. Hylton. "Interorganizational Analysis: A Hypothesis
   1962   on Co-ordinating Agencies." *Administrative Science Quarterly*, 6:395–420.
Merton, Robert K.   "Bureaucratic Structure and Personality." In Robert K. Merton
   1957   (ed.), *Social Theory and Social Structure* (rev. ed.). New York: The Free
             Press of Glencoe.
Miller, J. G.   "Toward a General Theory for the Behavioral Sciences." *American
   1955   Psychologist*, 10:513–51.
Negandhi, Anant R.   *Organization Theory in an Open System*. New York: Dunellen.
   1974
Negandhi, Anant R., and S. B. Prasad.   *Comparative Management*. New York:
   1971   Appleton-Century-Crofts.
Rosengren, W. R., and M. Lefton. *Hospitals and Patients*. New York: Atherton
   1968   Press.
Thorelli, Hans B.   "Organizational Theory: An Ecological View." *Proceedings of
   1967   the Academy of Management*:66–84.
Thompson, James D.   *Organizations in Action*. New York: McGraw-Hill.
   1967
Warren, Roland.   "The Interorganizational Field as a Focus for Investigation."
   1967   *Administrative Science Quarterly*, 12:396–419.
Warren, Roland L., Stephen M. Rose, and Ann F. Bergunder.   *The Structure of
   1974   Urban Reform*. Lexington, Mass.: D. C. Heath and Company.

Warren, Roland L., et al.   "The Interactions of Community Decision Organizations:
  1973   Some Conceptual Considerations and Empirical Findings." In Anant R.
          Negandhi (ed.), *Modern Organizational Theory*. Kent, Ohio: Kent State
          University Press.

Webster's Seventh New Collegiate Dictionary:895. Springfield, Mass.: G. C. Merriam
  1967   Company.

PART I

Theoretical and Conceptual
Issues in Interorganization Theory

2

Frameworks for Interorganizational Analysis

ANDREW H. VAN DE VEN, DENNIS C. EMMETT, RICHARD KOENIG, JR.

Recently, there has been a rapid growth of interest in interorganizational analysis (hereafter IA). As the literature on IA continues to expand (with new and sometimes conflicting theoretical perspectives and empirical findings), the absence of an overall systematic framework on IA emerges as a serious problem. At present, most of the work in this area consists of an eclectic smattering of theory and research devoted to selective topics within the field, but without much consideration for how these theoretical and empirical bits of knowledge relate and contribute to a developing interorganizational theory. The purposes of this paper are to review this literature, identify the alternative frameworks that have been advanced in IA, and examine the conceptual boundaries and empirical referents within each framework. Achieving this, the development and integration of the frameworks on IA may be advanced, and future research may be systematically focused.

THREE-DIMENSIONAL VIEW OF ENVIRONMENT

The literature on IA generally begins with an analysis of the environment, a clear understanding of which is required in order to examine how organizations function and interact within it. At least three basic approaches have been taken for conceptualizing the environment: (1.) as an external constraining phenomenon; (2.) as a collection of interacting organizations, groups, or persons; and particularly (3.) as a social system.[1] The next three sections will analyze the literature on IA in terms of these three approaches.

---

[1] This three-dimensional classification of the literature on IA was prompted by, and is analogous to Sanders' (1972:408–17) three-dimensional view of the health community.

The Environment as an External Constraining Phenomenon

A number of theorists and researchers view the environment as a social constraining phenomenon that exists external to the organization, but within which the organization must function. The environment as an external organizational phenomenon is illustrated in studies that examine first, the characteristics of the environment; second, its effect upon the internal design of the organization; and third, the strategies and tactics used by an organization to effect the environment in efforts to achieve certainty and rationality in its domain. While much of the literature that views the environment as a social phenomenon surrounding organizational behavior is formally intraorganizational in scope, we shall briefly review it because it serves as a basis for IA.

Hall (1972:297–324) defines the environment as the *general* and *specific* influences on the organization. The *general* environment includes those conditions that indirectly affect an organization, including technological, legal, political, economic, demographic, ecological, and cultural conditions. For example, Black and Kase (1963) examine the general environment of mental health rehabilitation agencies in terms of changing population and need for services, disease categories encountered, medical technology, and concepts of professional practice. In their study of innovation in public housing, Aiken and Alford (1970) measure the general environment as the political culture, concentration of community power, degree of poverty, and community differentiation, continuity, and integration. At a broader level, Emery and Trist (1963) describe four causal textures of the environment in terms of the turbulence and interconnectedness of its elements.

The *specific* environment is also often called the task environment (Thompson, 1967), or the relevant environment (Dill, 1958). It refers to the organizations, groups, and persons with which the organization is in direct interaction. In his summary of the literature, Child (1972) suggests that environmental variability, complexity, and threat are three major dimensions for empirically measuring the task environment. Environmental variability includes the frequency, degree, and irregularity of changes in environmental activities relevant to an organization's operations. Environmental complexity refers to the heterogeneity and range of external activities, while environmental threat refers to the external sources of stress faced by organizational decision makers. Perceptions about the task environment are also important. In his comparative case study of two Norwegian firms, Dill (1958), for example, describes how the decision-making autonomy of Alpha and Beta top managers is influenced by the nature of the environment, the accessibility of information about the environment, and by managerial perceptions about the meaning of environmental information.

Most writers who adopt an open-system perspective on intraorganiza-

tional analysis view the environment in terms of these external social phenomena and examine how the characteristics of a given organization are
affected or effected by the environment. The analysis begins with an examination of the organization's domain, which designates its specific goals in
terms of the functions performed, the population served, and the services
rendered (Levine and White, 1961). To achieve these goals, organizations
depend upon the environment in varying degrees for personnel, information,
monetary and physical resources, and clients, customers, or markets (Levine,
White, and Paul, 1963; Aiken and Hage, 1968; Aldrich, 1972; Clark and
Wilson, 1961). Indeed, Seashore and Yuchtman (1967 : 393–94) empirically
define organizational effectiveness in terms of its ability to exploit the
environment in the acquisition of scarce and valued resources to sustain
organizational functioning over time. In this sense, Guetzkow (1966)
notes that the roots of interdependence with the environment are internal
to each organization, while Aiken and Hage (1968) state that organizations
are pushed into joint-program interdependencies.

This resource dependency upon the environment imposes constraints
on organizational behavior and directly affects the internal functioning of
organizations. The greater the organizational interdependence with the
environment, the greater the complexity, decentralization, and program
innovativeness (Aiken and Hage, 1968). The greater the environmental
uncertainty experienced by an organization: (1.) the more adaptive and
organic the organizational structure (Burns and Stalker, 1961; Simpson
and Gulley, 1962; Terreberry, 1968); (2.) the more differentiated the orientation of managers (Lawrence and Lorsch, 1967; Dill, 1958); (3.) the greater
the lateral communications and participativeness in decision making by
employees (Aiken and Hage, 1968; Thompson and McEwen, 1958); and
(4.) the greater the internal problems of coordination and control (Aiken
and Hage, 1968; Galbraith, 1970; Thompson, 1967; Bales, 1965).

In reaction to these external influences, organizations "strain toward
autonomy" (Guetzkow, 1966). Autonomy implies that organizations are
capable of choosing the course of action they desire to pursue (Levine and
White, 1961; Clark and Wilson, 1961). Child (1972) argues that organization
decision makers have opportunities to select the types of environments
in which they will operate. For example, Thompson (1967) indicates that
organizational decision makers will perceive themselves as operating in
segmented markets and utilizing only selected input sources —— and regard
success in these areas as particularly vital for the organization's survival.
Further, Child (1972 : 4) states that "large organizations may command
sufficient power to influence the condition prevailing within environments
where they are already operating."

A number of strategies and tactics are available to the organization to
effect its chosen environment and achieve bounded rationality and certainty

within its domain (Thompson, 1967). An organization may adopt a variety of buffering mechanisms to protect its technical core from environmental influences by: (1.) adding on input and output components; (2.) anticipating external fluctuations through planning, forecasting, and scheduling; and, as a last resort (3.) by rationing (Thompson, 1967:20–24). Additionally, the organization can attempt to influence the processes for interaction with environment in terms of competition or cooperation, which includes bargaining, developing coalitions, and cooptation (Thompson and McEwen, 1958; Levine, White, and Paul, 1963; Yuchtman and Seashore, 1967; Morris and Binstock, 1966; Morris and Rein, 1967). Finally, the organization can protect and hedge its position in the environment through the alternative prestige-generating mechanisms discussed by Perrow (1961), Blankenship and Elling (1962), Caplow (1964), and Young and Larson (1966).

In summary, the studies that view the environment as an external constraining phenomenon examine the properties of organization structure and process as they affect or effect external environmental conditions. Formally, then, the organization is the unit of analysis, and studies in this vein are more appropriately classified as intraorganizational utilizing an open-system perspective. These studies are important for IA because they provide the underlying rationale for the existence of interorganizational activity. In varying degrees, all organizations are dependent upon their environment for the elements or inputs which are vital to their functioning (Perlman and Gurin, 1972:161). If organizations were self-sustaining entities, as Clark (1965) and O'Toole, et al. (1972), have suggested, there would be little need for IA.

The Environment as a Collection of Interacting Organizations,
Groups, and Persons

Most of the studies that can be formally classified as interorganizational view the environment as a collection of interacting organizations, groups, and persons. The analysis generally begins where studies in the previous sections conclude. Because organizations can seldom marshall the necessary resources to attain their goals independently, they must establish exchange relationships with other organizations. "Organizational exchange is any voluntary activity between two or more organizations which has consequences, actual or anticipated, for the realization of their respective goals or objectives" (Levine and White, 1961:588). Thus, in efforts to obtain resources, organizations develop greater interdependencies with a network or set of other organizations, groups, and parties (Evan, 1966).

Writers who view the environment as a collection of interacting parties examine the *comparative* and *relational* properties of an interaction network (Marrett, 1971). The distinction between comparative and relational properties of a collection of organizations is in the unit of analysis. In the latter, the focus is on the linkage mechanisms between the parties; in the former, it is focused on the parties themselves, which are then compared on certain attributes (Marrett, 1971 : 86).

Researchers have developed a number of dimensions to compare the properties of organizations which belong to an interaction network. These include:

1. Homogeneity—the functional and structural similarity of organizations (Levine and White, 1961; Evan, 1966; Zald, 1966; Thompson, 1967; White, Levine, and Vlasak, 1973; Aldrich, 1972).

2. Domain Consensus—which includes the following comparative characteristics among parties: (a.) the degree to which an organization's specific goals are disputed (Levine and White, 1961; Aldrich, 1972); (b.) the compatibility of organizational goals, philosophies, and reference orientations (Levine, White, and Paul, 1963; Evan, 1966; Miller, 1958; Rein and Morris, 1962); and (c.) the amount of goal overlap (Reid, 1969; Evan, 1966).

3. Awareness of Other Parties—the degree of knowledge or ignorance of the goals, services, and resources of other parties in the network (Litwak and Hylton, 1962; White, Levine, and Vlasak, 1973).

4. Stability—the length of time organizations are a member of the network, and the degree of turnover of the parties (Caplow, 1964; Thompson, 1963; Aldrich, 1972).

5. Resource Distribution—the amount and type of resources held by each party, and the amount and type of resources needed by each party (Evan, 1966; Aiken and Hage, 1968; Aldrich, 1972), or the balance of power among parties (Thompson and McEwen, 1958).

6. Number of Resource Sources—the number of alternative sources from which an organization can obtain its necessary resources (Levine and White, 1961; Litwak and Hylton, 1962; Evan, 1966; Zald, 1966; Aldrich, 1972).

7. Size of Network—the number of organizations in the network (Evan, 1966; Litwak and Hylton, 1962).

8. Overlap in Membership—the number of actors representing multiple organizations in the network.

Two approaches exist in the literature for examining the relational properties between organizations. One examines the *dimensions* of interaction or exchange between organizations, while the other analyzes the *mechanisms* for coordination between organizations.

The first approach is more general and is exemplified by Marrett's (1971) specification of the dimensions of interorganizational exchange. In an excellent synthesizing article on the works of others, Marrett (1971 : 89–97) presents four key dimensions for examining the linkage relationship between organizations:

1. Formalization—the degree to which exchanges between organizations are given official sanction or agreed to by the parties involved, and the extent to which an intermediary coordinates the relations (Hage and Aiken, 1967).

2. Intensity—the amount of involvement required by parties to the exchange in terms of the size of resource investment required, and the frequency of interaction (Johns and Demarche, 1957; Reid, 1964; Mayhew, 1971).

3. Reciprocity—the directions of the exchange (unilateral, reciprocal, or joint), and the extent to which terms on the bases and conditions of the exchange are mutually reached (Levine and White, 1961; Guetzkow, 1966).

4. Standardization—some reliable determination or fixedness of the units of exchange and procedures for exchange between organizations (Litwak and Hylton, 1962).

Studies that examine relational properties in this vein generally examine the mechanisms for interorganizational linkage in terms of one or more of these four dimensions. Marrett (1971) cites Reid's (1964) and Litwak and Hylton's (1962) analyses of structured (mediated) and unstructured (unmediated) coordination mechanisms as examples. Structured mechanisms (where an intermediary handles the interaction) are hypothesized to exist when the dimensions of the exchange are high in formalization, intensity, reciprocity, and standardization.

Alternatively, a second approach used to examine relational properties focuses on the linkage mechanisms themselves, and attempts to determine the contextual circumstances in which a variety of alternative coordination mechanisms are utilized. Studies following this approach examine the comparative properties (outlined above) as independent factors, and the coordination mechanisms as the dependent variables. Litwak and Mayer (1966), for example, suggest that when there are many overlapping memberships, common messengers are frequently used to coordinate between organizations. Similarly, Levine and White (1961), Gilbert (1969), Burke (1965), Reid (1964), and Warren (1967) suggest a number of comparative property prerequisites to the existence of a coordination agency, including domain consensus, complementarity of resources, homogeneity of structure, mutual awareness, and stability between the organizations in the exchange relationship. Also closely related to studies in this vein are Guetzkow's (1950) study of interagency committee usage, the alternative modes for interagency coordination by Black and Kase (1963), and the studies that examine determinants of cooperative versus competitive relationships between organizations (Barth, 1963; Clark, 1968; Aldrich, 1972).

To summarize, literature that views the environment as a collection of interacting organizations focuses upon the network of relationships occurring between the parties in the exchange. Considerable strides have been made recently to operationally define the variables and analytically identify the relationships between the comparative and relational properties of a given collection of interacting organizations. Considerably more empirical research is required before one can discuss the relationships between the comparative and relational properties in greater detail. It is encouraging to note, however, the increasing number of research studies either in progress or currently being published in this area.

The Environment as a Social System

A third way to view the environment is as a social system. Many efforts are currently being made to distinguish between behavior that occurs between a collection of organizations, groups, and people that make up the environment, and the behavior within and among collectivities of organizations functioning as social systems within the aggregate environment system. Levine and White (1972:379) suggest a need to shift the focus of research from the relationships *between* agencies to relationships *among* the agencies themselves as an exchange network. Warren has adopted Lewin's (1961) concept of "field" (which refers to the "totality of coexisting facts that are mutually interdependent"), and defines the interorganizational field as the "properties of the individual organizations themselves" (Warren, et al., 1973:145–59). In discussing the manpower training system, Aldrich suggests that the scope of analysis among a set of organizations is something more than the pairwise relationships between organizations. "Here emphasis is on ... an aggregate of emergent outcome of the interaction of many paired interactions" (Aldrich, 1972:17). In a similar vein, Sanders (1972:411) summarizes a number of current efforts being made to define and examine the collection of health organizations and groups in a community as a social system.

As can be inferred from the above discussion, the notion of viewing the environment as a social system is, at best, suggestive. With the notable exception of the general theory of social systems by Talcott Parsons (1962), no systematic theory has been developed for analyzing the environment as a social system. The remainder of this paper will attempt to apply Parsons' general theory to IA by examining the properties of an interorganizational collectivity (a subsystem within the aggregate environmental system).

THE INTERORGANIZATIONAL COLLECTIVITY

Interorganizational analysis can be defined as the study of interorganizational collectivities as social action systems. A brief elaboration of the key components in this definition is in order.[2]

The *action system* is a set or series of goal-directed behavioral acts. The acts are directed toward the attainment of some ends of the system, and between acts there are cause and effect relations (Parsons, 1949 : 78).

As a *social system*, the interdependent actions are performed by various participants in interaction with each other (Parsons, 1964 : 29). Over time, the participants take on specialized roles and necessarily develop normative behavioral expectations of each other (Homans, 1960). If the *social system* is to remain stable for any length of time, the role occupants must have some shared norms and values regarding the rights and obligations of participants vis-a-vis other participants.

As a *collectivity*, the role structure of the social action system is such that it is able to act as a unit (Parsons, 1964 : 96–101). This implies: (1.) that occupants of one or more roles of the collectivity can make decisions that are binding for the *collectivity* as a whole; (2.) that the participants in the *collectivity* are interdependent in terms of the unit's decision; (3.) that the *collectivity* can perform actions (i.e., pursue goals) in a manner similar to an individual participant; and (4.) that the *collectivity* can participate in, and must adapt to, other collectivities or other social systems more encompassing than itself, just as an individual participant does by being a member of the *collectivity* (Lessnoff, 1968 : 186).

As an *interorganizational collectivity*[3] (hereafter IC), the primary participants in the collectivity are two or more organizations. These organizations join together as an action system to attain a specific objective by

---

[2]Space limitations do not permit a thorough elaboration of the full meaning Parsons intends in the use of the words in the definition. At the risk of oversimplification, we will attempt to define these concepts as they relate to the framework for IA.

[3]Unfortuantely, the word "collectivity" has a variety of meanings and is used quite loosely in the literature. It is therefore important to recognize that the strict Parsonian definition of collectivity, as defined above, is used throughout this paper.

performing a set or series of goal-directed behavioral acts. For example, Litwak and Hylton (1962), and Levine, White, and Paul (1963), suggest a number of ends for organizations to join together as an action system: (1.) to communicate pertinent information by forming a social service exchange; (2.) to promote areas of common interest through such groups as a Chamber of Commerce; (3.) to jointly obtain and allocate a greater amount of resources than would be possible by each agency independently through a community chest; and (4.) to protect areas of common interest and adjudicate areas of dispute (e.g., a professional sport's league).

As a social system, the actions of the organizations are interdependent and, over time, member organizations or representatives thereof take on specialized roles and develop behavioral expectations of each other regarding the rights and obligations of membership in the collectivity. In this sense, Clark (1965:234) suggests that two or more interdependent organizations bind themselves together by performing specialized activities to attain a specific objective for a limited period of time, often by the terms of a contract. As a *collectivity*, this role structure is such that the IC can *act as a unit* and make decisions to attain the goals of the system. Generally, decisions are allowed to emerge out of the interaction among various role occupants. Modifications and changes which are necessary in making a joint decision "occur incrementally through the waxing and waning of the resource allocation mechanism, and through changes in legitimation or shifting domains" and roles of members within the IC (Warren, 1967:413).

Through such a process, the decisions made are binding for the collectivity as a whole. The IC decisions, however, may have unanticipated consequences for certain member organizations and may not result in the attainment of their suboptimized objectives. Wood (1972) illustrates the case of how a council of churches' decision to be involved in the civil rights movement resulted in dwindling memberships and fund-giving to the council's southern churches. In spite of the unanticipated consequences for the southern churches, Wood suggests they continued to participate as members of the council, possibly because of a shared higher moral objective.

As the above discussion suggested, the IC is a particular social system that can be distinguished from other collectivities existing in a hierarchy of systems of social orders (Parsons, 1960). The dimensions that appear to distinguish the IC from lower level systems (e.g., intraorganizational collectivities), and higher collectivities (e.g., interorganizational collectivities), and eventually the societal collectivity, are its primary orientation toward the attainment of a unique level of goals and its basic unit of analysis.

The primary goals of the IC are such that no single organization can achieve them individually. Thus, while intraorganizational collectivities strain toward autonomous goal attainment (Guetzkow, 1966), there are a number of higher level goals that are unachievable without coordinated action between quasi-autonomous intraorganizational collectivities. The latter goals are the proper realm of the IC.

Although the IC can act as a unit, it does not include all the actions necessary to its own existence. Only society, which Parsons (1966:17–18) defines as a "total social system," includes all the actions necessary to its own existence. Therefore, while it would be expected that ICs strain toward autonomy, there again are a number of higher level goals and requirements that are unachievable by individual ICs and fall into the realm of the next higher level system. Warren's (1967) analysis of decision making between ICs (which he calls community decision organizations) is an example of this next higher inter-interorganizational collectivity.

At a more operational level, the specification of the boundaries of the IC are admittedly obscure. Since the IC is an open-system model, it is subject to this conventional limitation when attempting to apply it generally for IA. At a more situation-specific level, it can be shown by illustration that the IC requires a very selective, analytic perspective on IA.

Figure 1 illustrates a very simple environmental social system. The circles represent a collection of organizations (0) in the environment. The straight lines represent interdependent linkages between the organizations. Five ICs can be distinguished in the aggregate environmental system. IC 1

Figure 1
ILLUSTRATION OF SIMPLE ENVIRONMENT

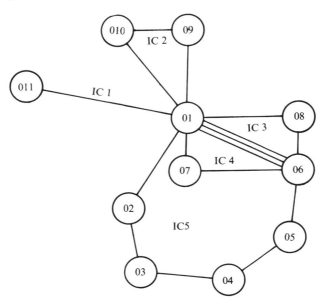

is the simplest case of two organizations that may have joined together to develop a joint program as discussed by Aiken and Hage (1968). IC 2 is like IC 1, except that the collectivity contains a greater number of members. ICs 3, 4, and 5 illustrate cases where some of the same organizations may be joined together in different collectivities. For example, Sanders (1972) discusses how the same health institutions within a community may be linked with other agencies and groups for clearly different purposes: to obtain resources by membership in a community chest (e.g., IC 5); to be a member of a joint case referral program with other agencies in order to treat patients with a variety of diseases that cannot be treated by a single member agency (e.g., IC 3); and to coordinate and plan the health services in a community through a regional medical program (e.g., IC 4).

Two important observations can be drawn from this example. While the IC may be interrelated and overlapping in membership: (1.) the structure and process within each IC may be different and may be influenced by its unique collective objective;[4] and (2.) the role behavior and specialized activities of a given organization with membership in more than one IC are different in each IC.

It is important to clarify that an IC is not an interorganization-set (Caplow, 1964; Evan, 1966). If 01 in Figure 1 is chosen as a focal organization, by Evan's (1966) definition the collection of organizations directly linked with 01 constitutes a set. From our perspective, it can be seen that 01 is a member of five ICs. Further, it would be expected that 01 has different motivations for membership in each IC, and that it adopts differential role behaviors in each IC. As Thompson (1967) and Child (1972) suggest, a given organization does not treat its task environment as a set. Rather, it isolates different segments of its task environment by distinguishing between the collectivities of organizations in its set, and utilizes unique strategies to deal with each IC. Interorganizational analysis in terms of ICs is therefore a very focused perspective. It requires that the researcher identify and isolate a given environment to specific clusters of independent organizations that join together and act as a collectivity to achieve special-purpose objectives. Membership in these collectivities may overlap, just as membership of personnel in different organizations may overlap. However, ICs, like organizations, are not distinguished by membership but by their functional goals, role structure, and behavior as a social action system. It should also be recognized that two or more collectivities that are composed of the same member organizations may exist in a given environment. For example, within a small community, the retail business organizations may, by nature of their trade and a limited sales market, be forced together into

---

[4]This observation will be discussed later in this paper when we examine the overall configuration of the IC.

a cut-throat, competitive IC. At the same time, they may be joined together in a cooperative Chamber of Commerce IC.[5]

The basic unit of analysis for IA is generally considered to be the organization (Levine and White, 1961; Litwak and Hylton, 1962; Evan, 1966). Since the IC can act as a unit, however, this suggests, as Durkheim (1947) does, that many behavioral acts and events of the IC cannot be explained simply in terms of analyzing the behavior of individual organizations that are members of the IC. Rather, these observable social facts are collective events that arise out of the actions of the social system and are formally a property of the IC itself (Timasheff, 1967:108). For example, Warren, et al. (1973:145–59), recently reported that "one can describe and analyze as a single system of interaction any group of organizations whose properties may differ from those of the interacting organizations themselves and cannot be reduced to properties of these individual organizations." The appropriate unit of analysis for examining the IC must, therefore, include the social action system itself.

Functional Levels within the
Interorganizational Collectivity (IC)

In his general theory of social systems, Parsons (1957:4) warned against undertaking "complicated analyses of the dynamic process (within the IC) without adequately clarifying the structural reference points that describe the system in which the process takes place and its situation." Therefore, we will now define the major structural levels within the IC that can be identified by the qualitatively different functional orientations within the social action system.

All social systems, if they are to survive, must solve at least four functional problems: goal attainment, or enabling system participants to attain their goals; integration, or articulating together the actions of system members; adaptation, which refers to the boundary maintenance relationship between the system and its environment; and instrumental pattern maintenance, or ensuring that the task activities, norms, and values of participants are consistent with those of the system (Parsons and Smelser, 1956:14–16).

Participants in small ICs (e.g., an IC consisting of two organizations) necessarily have to perform the four requisite functions simultaneously. Given sufficient size, however, under norms of rationality the IC will attempt to achieve the benefits of process specialization (Thompson, 1967) by

---

[5]This example also suggests that the seemingly inconsistent relationship often observed between organizations can be explained by the overlapping or multiple memberships in various ICs. Each IC exists to attain a specific objective, and its members assume specialized roles and develop normative behavioral expectations that facilitate IC goal attainment.

dividing the primary performance of these functions by levels within the collectivity. Analogous to Parsons' (1957:3–16) three levels of hierarchical structure with the intraorganizational collectivity (technical, managerial, and institutional levels), there are at least three functionally differentiated levels, or subsystems, within the IC. We shall simply label these Levels I, II, and III of the IC. These levels provide empirical referents to guide the researcher in investigating the properties of the IC.

Level I of the IC.—The Level I subsystem consists of the primary instrumental productive units or organizations that are members of the IC. The major functional orientation of the quasi-autonomous organizations at Level I is attainment of suboptimized goals when the resources necessary to attain instrumental ends exist external to each organization. This organizational dependence upon other units within the IC serves as the necessary motivation for organizations to participate in the IC.

Research at Level I would focus on the member organizations of the IC, and would compare the inputs, outputs, and instrumental activities of each member organization in specific relation to the IC. As discussed above, many organizations hold membership in a number of ICs. If one is to identify cause and effect relationships, this suggests that the researcher must isolate those inputs, outputs, and instrumental functions of organizations which relate directly to the IC under investigation. The eight dimensions set forth earlier in this paper could be chosen to empirically explore the comparative properties of organizations that are members of the IC.

Level II of the IC.—The major functional orientation of the Level II subsystem is integration of the differentiated, but interdependent, Level I organization members of the IC. Analogous to the managerial level in the intraorganizational collectivity (Parsons, 1957:11), the major functional requisites of Level II are coordination, control, and procurement. The units of analyses at Level II are the "relational linkage" (Marrett, 1971:86), or the mechanisms used for integration between the constituent members of the IC.

The two approaches outlined earlier for examining the relational properties between organizations could be adapted to empirically examine the coordination, control, and procurement functions at Level II of the IC. The researcher could examine the four *dimensions* of interaction or exchange within the IC, and relate them to the *mechanisms* used to coordinate, control, and procure activities among the differentiated member organizations. Alternatively, the researcher might systematically examine the relationships between the Level I and Level II subsystems of the IC by examining the Level I comparative properties of member organizations as independent factors, and the integration mechanisms used at Level II as the dependent variables.

Level III of the IC.—Level I member organizations are concerned with

primary instrumental goal attainment, while the integration function is
the relevant concern at Level II. Generally speaking, the overall goals,
policies, and domain of the IC which govern the functions performed at
Levels I and II are determined and institutionalized at a level higher than
Level II (Parsons, 1960:13). For example, in paraphrasing Levine and
White (1972:378), there are indeed crucial points of articulation between
governing boards at Level III and the member agencies of the IC, such as
the allocation of funds and other resources which establish the limits within
which the IC operates. Once the policy makers establish the objectives
and functions of Levels I and II, however, these objectives and functions
largely determine the mode of operation within the IC and the interaction
patterns between member organizations. The governing board of the IC
is generally composed of representatives from the member organizations.
In this sense, the goals, policies, and domain of the IC are generally developed
out of the interaction within the IC itself, as well as with its external environment. Since the IC is not a self-sustaining unit (as discussed above), it is
dependent upon the outside environment for some of the actions necessary
for its continued existence.

The principle functions of the Level III subsystem, therefore, are
governance of overall goals and policies, and external legitimation and
support of the IC domain with other social collectivities. Generally, the
unit of analysis at Level III is some kind of fiduciary board of directors or
trustees, the members of which are given certain responsibilities and prerogatives vis-a-vis the IC (Parsons, 1960:14). Alternatively, in the less
formalized ICs, the fiduciary functions may be performed by principle role
occupants.

Research on the Level III functions of the IC must first, seek answers
to the questions Clark (1968) asks: "Who governs, when, where, and with
what effects?" Similarly, Rossi (1957) asks: "Who influences what?"
By utilizing the methodologies for examining community power structures
(Perrucci and Pilisuk, 1970), empirical answers to these questions can
provide a basis for determining the decision-making structure and the
locus of power and authority within the IC.

Rossi (1957) suggests that three classes of variables seem important
for research on the decision-making structure at Level III: the characteristics of the decision makers; the range of issues being decided upon; and
the decision-making process itself. An aspect of the decision-making
structure is the power structure which resides in the web of interconnections
between member organizations within the IC, as well as in the network
that links the IC with other collectivities in the environment (Perrucci and
Pilisuk, 1970; Warren, 1967; Aldrich, 1972; Turk, 1973).

An examination of the decision-making and power structures may
provide some insight into the complex phenomenon that Warren, et al.

(1973 : 145–59) identified and labeled the "institutionalized thought structure," consisting of the aggregate system of interaction within the IC that "serves to reduce uncertainty to controllable dimensions, to minimize contest, to resist change, and to insure organizational viability ... This institutionalized thought structure is reflected in the technological and administrative rationales of the (IC), the source of their legitimation and their relation to power configurations" of the environment external to the IC. Considerably more exploratory research is required to clearly understand this intriguing but complex phenomenon.

The Overall Configuration of the IC

Research is also needed to investigate the overall structure and process of the IC. Warren's (1967) conceptualization of four types of CDOs is a major contribution in this direction. The unitary, federative, coalitional, and social choice contexts can serve as a guide for an exploratory comparison of alternative IC configurations. These configurations could be distinguished from each other in terms of the following dimensions: relation of member organizations to an inclusive goal; locus of inclusive decision making; locus of authority; structural provision for division of labor; commitment to a leadership subsystem; and prescribed collectivity orientation of member organizations (Warren, 1967 : 404).

The IC as a Framework for IA

This section has defined IA as the study of ICs. In summary, the IC is a social action system that can be differentiated from other social collectivities in terms of (1.) its unit of analysis, a collectivity of primary, productive organizations that are dependent upon one another in some fashion; and (2.) its orientation toward the attainment of goals that are unachievable by organizations independently and require coordinated action by the member organizations in the collectivity. As a social action system, the IC must solve four functional problems if it is to survive: goal attainment, integration, adaptation, and instrumental pattern maintenance. To achieve the benefits of process specialization, the larger ICs will divide the primary performance of these functions to subsystem Levels I, II, and III.

Although the three levels constitute a continuous system-subsystem hierarchy that is articulated together by each next higher level, Parsons (1957 : 16) underscores that there is a qualitative discontinuity in functional orientation and categories of activities at each point in the transition between levels. The requisite functions at primary Level I are instrumental goal attainment and pattern maintenance of the productive units or member organizations. Level II performs the major integration function and includes the mechanisms used to coordinate, control, and procure activities between differentiated Level I organizations. The principal functions of external adaptation, domain governance, and overall system goal attainment are performed by fiduciary boards or principal role occupants at Level III.

According to Marrett (1971 : 89), "A total analysis of interorganizational relations requires a thorough understanding of the interplay between variables operating on all levels. But such an analysis is dependent upon the delineation of these variables." Therefore, an attempt has been made to outline some directions for research on the IC by abstracting from the literature the empirical dimensions that might be used to explore variations in structure and process within each subsystem level of the IC, as well as variations in overall configurations between ICs.

CONCLUSION

The ability to understand and critically evaluate the literature on interorganizational analysis requires a theoretical framework. A number of such frameworks are available to guide one's investigation and this paper has presented three. The three frameworks emerged from the observation that at least three basic approaches have been taken for conceptualizing the environment: as an external constraining social phenomenon; as a collection of interacting organizations, groups, and persons; and as a social system. The studies that view the environment as an external constraining phenomenon examine the properties of organization structure and process as they affect or effect external environmental conditions. Studies in this vein are most appropriately classified as intraorganizational and utilize an open-system framework. Most of the literature on IA views the environment as a collection of interacting organizations, and utilizes a contingency framework that focuses on the network of relationships between the parties in the exchange. The most recent way is to view the environment as a social system. Based upon the general theory of Talcott Parsons, the interorganizational collectivity was presented as a framework for IA from a social system perspective.

While rudimentary in its present form it is believed that the interorganizational collectivity (IC) provides a framework for interorganizational analysis (IA) that can: (1.) incorporate most of the theoretical and empirical studies on IA (and in this sense builds upon a growing body of knowledge); and (2.) serves as a basis for the systematic comparison and linking of social systems in a hierarchy of social orders. A one-for-one proportional correspondence may not exist between the intraorganizational collectivity. However, in the interorganizational collectivity, as well as in higher level collectivities, we would expect, as Parsons (1962) suggests, that each level of collective behavior will exhibit the same major properties of a social action system.

REFERENCES

Aiken, Michael, and Robert Alford. "Community Structure and Innovation: The
1970   Case of Public Housing." *The American Political Science Review*, 64:843–64.

Aiken, Michael, and Jerald Hage. "Organizational Interdependence and Intra-
1968   Organizational Structure." *American Sociological Review*, 3:912–30.

Aldrich, Howard. "Cooperation and Conflict between Organizations in the Man-
1972   power Training System: An Organization-Environment Perspective." In
        Anant R. Negandhi (ed.), *Conflict and Power in Complex Organizations:
        An Inter-Institutional Perspective*. Kent, Ohio: Comparative Administration
        Research Institute, Center for Business and Economic Research, Kent
        State University.

Bales, Robert. "The Equilibrium Problem in Small Groups." In T. Parsons, R.
1965   Bales, and E. Shils (eds.), *Working Papers in the Theory of Action*. New
        York: The Free Press.

Barth, Ernest. "The Cause and Consequences of Interagency Conflict." *Sociological
1963   Inquiry*, 33:31–33.

Black, Bertram, and Harold Kase. "Interagency Cooperation in Rehabilitation
1963   and Mental Health." *Social Service Review*, 37:26–32.

Blankenship, Vaughn, and Ray Elling. "Organizational Support and Community
1962   Power Structure: The Hospital." *Journal of Health and Social Behavior*,
        3:257–69.

Burke, Edmund. "The Road to Planning: An Organizational Analysis." *Social
1965   Service Review*, 39:261–70.

Burns, Thomas, and G. M. Stalker. *The Management of Innovation*. London:
1961   Tavistock Publications.

Caplow, Theodore. *Principles of Organization*:201–28. New York: Harcourt,
1964   Brace.

Child, John. "Organizational Structure, Environment, and Performance: The
1972   Role of Strategic Choice." *Sociology*, 6:1–22.

Clark, Burton. "Interorganizational Patterns in Education." *Administrative Science
1965   Quarterly*, 10:224–37.

Clark, Terry. "Community Structure, Decision-Making, Budget Expenditures and
1968   Urban Renewal in 51 American Communities." *American Sociological
        Review*, 33:546–93.

Clark, Peter, and James Wilson. "Incentive Systems: A Theory of Organizations."
1961   *Administrative Science Quarterly*, 6:29–166.

Dill, William R. "Environment as an Influence on Managerial Autonomy." *Adminis-
1958   trative Science Quarterly*, 2:407–43.

Durkheim, Emile (trans. by George Simpson) *Division of Labor in Society*. Glencoe,
1947   Ill.: The Free Press.

Emery, F. E., and E. L. Trist. "The Causal Texture of Organizational Environments."
1963   Presented at the 17th International Congress of Psychology, Washington,
        D. C.

Evan, William M. "The Organization-Set: Toward a Theory of Interorganizational
1966   Relations." In James Thompson (ed.), *Approaches to Organizational Design*.
        Pittsburgh: University of Pittsburgh Press.

Galbraith, Jay. "Environmental and Technological Determinants of Organizational
1970   Design." In Jay Lorsch and Paul Lawrence (eds.), *Studies in Organization
        Design*: 133–39. Homewood, Ill.: Richard D. Irwin, Inc.
Gilbert, Neil. "Neighborhood Coordinator: Advocate or Middleman?" *Social
1969   Service Review*, 43.
Guetzkow, Harold. "Relations Among Organizations." *Studies in Organizations*:
1966   13–44. Athens, Ga.: University of Georgia Press.
————. "Interagency Committee Usage." *Public Administration Review*, 10:
1950   190–96.
Hage, Jerald, and Michael Aiken. "Relationship of Centralization to Other Structural
1967   Properties." *Administrative Science Quarterly*, 12:72–92.
Hall, Richard H. *Organizations, Structure and Process*. Englewood Cliffs, N. J.:
1972   Prentice Hall, Inc.
Homans, George. *The Human Group*. New York: Harcourt, Brace, and World.
1960
Johns, Ray, and David Demarche. *Community Organization and Agency Responsibi-
1957   lity*. New York: Associated Press.
Lawrence, Paul, and Jay Lorsch. *Organization and Environment: Managing Dif-
1967   ferentiation and Integration*. Boston: Division of Research, Graduate School
        of Business, Harvard University.
Lessnoff, M. H. "Parsons' System Problems." *Sociological Review*, 16:185–215.
1968
Levine, Sol, and Paul White. "The Community of Health Organizations." In Howard
1972   E. Freeman, Sol Levine, and Leo Reader (eds.), *Handbook of Medical Sociol-
        ogy*. Englewood Cliffs, N.J.: Prentice Hall, Inc.
————. "Exchange as a Conceptual Framework for the Study of Interorganization-
1961   al Relationships." *Administrative Science Quarterly*, 5:583–601.
Levine, Sol, Paul E. White, and Benjamin D. Paul. "Community Interorganizational
1963   Problems in Providing Medical Care and Social Services." *American Journal
        of Public Health*, 53:1183–95.
Lewin, Kurt. *Field Theory in Social Science: Selected Theoretical Papers*. New
1961   York: Harper and Row.
Litwak, Eugene, and Lydia F. Hylton. "Interorganizational Analysis: A Hypothesis
1962   on Coordinating Agencies." *Administrative Science Quarterly*, 6:395–420.
Litwak, Eugene, and Henry Mayer. "A Balance Theory of Coordination between
1966   Bureaucratic Organizations and Community Primary Groups." *Adminis-
        trative Science Quarterly*, 11:31–58.
Marrett, Cora Bageley. "On the Specification of Interorganization Dimensions."
1971   *Sociology and Social Research*, 61:83–99.
Mayhew, Leon. *Society: Institutions and Activity*. Glenview, Ill.: Scott, Foresman
1971   and Company.
Miller, Walter. "Interinstitutional Conflict as a Major Impediment to Delinquency
1958   Prevention." *Human Organization*, 17.
Morris, Peter, and Martin Rein. *Dilemmas of Social Reform: Poverty and Community
1967   Action in the United States*. Chicago: Aldine Publishing Company.
Morris, Robert, and Robert Binstock, with Martin Rein. *Feasible Planning for
1966   Social Change*. New York: Columbia University Press.

O'Toole, R., et al. *The Cleveland Rehabilitation Complex: A Study of Interagency*
1972 *Coordination.* Cleveland, Ohio: Vocational Guidance and Rehabilitation
Services.

Parsons, Talcott. "The Political Aspect of Social Structure and Process. In D. Easton
1966 (ed.), *Varieties of Political Theory.* Englewood Cliffs, N.J.: Prentice-
Hall.

——————. *The Social System.* New York: The Free Press.
1964

——————. *Toward a General Theory of Action.* New York: Harper and Row.
1962

——————. *Structure and Process in Modern Societies.* New York: The Free Press.
1960

——————. "General Theory in Sociology." In R. K. Merton (ed.), *Social Theory*
1957 *and Social Structure*:3–17. rev. ed., New York: The Free Press.
——————. *The Structure of Social Action.* New York: The Free Press.
1949

Parsons, Talcott, and N. J. Smelser. *Economy and Society.* New York: Routledge
1956 and Kegan Paul.

Perlman, Robert, and Arnold Gurin. *Community Organization and Social Planning.*
1972 New York: John Wiley and Sons.

Perrow, Charles. "Organizational Prestige: Some Functions and Dysfunctions."
1961 *American Journal of Sociology,* 71:335–41.

Perrucci, Robert, and Marc Pilisuk. "Leaders and Ruling Elites: The Interorganiza-
1970 tional Bases of Community Power." *American Sociological Review,* 35:
1040–57.

Reid, William. "Interagency Coordination in Delinquency Prevention and Control."
1964 *Social Service Review,* 38:418–28.

——————. "Interorganizational Coordination in Social Welfare: A Theoretical
1969 Analysis and Intervention." In R. M. Kramer and H. Specht (eds.), *Readings
in Community Organization Practice.* Englewood Cliffs, N.J.: Prentice-Hall.

Rein, Walter, and Robert Morris. *Social Work Practices.* New York: Columbia
1962 University Press.

Rossi, Peter. "Community Decision Making." *Administrative Science Quarterly,*
1957 1:415–43.

Sanders, Irwin. "Public Health in the Community. In Howard Freeman, Sol Levine,
1972 and Leo Reader (eds.), *Handbook of Medical Sociology.* Englewood Cliffs,
N.J.: Prentice-Hall.

Seashore, Stanley, and Ephraim Yuchtman. "Factoral Analysis of Organizational
1967 Performance." *Administrative Science Quarterly,* 12:377–95.

Simpson, Richard, and William Gulley. "Goals, Environmental Pressures, and
1962 Organizational Characteristics." *American Sociological Review,* 27:344–51.

Terreberry, Shirley. "The Evolution of Organizational Environments." *Adminis-
1968 trative Science Quarterly,* 12:590–613.

Timasheff, Nicholas. *Sociological Theory: Its Nature and Growth.* New York:
1967 Random House.

Thompson, James. "Organizations and Output Transactions." *American Journal
1963 of Sociology,* 68:309–24.

———. *Organizations in Action.* Chicago: McGraw-Hill.
1967

Thompson, James, and W. J. McEwen.   "Organizational Goals and Environment:
1958   Goal-Setting as an Interaction Process." *American Sociological Review*,
        23:23–31.

Turk, Herman.   "Comparative Urban Structure from an Interorganizational Perspec-
1973   tive." *Administrative Science Quarterly*, 18:37–55.

Warren, Roland.   "The Interorganizational Field as a Focus for Investigation."
1967   *Administrative Science Quarterly*, 12:396–419.

Warren, Roland, et al. "The Interactions of Community Decision Organizations:
1973   Some Conceptual Considerations and Empirical Findings. In Anant R.
        Negandhi (ed.), *Modern Organizational Theory*. Kent, Ohio: Kent State
        University Press.

White, Paul, Sol Levine, and George Vlasak. "Exchange as a Framework for Under-
1973   standing Interorganizational Relationships: Applications to Non-Profit
        Organizations." In Anant R. Negandhi (ed.), *Modern Organizational Theory*.
        Kent, Ohio: Kent State University Press.

Wood, James. "Unanticipated Consequences of Organizational Coalitions: Ecumeni-
1972   cal Cooperation and Civil Rights Policy." *Social Forces*, 50:512–21.

Young, Ruth, and Olaf Larson. "The Contribution of Voluntary Organizations
1966   to Community Structure." *American Journal of Sociology*, 71:178–86.

Yuchtman, Ephraim, and Stanley Seashore. "A System Resources Approach to
1967   Organizational Effectiveness." *American Sociological Review*, 33:891–903.

Zald, Mayer. "Organizations as Policies: An Analysis of Community Organization
1966   Agencies." *Social Work*, 2:56–65.

3

Interorganizational Relationships and Social Structure: A Critique of Some Aspects of the Literature

GERALD ZEITZ

In the recent study of formal or complex organizations, two claims have appeared with increased frequency. The first is that organizations are open rather than closed systems, and accordingly, that we must bring into our analysis of organizations various factors external to the structural properties of the organization itself. However, to the extent that hypotheses have been suggested applying to environmental and interorganizational relationships, we have heard the second claim that this new field of study is fragmented and in need of better theoretical underpinnings. Yet attempts to develop such theory have been few and only marginally successful.

I would like to suggest that perhaps researchers have not always searched in the right places. Starting with the assumption that the organization is a functionally autonomous unit of analysis, the field has made rather little use of community or societal literature to help develop such a theoretical framework. My comments here will suggest that the interorganizational field should make further use of this literature and also provide some reasons why it has not. The work of Turk (1970) is, of course, a step in this direction.

There is a good deal of variability in the way specific relationships between the (focal) organization and the other components of its environment are conceptualized. There are examples of (a.) organizational relationships as relational properties of the focal organization itself, with no specific description of the other pole of the relationship (Aiken and Hage, 1968); (b.) there are relationships conceptualized as a series of dyads between specific organizations (Hall and Clark, 1973); (c.) there are examples of relationships between the focal organization and the general field or environment in which some specific knowledge of that environment or field is assumed to be known; this generally involves the effects the environment has on the focal organization (Lawrence and Lorsch, 1967); and (d.) there are examples of field to field relationships in which relational or analytic properties of the field are related to other relational or analytic properties (Guetzkow, 1966).

It seems imperative that the study of interorganizational relationships should consider this fourth level of analysis: relationships at the field level. Further, these field level relationships are in themselves constitutive of community and societal relationships rather than just being placed or located in community or societal contexts. While many case studies provide rich and detailed analyses of organizations operating in community and societal contexts (Selznick, 1949), when it comes to formulating general models (Evan, 1966; Guetzkow, 1966), the tendency has been to adopt an atomistic approach to interorganizational relationships. Organizations have been assumed to be functionally autonomous. This claim is somewhat problematic so it will be developed further.

In response to what was thought to be an oversocialized concept of man and an overintegrated concept of the social system in sociology, Wrong (1961) and Gouldner (1959) felt it necessary to argue for the functional autonomy or independence of the parts, the subunits of social systems. The functional autonomy of a system part was operationally defined by Gouldner (1959:254) as "the probability that it (the part) can survive separation from the system." It seems that the opposite tendency is now apparent in the interorganizational field. Of course, almost nowhere in the literature is it stated that organizations are functionally autonomous. In fact, it is the point of much literature that the autonomy of the organization is limited in specified ways (Aiken and Hage, 1968; Emery and Trist, 1965; Clark, 1965). But the tendency is to assume that the organization is an already constituted, independently functioning unit. Environmental factors are brought into the analysis one by one, which set constraints on this functioning. Autonomy is assumed unless otherwise demonstrated. Thus, substantive assumptions are made about the behavior of organizations which are not consistent with the findings of macrosociological research. More importantly, such assumptions have not encouraged the utilization of techniques and perspectives already applied in community and societal research. Highly abstracted conceptualizations of the environment of interorganizational networks often cannot be compared with concepts in the macrosociological literature. For instance, in the interorganizational literature we know that "uncertainty" or "hostility" or "turbulence" lead to reactions in organizations; but we don't know (theoretically) what effects rapid economic change, or socialist government, or high rates of social conflict have on organizational behavior.

It is noteworthy that one of the few theoretical frameworks suggested for interorganizational relations is exchange theory (Levine and White, 1961). In exchange theory, dyadic relationships between actors originate from the rational desire of each party to maximize his utilities. While stable networks of relationships develop according to this model, possibly even characterized by unequal or dominance relations, it seems that exchange theory postulates a basic functional autonomy of the actors. Actors are assumed to be already constituted, rational, and functioning entities who enter into exchanges to make up for specific deficiencies through exchanges. It is instrinsic to exchange theory that actors have a basic functional autonomy, such that they may evaluate exchange alternatives and (rationally) select the most optimal ones in terms of their own values. Exchange theory seems less useful for explaining bureaucratic encrustations which may dominate behavior, for explaining power and resource structures which may impose alternatives, or for explaining established ideologies which may determine individual values.

But apart from some suggestive essays (Kaufman, 1959; Turk, 1970, 1973; Warren, 1967a), there has been a reluctance to see interorganizational networks as constitutive of community and societal structure. Part of the reason for this is simply organizational theory's commitment to the organizational level of analysis. Part is also due to a quite reasonable research strategy, namely to focus on only one level of analysis because of the pragmatic limitations of what can be accomplished with limited resources. But I would like to suggest another possible reason: the pragmatic concerns of those groups who primarily fund this research and who have an interest in certain kinds of results.

It seems that the bulk of interorganizational research has come from two traditions. One is a sociological tradition in which primarily government agencies have funded research projects trying to discover how best to achieve "coordination" between a fragmented set of health or social service agencies. In most cases the government did not want, or was not able to utilize funding or legal power sufficiently to challenge the inherent autonomy of a multiplicity of public and private agencies under diverse auspices. The result was to try to discover various mechanisms which could help induce, persuade, cajole, or trick agencies into some measure of increased integration. What I suggest is that given the current distribution of power, resources, and influence, the overall structure of the community of society was seen as a constant, while various organizational or interorganizational characteristics (data banks, planning boards, etc.) were seen as the relevant, manipulable variables. I am suggesting, then, that it is not accidental that interorganizational theory has failed to consider a fuller, more systematic theory of society to be relevant to interorganizational problems. The larger structure itself has been accepted as merely part of the natural environment, an unchanging set of constants in which manipulation of interorganizational networks might take place.

The other tradition is the management tradition, which has been concerned with the practical problems of the managers (and owners) of business firms. As environments themselves moved from states of "randomness and placidity" to "turbulence," managers (meaning all managerial functions, including "External Affairs") have found it increasingly impossible to manage using only those management principles concerning internal or technological variables. The increasing interdependence and complexity of society forced them (and organizational theory) to consider more systematically the effects of environment, i.e., the open-systems perspective. But the concern was not to understand the social structure in which firms were embedded, and which firms sometimes manipulated. It was to discover which aspects of the environment could be better predicted and controlled in order to achieve management objectives, whatever those objectives might be. This may be seen as an extension of the Weberian notion of rationalization to external relationships. Thus relevant aspects of the environment were conceptualized in such general terms as stability/change, certainty/uncertainty, hostile/friendly, etc. These are characteristics of the environment, but from a point of view especially relevant to the practical concerns of management.

Thus, those community and societal variables accepted as constant by the funding sources were accepted as nonproblematic constants in the research literature. Those variables seen as manipulable are selected as the variables for analysis. Boddewyn (1974) presents a good example of a theoretical problem being couched in terms of the concerns of management. He convincingly argues that the external affair function is a unique, important, and growing function with its own task environment. However, it is significant that, in the end, no adequate theoretical structure can be readily pointed to. Studies such as Mills' *Power Elite* (1956) demonstrate how such upper-level boundary spanning personnel are integral parts of the larger national and international dynamics. In order to develop a theory of the external affairs function, I think that one should account for the fact that multinational corporations are large profit-making firms, often based in the U.S., backed up by the military and diplomatic power of the U.S., engaged in competitive and monopolistic quests for new sources of raw materials and markets, and are usually managed by high-status personnel who themselves often have extensive stockholdings and upper-class family backgrounds. Further, these firms are themselves constitutive parts of national and international political economies, both in the U.S. and in the host country. Unless variables like these are brought into the analysis, I'm not sure what more one can say theoretically about the external affairs role.

Three papers in this volume are concerned more with interorganizational networks within societal or community settings. The paper by Professors Richard Hall and John Clark has made use of a most promising methodological technique: the analysis of specific dyads in an organizational network. It will be interesting to discover, for instance, whether these relationships will be the same in other communities studied. I suspect even the basic organization sets will be quite different. At any rate, the strategy of using the same measures systematically will allow for some interesting covariance analyses. I believe the study design also included measures of field-level properties using the same perceptual measures.

In general, I am uneasy about using only perceptual measures for organizational properties. They do not necessarily correlate highly with behavioral or global measures. This uneasiness applies even more to the use of perceptual measures for field-level variables. I would suggest that my characterization of interorganizational studies is applicable to this paper. There is a certain abstractness in these organizational measures of the community context. We really don't know very much about the actual relations between these organizations, or about the community context. We really don't know very much about the community determinants of these relationships. Further, coordination would seem to have something to do with efficient and effective exchange of clients; yet we know nothing of the experience of these clients in this system. The clients are in fact most firmly embedded in a community structure. They are likely to be concentrated in certain neighborhoods, to be disproportionately lower-income, with perhaps a sprinkling of alienated middle-class youths from suburbs. In addition, legal and funding structures have been alluded to, but we don't know much about how they affect the organization. I suspect that data like this is known to the researchers, but I think analysis would benefit from having it reported.

My comments on Professor Jerald Hage's paper should be suspect, since I was directly involved with the research project it reports. But I will try to be impartial. The study of mental retardation projects (out of which that paper grew) made one lesson clear to all of us involved: networks of interorganizational relationships are integrally embedded in community and societal structures. The prescriptive model suggested is an attempt to take cognizance of the fact. I think a basic principle involved in this recommendation was not to create just another agency, which would then have to be integrated with all the rest, but to try to link together those agencies at those points of greatest need by making use of the major interest groups in the community. There is still a certain vagueness in the basic recommendation to create jointly funded, domain-specific partial coalitions between agencies. On the one hand, the boards of these joint programs, composed of the three major "estates"—clients, professionals, and influentials—are supposed to exert pressure on legislatures (one wonders at what level) to fund such boards adequately. But then what can account for the creation of such boards in the first place? Perhaps like Topsy, they just grow from voluntarily federated programs or elaborate joint programs. One wonders what would lead the constituent organizations to surrender autonomy to such a semi-autonomous joint board. On the other hand, the lesson of the mental retardation projects seemed to suggest that the federal government could initiate such projects. With enough determination, it seems reasonable to assume that partial coalitions, such as the ones suggested by Professor Hage, could have been successfully implemented by making them a condition of receiving funds and by committing such funds on a permanent basis. A host of political problems are stirred up in the proposal, but none are analyzed or resolved.

Having done the field research on the Cleveland project, I would like to summarize briefly some of the special lessons of that project as I saw them. The project in Cleveland was first conceived in 1963 when it became apparent to elites at the national and community levels that services for the retarded were highly fragmented and largely inadequate. The mental retardation field was an especially fragmented one, not only in the Cleveland area, but also nationally. There was a multiplicity of funding sources, ethnic and religious auspices, class bases, traditions, philosophies, regions, and governmental jurisdictions. These factors have often been recognized as leading to community decentralization and fragmentation. In this context, the Vocational Rehabilitation Agency decided to include Cleveland as one of five cities to receive approximately $100,000 a year for five years for a demonstration project. The purpose was to achieve coordination between community services for the retarded and to increase the overall level of services.

It is interesting to note that the Mental Retardation Project, as it was called in Cleveland, consciously styled itself as a "community organization" project adhering to classic community organizing principles, especially as summarized by Dunham (1970). This ideology, containing both substantive assumptions about the nature of communities, as well as prescriptive recommendations for action, could be termed an "ideology of decentralization." This ideology held, among other things, that both communities and the organizations and groups within them were characterized by a relatively high degree of autonomy; that changes originated from the actions of individuals at the grass roots levels; that governmental bureaucracies were often inefficient and oppressive; that, in order to accomplish community coordination, one should steer as clear of political issues as possible; and that an organizing effort should be decentralized and rely on persuasion since this guarded the individualism and freedom so valued within American culture. I would suggest that these substantive assumptions about the autonomy of organizations are consistent with the assumptions of the interorganizational literature. Both orginated within the same societal and intellectual context, and in many cases, no doubt, there has been diffusion from one discipline to the other.

Thus, the Mental Retardation Project set out to use communication and moral persuasion, implemented through planning committees and planning documents, to induce agencies and individuals to voluntarily adjust their services to one another. This voluntary compliance would fill out a "mosaic" of services, the overall design for which was sketched out in several planning blueprints.

While the project increased awareness of services for the retarded and helped educate many persons about the situation, I think in the end (by 1972) it was apparent that the overall structure of services had not been radically "integrated" by the project's efforts. Important structural changes in services had taken place, but these occurred as a result of systematic state legislation (the 648 and 169 bills passed in 1967). These bills themselves were the product of both federal enabling legislation and the efforts of a complex array of interest groups. Not even this legislation disturbed the power of certain segments of the system of services for the retarded. In many ways, the efforts of the project and of state legislation helped strengthen and integrate several networks of organizations and agencies. These networks, eight of which I have identified, are good empirical examples of "interorganizational collectivities" (ICs), or "community decision organizations" (Warren, 1967b). However, the strengthening of these ICs, in particular their funding bases, made them as collectivities even more resistant to systematic community-wide coordination. Understanding the roots of these cleavages brings us into the thick of community and societal structure.

I think this example points to the usefulness of Professor Van de Ven's concept of interorganizational collectivities. Yet I think it underlines that such ICs themselves are not "social structures" but are historically specific constellations of organizations and individuals whose overall functions and operations must be understood as constituent parts of a larger social system. Further, it seems that the integration of these ICs has been merely assumed. Gouldner's (1959) critique of Parsons seems relevant here. In this case the functional autonomy of the parts of the IC is underplayed. Integration of the IC is seen as a constant, not as a variable which is the product of a complex dialectical interplay between the strains of the actor for autonomy and the attempt of the system to control its members. Thus what is problematic, the degree of integration, is merely assumed. Organizations lose autonomy in the IC; the IC is then seen as a functionally autonomous unit in society, though we have little idea of how it articulates with society.

Clearly, a lot of work remains to be done in order to develop a theory of interorganizational relationships which takes full account of the integral place they have in community and societal structure. Such a synthetic theory would have implications both for organizational theory and for macrosocietal theory. Organizations are seen not as deterministic atoms operating in a generalized field. Rather, they are, to a greater or lesser extent, instruments of social control and social action serving the interests of some groups or individuals and perhaps hurting the interests of others. At the same time, organizations themselves are real social units with their own internal dynamics, with power, and with survival needs which can threaten to subvert the utility of organizational instruments for any rational social ends.

Organizations interact with other organizations, but this interaction is conditioned by the power of groups who control or who are affected by organizations, and by established political, legal, and administrative structures. Individuals or groups which may "control" organizations do not do so voluntarily. They are themselves acting as the result of their positions as individuals or groups in a societal system. Sociologists have tended to look on socioeconomic class as the most important explanatory variable in society; and I think its use is relevant here. Thus, while organizations may be increasing the effective units of action in society, one should not reify the organization and disregard individuals and groups. For instance, in the study of organizational boundary spanners in a community context, their organizational roles could be related to their positions as community influentials, using reputational techniques (Perrucci and Pilisuk, 1970). A similar analysis might be utilized for large business firms. The interrelationships of major organizations and institutions at the national level have been analyzed by several researchers, and the interorganizational affiliations have been shown to be buttressed by familial, social, and school connections (Mills, 1956; Baltzell, 1966).

Community and societal theory, on the other hand, will benefit by incorporating an interorganizational perspective. Turk (1970) has done empirical work in this area, but the idea of the "organizational" society was developed earlier (Etzioni, 1968). The classical societal analysis of both Weber and Marx have emphasized that organizations are important actors in modern society. Even Marx had an implicit theory of interorganizational relationships, though he emphasized always the particular type of organization and its particular time-specific and historically-specific function in the societal system. Thus, the system of relationships which builds up between organizations should be seen not as just a process which takes place *within* a societal context, but as a part of the process of society itself. The system of interorganizational relationships can be a driving force which can lead to fundamental changes of the social system itself.

While the search for legitimation in terms of the cultural values of a given society is one of the major functions of organizations, and presumably this function is served by the external affairs role, another major activity of organizations, and of the interest groups which stand behind them, is the manipulation of those cultural values and the creation of new cultural values in such a manner as to serve their own interests. In other words, there is not a beneficent "group mind" which sees to society's interests handing out certificates to those organizations which serve one of its several necessary functions. Nor is the value structure of society an unchanging and universally valid fact to which organizations must necessarily defer. The value structure is at least partially *responsive* to the interests of individuals, groups, and organizations. Most every large organization worth its salt spends a good deal of money on public relations and lobbying, etc., trying to *create* legitimation rather than just win it.

To summarize briefly, I have suggested that the analytical focus on organizations as the unit of analysis has led to a substantive assumption that organizational units are functionally autonomous. This assumption has been reinforced by the practical concerns of government and business, both of whom have accepted the existing societal structure as given, and have been concerned primarily with manipulating the individual organization or sets of organizations within that structure. However, researchers have increasingly looked for a more comprehensive theoretical framework through which to comprehend interorganizational relationships. The assumption of functional autonomy has hampered the efforts of theorists by diverting their attention away from the "field" level of analysis. While interorganizational networks are themselves constitutive of community and societal structure, researchers have tended not to use models and techniques already developed for those levels. An attempt to synthesize the interorganizational and the community and societal literatures would be mutually enriching. The end result might not only be a better understanding of the environmental constraints on organizations, but an organizational conception of communities and societies in which organizations would be seen as important actors in societal systems.

REFERENCES

Aiken, Michael, and Jerald Hage. "Organizational Interdependence and Intra-
1968   Organizational Structure." *American Sociological Review*, 30:912–30.
Baltzell, E. Digby. *The Protestant Establishment*. New York: Vintage Books.
1966
Boddewyn, J. J. "External Affairs: A Corporate Function in Search of Conceptualiza-
1974   tion and Theory." *Organization and Administrative Sciences*, 5:67–112.
Clark, Burton. "Interorganizational Patterns in Education." *Administrative Science*
1965   *Quarterly*, 10:224–37.
Dunham, Arthur. *The New Community Organization*. New York: Crowell.
1970
Emery, F. E., and E. L. Trist. "The Causal Texture of Organizational Environments."
1965   *Human Relations*, 18:21–32.
Etzioni, Amitai. *The Active Society*. New York: The Free Press.
1968
Evan, William M. "The Organization-Set: Toward a Theory of Interorganizational
1966   Relations." In J. D. Thompson (ed.), *Approaches to Organizational Design*:
        173–91. Pittsburgh: University of Pittsburgh Press.

Gouldner, Alvin W.   "Reciprocity and Autonomy in Functional Theory." In L. Gross
1959   (ed.), *Symposium on Sociological Theory*. Evanston, Ill.: University of
   Illinois Press.
Guetzkow, Harold.   "Relations Among Organizations." In Raymond V. Bowers
1966   (ed.), *Studies on Behavior in Organizations*: 13–44. Athens, Georgia: University of Georgia.
Hage, Jerald.   "A Strategy for Creating Interdependent Delivery Systems to Meet
1974   Complex Needs." *Organization and Administrative Sciences*, 5:17–44.
Hall, Richard H., and John P. Clark.   "Problems in the Study of Interorganizational
1973   Relationships." *Organization and Administrative Science*, 5, 1:45–60.
Kaufman, Harold F.   "Toward an Interactional Conception of Community." *Social
1959   Forces*, 38:8–17.
Lawrence, Paul R., and Jay W. Lorsch.   *Organization and Environment*. Boston:
1967   Graduate School of Business, Harvard University Press.
Levine, Sol, and Paul E. White.   "Exchange as a Conceptual Framework for
1961   the Study of Interorganizational Relationships." *Administrative Science
   Quarterly*, 5:583–601.
Mills, C. W.   *The Power Elite*. New York: Oxford University Press.
1956
Perrucci, Robert, and Marc Pilisuk.   "Leaders and Ruling Elites: The Interorganiza-
1970   tional Bases of Community Power." *American Sociological Review*, 35:
   1040–57.
Selznick, Philip.   *TVA and the Grass Roots*. Berkeley, Calif.: University of California
1949   Press.
Turk, Herman.   "Comparative Urban Structure from an Interorganizational Perspec-
1973   tive." *Administrative Science Quarterly*, 18:37–55.
————.   "Interorganizational Networks in Urban Society: Initial Perspectives
1970   and Comparative Research." *American Sociological Review*, 35:1–18.
Van de Ven, Andrew, Dennis C. Emmett, and Richard Koenig, Jr.   "Frameworks
1974   for Interorganizational Analysis." *Organization and Administrative Sciences*,
   5:113–30.
Warren, Roland.   "The Interorganizational Field as a Focus of Investigation."
1967a   *Administrative Science Quarterly*, 12:396–419.
————.   "The Interaction of Community Organizations: Some Basic Concepts
1967b   and Needed Research." *Social Service Review*, 41:261–70.
Wrong, Dennis.   "The Oversocialized Conception of Man in Modern Sociology."
1961   *American Sociological Review*, 26:183–93.

4

An Organization-Environment Perspective on Cooperation and Conflict between Organizations in the Manpower Training System

HOWARD ALDRICH

Organizational theorists have been concerned for some time with conflict within organizations, e.g., conflict between staff and line (Dalton, 1959), between departments (Crozier, 1964), and between labor and management (Kerr and Seigel, 1954). Conflict between organizations has received less attention, and most of it has been at the theoretical rather than empirical level (Litwak and Hylton, 1962; Warren, 1967; and Ridgeway, 1957). The problem of studying conflict between organizations is part of the larger problem of investigating relations between organizations; thus, progress in the former awaits new developments in the latter (Aldrich, 1971). In this paper I wish to argue that an open-systems perspective, which focuses on a population of organizations in interaction with its environment, provides an approach to the study of conflict between organizations that is theoretically sound and feasible for empirical testing.

After summarizing the major components to an organization-environment perspective on organizational behavior, I will present typologies of environmental dimensions and interorganizational dimensions. Since my current research involves the study of manpower training and related organizations, examples used in these sections will be taken from the manpower training system. The final section of this paper is a brief discussion of propositions about conflict and cooperation between organizations, based upon an organization-environment perspective.

THE ORGANIZATION-ENVIRONMENT PERSPECTIVE

We require a model of the organizational and environmental factors that affect the potential for forming cooperative or competitive relations within organization-sets or interorganizational fields to predict which outcome will be observed. This section will summarize the open-systems model of organizations previously discussed (Aldrich, 1971), describe the population of manpower organizations being studied, and then discuss two alternative models of an organizational population's structure.

There are two major differences between an organization-environment approach and the more traditional approach to organizational analysis: (1.) an emphasis on factors making for intraorganizational conflict and variation as opposed to a concern for internal cooperation and stability; and (2.) an emphasis on turnover and conflict within a population of organizations as opposed to the study of individual organizations. There are a great number of disintegrative or independence-generating forces at work within organizations, as Sjoberg (1960), Gouldner (1959), and others have noted. Within organizations, there are conflicts over priorities in maximizing values, and over the structure and consequences of the distribution of authority. There are conflicts between internal organizational objectives and external sources of demand. The environment itself sometimes makes multiple and conflicting demands on the organization (Dill, 1958).

The occurrence of internal variations is essential if organizations are to respond to environmental changes. Sources of variation act as "a potential pool of adaptive variability to meet the problem of mapping new or more detailed variety and constraints in a changeable environment" (Buckley, 1967:63). Those aspects of organizational variability that most closely map the environment are selectively chosen or reinforced through both internal and external selection mechanisms. Internally, the selection mechanism can either be formalized in the planning process or left informal through the acts of boundary personnel and others who deal directly with environmental influences (Aldrich and Reiss, 1971). Externally, the selection function is performed by the organization's environment by selective reinforcement of organizational activities.

An emphasis on turnover and conflict within a population of organizations is required because the problem with traditional approaches has been that organizational properties have been investigated without regard to their contributions to fitness in varying or diverse organizational environments. We have not investigated the question of what particular combinations of internal characteristics are most effective in permitting organizational survival and growth, and we have only recently begun to make distinctions between major classes of organizations, e.g., on the basis of technology (Perrow, 1967; Woodward, 1965).

Organizations, from our perspective, will be treated as goal-directed, boundary-maintaining, information-processing activity systems. As such, organizations are characterized by internal variation and diversity, and their survival and growth is dependent on their ability to adapt to environmental contingencies and constraints. Other key concepts in this approach include the idea of task environment, domain, and organizational subsystems.

The task environment of an organization concerns those parts of the environment which are relevant or potentially relevant to the goal setting, goal attainment, survival, or effectiveness of the organization (Dill, 1958; Thompson, 1967). This definition brings into the organization's environment both the general conditions that affect all organizations and the specific influences that have a direct effect on particular organizations (Hall, 1972: 298). Hall, by making a distinction between general and specific environments, brings to the surface a problem that plagues this area of study: to what extent need the theorist be concerned with demonstrating a concrete link between something in the organization's environment, and change or reaction in the organization's behavior? In my research, I have tried to make such a link as explicit as possible. Hall describes the specific environment as being composed of the organizations and individuals in direct interaction with the organization, a definition very close to the idea of "domain" (as will be discussed below).

An organization's task environment is defined in my research as consisting of all parts of the environment potentially or actually relevant to the organization's behavior. This emphasizes the fact that an organization need not be aware of its environment—in the sense of monitoring all important aspects—for the environment to have an effect on the organization. Open-systems theory makes problematic the extent to which the information-gathering and processing units for the organization do, in fact, recognize and react to the significant parts of the task environment. Regardless of its level of awareness, the organization is still in contact with its environment at many points, given that practically all organizations by definition are open systems and are open to exchanges or transactions with their environment. It is through these boundary-crossing transactions that organizations obtain needed resources and dispose of the products or services they offer.

The domain of the organization is a subset of the task environment and refers to the range of activities claimed by the organization for itself as its particular arena of operation (Levine and White, 1961). Defining domain as the "claimed" environment emphasizes the fact that the organization may find its claim resisted by other elements in its task environment, and conflict may arise over the question of domain legitimacy. The input domain consists of those points at which the organization is dependent on inputs from the environment, and can be broken down into two dimensions: (1.) the range of products or services needed and the means (technology) used to acquire them; and (2.) the population of suppliers, which may be called the domain population. The output domain consists of those points at which the organization is dependent upon exchanging its products or services for resources from the environment. What Katz and Kahn

(1966) call the "through-put" of the organization is exchanged for the generalized resources needed to acquire the more specific resources required by the input domain. Two dimensions are important: (1.) the population served, or the domain population; and (2.) the range of products or services produced, along with the means used by the organization to dispose of them.

In focusing on the relationship between organizations and their environments, the investigator is alerted to the need to determine what it is that flows between the organization and the environment or other organizations. To this point I have conceptualized the environment in terms of input and output domains within a larger task environment. In a subsequent section I will list some dimensions of the environment that refer in a general way to "elements" in the organization's environment. Here, however, I will define these elements as either the resources sought after by the organization, or the units that possess or control resources.

A general definition of *resources* is "the generalized means, or facilities, that are potentially controllable by social organizations, and that are potentially usable—however indirectly—in relationships between the organization and its environment" (Yuchtman and Seashore, 1967:900). This definition has several advantages, as noted by Yuchtman and Seashore. First, it does not attribute directionality as an inherent quality of resource, leaving open the question of whether the resource is acquired in a competitive or cooperative situation. Second, this definition does not limit the concept of resources to physical or economic objects or states; hence, information can be a resource. Third, this definition implicitly recognizes the importance of organizational boundaries by use of the term "potential control" over resources.

I have found it useful to think of four types of resources: (1.) personnel; (2.) information; (3.) products and services; and (4.) operating funds, including accumulations of capital. Resources are most valuable when they are: (1.) highly liquid and thus can be quickly converted into something else needed by the organization; (2.) stable, and thus can be accumulated or stored; (3.) universal and required by many or all types of organizations; and (4.) unique, in the sense that other resources cannot readily be substituted in their place. Yuchtman and Seashore (1967) define effectiveness as the organization's ability to exploit its environment in the acquisition of resources. Effectiveness is thus a function of an organization's bargaining position in its environment.

ORGANIZATIONS IN THE MANPOWER TRAINING SYSTEM

The population of organizations currently under investigation (in the context of the above perspective) is the set of manpower programs and associated organizations that have been created by the federal government, with the involvement of state and local governments, in the past ten years. Manpower development programs in the ad hoc and evolving systems focus on providing or upgrading the work-related skills of individuals and/or instilling or improving attitudes and beliefs that are assumed to make individuals employable. Although these objectives appear straight-forward, their implementation has been problematic, as "we still have a cumbersome network of channels administering fragmented, overlapping, and sometimes competitive programs, often with gaps served by no pro-grams, and without clearcut allocation of responsibility or sufficient flexibil-ity to reform itself" (Lovell, 1972). Programs have been created by separate legislation to meet specific perceived needs of individuals in the work force, with authority over the programs being given to a variety of federal level units and delegated in differing ways to the state and local levels.

The rapid growth of the manpower sector, from $56 million in appro-priations in 1963 to about $3.1 billion in 1973, has left organizational domains, lines of authority, manpower development technology, and other organizational matters in a state of flux. Along the way, a number of attempts have been made to rationalize the "system," e.g., the Cooperative Area Manpower Planning Systems (CAMPS) which was begun in 1967. CAMPS attempted to bring together state and local manpower program personnel at a regional level in order to coordinate manpower programs in the area. However, as Lovell points out (1972:4), "it proved to be a useful informa-tion-sharing device, but was not adequate to overcome constraints of program categorization and divided lines of responsibility for different programs."

The manpower training system (or nonsystem) that has evolved as a result of federal and state legislation thus provides an ideal context for an investigation of propositions concerning conflict within a population of organizations. First, although programs are derived from federal legislation in most cases, the constraints on local community manpower organizations are fairly general policy-type directives which leave a great deal of freedom for the organizations to respond to state and local conditions. Indeed, regardless of the various federal (and state) policy constraints on program operations, the fact is that employment problems are implicitly treated as local problems in the present system because of the way programs are structured. Consequently, local conditions are important determinants of actual behavior of the network of manpower and related organizations. These considerations suggest that the relevant level of analysis is the com-munity, or metropolitan area, therefore reducing the problem of data collection and aggregation to a manageable level and also bringing into relief an important set of contextual variables.

Second, the manpower training system at the community level is made up of a highly heterogeneous group of organizations. Included are the manpower organizations themselves (generally sponsored by the Employment Service, a local OEO agency, the Chamber of Commerce, the Board of Education, or other nonprofit community organizations); private businesses and nonprofit organizations that send or receive persons to and from manpower organizations; the State Employment and Testing Service, which may function as a linking point between manpower and other organizations; community or neighborhood "action" groups that are interested in economic and political benefits for their constituency; and other local organizations that may at one time or another have some contact with one of the organizations in the system. The heterogeneity of the population of organizations to be studied means that there is a great deal of variation in the variables I will be using as operational indicators of the concepts making up the perspective.

TWO MODELS OF THE ORGANIZATIONAL POPULATION'S
STRUCTURE

The variance of two major dependent variables will be accounted for in this study. Both concern relations between organizations, but are at different levels of analysis. The first is the nature of the relationship between a particular organization and other organizations in its organization-set. (The characteristics of the relationships to be examined will be discussed later.) Most interorganizational analysis deals with this level, i.e., the relationship of individual organizations to one another. The second outcome to be accounted for is the nature of the relationship between the entire set of organizations in the environment studied. Here, emphasis is on the state of the network of relations in the population of organizations, i.e., an aggregate or emergent outcome of the interaction of many paired interactions.

The first dependent variable concerns the organization-set, viewed from the perspective of a focal organization; the second dependent variable concerns the interorganizational field, viewed from the perspective of the intersection of many organization-sets. In each case, we can visualize the properties of the organizational network in terms of a continuum with two extremes:

A. A network of complementary and supplementary relationships between manpower and other types of organizations; or

B. A network of competitive and antagonistic relationships between manpower and other types of organizations.

Major problems of operationalizing these two outcomes confront us, but it is clear that we would begin at the level of specific properties of one-to-one relationships and work our way up. What these properties might be will be discussed later.

At this point it may be useful to briefly indicate the general outlines of the abstract argument for predicting one outcome or the other. Note again that we are speaking of two ideal types and that reality falls somewhere in between. The general argument is based upon the theory of functional differentiation and integregation, as discussed by Durkheim (1949), Hawley (1950), Mayhew (1971), Warren (1967), and others. Technology, ideology, and environment are the chief components of the theory that will be stressed here.

Outcome Type A

An expectation of a network of complementary and supplementary relationships is based upon the idea that "the division of labor and the differentiation of control over resources makes groups interested in forming stable relationships" (Mayhew, 1971 : 215). Technological differences and environmental constraints on organizational expansion lead to organizational interdependencies and the founding of complementary relationships (Aiken and Hage, 1968). Ideological similarities, e.g., common goals and shared definitions of the situation, and the drive for domain expansion and acquisition lead to coalition formation and supplementary relationships.

Linkages based upon complementary and supplementary interests can be considered investments made by organizations. Organizations have an interest in protecting and stabilizing their relations with others, and the resulting pattern of interorganizational relations can be thought of as a network of vested interests (Mayhew, 1971 : 215). In the manpower training interorganizational field, the technological and administrative rationales of the various organizations involved appear to be derived from a common and shared definition of the situation, i.e., that individual disabilities are at the root of employment problems. In addition, the legitimation and source of authority of the various organizations is based upon their relationship to the existing political structure of the local community and the state and federal governments (Warren, et al., 1973).

The resulting network of organization-sets would be highly stable, for as Mayhew points out, it is supported at three levels: first, at the level of individual organizations seeking certainty in their relations with their environments; second, at the level of vested interests between pairs of organizations; and third, at the level of institutional legitimacy of the normative and legal order in which relations are based upon the exchange of specialized services between interdependent organizations.

Outcome Type B

The above argument for expecting a network of complementary and cooperative relations in an organization-set or interorganizational field is quite persuasive; but an argument can also be made for expecting a network of competitive and antagonistic relations. We begin with the assumptions that manpower organizations are technologically very similar, have overlapping domains, and compete for public funds and clients. Being technologically very similar, in the sense of drawing upon a common pool of "manpower specialists" and "disadvantaged clients," such organizations are put into competitive positions vis-a-vis one another. Legislative definitions and prescriptions of manpower goals leave the questions of organizational boundaries ambiguous and thus make organizations anxious about protecting their boundaries and conserving or expanding their claimed domain. Ideological differences between publicly sponsored and privately sponsored organizations lead to battles over the form that public intervention into the labor market should take; and even subtle differences in ideology can provide occasions for conflict or coalition formation between the manpower organizations themselves.

Under these assumptions, accommodation and cooperation are simply tactics that are used in the long-run struggle for organizational autonomy and a better bargaining position in the organization-set or interorganizational field (Miller, 1958). As Perrow (1972) argues, organizations must be seen as tools, with men struggling for their control. Because organizations are powerful tools, the men who control them acquire power to shape the world as they wish it to be shaped. Similarly, control over an organization-set or interorganizational field is also an important resource and is equally contested.

Olson's (1965) work on the logic of collective action is highly relevant here, as he argues that it is theoretically implausible to expect to find a large set of organizations cooperating to take action on behalf of their collective self-interest. Interestingly enough, Warren, et al. (1973) began their study of model cities organizations with the expectation that they would find change, conflict, and in general a great deal of interorganizational activity, but found instead that mild cooperation in the field was the normal state of affairs. The present research effort can be seen as an attempt to replicate this study (and perhaps findings?) on a different set of organizations.

There are few a priori reasons for predicting one or the other outcome, given the weak state of development of the perspective discussed here. Nevertheless, it seems fruitful to attempt to specify the properties of the environment and the organizational characteristics that would prove most useful in making predictions. The following discussion is based upon the open-systems perspective on organization-environment interactions discussed in Aldrich (1971) and Aldrich and Reiss (1971), and based upon the work of Buckle (1967), Thompson (1967), Aiken and Hage (1968), and others. While we can make only weak predictions at present (i.e., the presence or absence of zero-order correlations), they will hopefully become stronger as research progresses.

DIMENSIONS OF ORGANIZATIONAL ENVIRONMENTS

The key requirement of our organization-environment perspective is a delineation of environmental dimensions. These dimensions will be operationalized to serve as the independent variables in a model that predicts the nature of relations between organizations in an organization-set or interorganizational field. I begin at the level of dimensions that are clearly relevant to relations between pairs of organizations. In keeping with my desire to include organized and unorganized elements of organizational environments in the model, I have searched for environmental characteristics that relate to both.

A search of the literature on organizations and their environments reveals seven dimensions that various investigators have identified as important. Organizations are conceptualized as open systems, internally differentiated into organizational subsystems which may be only loosely joined to one another. Thus, while one dimension of the environment may be of special significance for one organizational subsystem, it may have little relevance for another.

Each dimension should be viewed as a continuum rather than a dichotomy, and it is hoped that each can be operationalized in such a way as to preserve the full range of variation implied in describing the dimension as a continuum. The examples chosen to illustrate each dimension are drawn from the manpower study, from my study of small business organizations (Aldrich, 1969), and other areas. I will note, in passing, theorists who have contributed to the conceptualization of some dimensions. Examples of the operationalization of each concept will be given after each definition.

1. Stability (instability): the degree of turnover in the elements of the task environment, whether these elements are persons or organizations. Examples: (1.) clients—turnover in the domain population; (2.) organizations—turnover in the population of organizations which accept referrals from manpower programs.

A stable environment implies that organizations will be able to develop fixed sets of routines for dealing with environmental elements and consequently fairly formalized relations should develop (Thompson, 1967). Other things being equal, organizations will be positively selected on the basis of age when the environment is stable, i.e., the longer an organization is in the environment, the more it learns, and it thus acquires an advantage over new organizations. Conversely, when an environment moves from stable to unstable, established organizations should have more difficulty in coping with the change than new organizations. This dilemma is illustrated by the current problems of State Employment Service offices which are staffed by career civil servants and have evolved into a bureaucratic structure that apparently is highly resistant to change. The "new" manpower organizations complain that the Employment Service doesn't respond quickly enough to their requests and the newly militant (and sometimes organized) clients complain of the seemingly unsympathetic manner in which they are treated.

The small business study has found that turnover in a business's population of customers from white to black because of migration to the suburbs has a drastic affect on a business's ability to cope with its environment. The new customer population is highly unstable and traditionally entrepreneurial notions of "steady customers" are becoming inappropriate.

2. *Homogeneity (heterogeneity):* the degree of similarity between the elements of the population dealt with, including organizations as well as individuals. Examples: (1.) clients—the racial and educational distribution of the domain population; (2.) organizations—the organizational mix of the community in terms of the number of different industries represented.

A homogeneous environment rewards the development of standardized ways of treating the domain population and may lead to the development of an undifferentiated set of products or services (Thompson, 1967). Homogeneity simplifies organizational behavior because a small set of operating routines may suffice for a large population; however, homogeneity can be troublesome and can lead to conflict if an organization seeks to transform its rather homogeneous clients into highly differentiated outputs. For example, state universities that admit a homogeneously defined population, i.e., state high school graduates, have difficulty developing routines that transform this population into outputs specialized by subject matter. University systems adapt by differentiating themselves into campuses specialized by the nature of the client, e.g., junior colleges, four-year colleges, and universities, and by screening the population of inputs periodically so that the clients are soon recorded in the filing system of the university as differentiated by skill level, motivation, etc.

Manpower organizations by law are assigned quite heterogeneous client populations and thus we might expect them to adopt strategies for obtaining a more homogeneous population. At the level of the manpower training system as an interorganizational field, what we have observed in the past decade is a proliferation of programs that have had the implicit effect of expanding the range of clients covered while at the same time narrowing the range of any one program. Even within the range of clients and organizations assigned to a program, we still observe organizations making further attempts to obtain the most desirable elements. This process is called "creaming" when done to select the best qualified (but disadvantaged) clients.

3. Concentration (dispersion): the degree to which the population dealt with is evenly distributed over the range of the organization's domain (Emery and Trist, 1965). Examples: (1.) clients—the "ghettoization" of the domain population, e.g., in schools for the Neighborhood Youth Corps; (2.) organizations—the proportion of the labor force employed by the handful of large organizations in the area.

When resources are randomly distributed over a domain, little organizational learning is possible beyond the development of simple tactics for approaching the scattered resources. If, however, resources are concentrated in identifiable units, then strategies for exploiting the organization's position can be worked out. Position in the environment becomes important when elements are concentrated rather than dispersed in a random fashion.

In the case of small businesses, the migration of middle income whites from the central city to the suburbs has dispersed customers over the metropolitan area. Since many small businesses depend upon customers living near the site for their steady business, such dispersal makes survival problematic. Businesses can adapt by following population concentrations to the more affluent suburbs, or by locating in centrally located shopping centers, which in a sense concentrate the domain population by maximizing access to it. From the population's point of view, what is concentrated is a group of essential retail and service businesses at an easily accessible location.

Manpower organizations appear to adapt to concentrations of the relevant environment by first, changing their recruiting and intake procedures, and second, by taking more drastic steps. When the concentration is due to the presence of another organization, e.g., the schools in the case of the Neighborhood Youth Corps, the organization adapts by establishing a relationship with that organization, albeit generally a nonformalized one. Concentrations of scarce resources, such as professional educators skilled in vocational training, may attract a large number of manpower organizations with attendant competition for their services; e.g., in New York State the Boards of Cooperative Educational Services face this situation and adapt by attempting to ration their resources among the competing manpower organizations.

4. Environmental Capacity (rich/lean): the relative level of resources available to an organization within its domain. This dimension can be conceptualized as the degree to which an organization has to expand its domain to obtain the resources it requires, either to achieve stability or growth. Examples: (1.) clients—the mean education or income level of the domain population; (2.) organizations—the total number of different organizations represented in the community, including business and social welfare organizations.

Organizations have access to more resources in rich environments, but of course such environments also attract other organizations. Stockpiling and hoarding of resources is probably not as prevalent in rich as in lean environments. Lean environments also promote cutthroat competitive practices, and apart from rewarding organizations capable of stockpiling and hoarding, lean environments also reward efficiency as well as effectiveness of operation.

Two basic alternatives are open to organizations in lean environments: either leave or develop more efficient and effective operations. Effectiveness can be accomplished by improving efficiency, merging with other organizations, becoming more aggressive in soliciting business, or finding a protected subenvironment of resources, i.e., specializing. Organizational density is probably greater in rich environments and the organizational stratification hierarchy is also more pronounced.

Most manpower organizations operate in relatively rich environments, although they seem to have difficulty exploiting this fact. Rich environments can be seen on the one hand as a barrier to the formation of interorganizational relations, at least of the more formalized kind. According to Aiken and Hage (1968), the need for resources is an important determinant of the formation of linkages with others, and this "push" factor is missing for organizations in rich environments. On the other hand, a rich environment can be seen as a precondition to the formation of interorganizational linkages, since matters of domain protection and survival would not be as salient for organizations in rich as compared with lean environments. In rich environments we would expect more intense interaction, following the latter argument, and reciprocity would be less problematic than in lean environments.

5. *Domain Consensus (dissensus):* the degree to which the organization's claim to a specific domain is disputed or recognized by other organizations (Levine and White, 1961). This variable can be conceptualized at the institutional level or the interorganizational field level. Examples: (1.) organizations—instances of domain conflict reported; (2.) organizations—action that is taken when services are duplicated by two or more organizations.

The concept of domain consensus is a dynamic one and several hypotheses about organizational development can be derived from it. For example, organizations attempt to capture a domain by differentiating themselves from other organizations with highly similar goals. The achievement of domain consensus can be viewed as a process involving cooperation, conflict, negotiation, and so forth.

Small businesses appear to get involved fairly often in matters involving domain defense. One example is the process of advertising competition between businesses offering similar or substitutable goals. A less obvious example is the battle over zoning laws in developing suburbs, where (perceived) incompatible land users battle with one another over the right to locate at choice sites.

Manpower organizations are particularly sensitive to encroachment on their domain, and a great deal of interorganizational contact involves negotiations over claimed areas of competence. The CAMPS system, for example, involves a good deal of this type of interaction. Much of the conflict over domain takes place vertically, with manpower organizations and programs attempting to have their claimed domain statutorily defined by state or federal governmental intervention. In the recent history of disputes over CAMPS, such disputes go all the way up to the cabinet level.

6. *Turbulence (placidness)*: the extent to which the environments of the focal organization are being disturbed or changed by other external activities (Terreberry, 1968). This dimension can be conceptualized in terms of externally induced changes in the interorganizational field, e.g., through federal intervention in the local labor market. Examples: (1.) organizations—rapid increase in area manpower programs; (2.) organizations—businesses affected by state-wide economic trends, population movements, etc.

Manpower programs present one example of turbulence as far as small businesses are concerned. To the extent that institutional training and similar "hold-in-training" programs provide an attractive substitute to high-turnover, low-wage jobs in a community, such programs are a source of turbulence in the small business labor market.

Terreberry argues that organizational environments are becoming increasingly turbulent because of the complexity and rapidity of change in the causal interconnectedness of organizational environments. Indeed, this is an accurate description of the history of manpower training programs, as program has been piled on top of program with a geometric increase in the number of potential links between programs. Implied in this change is a decrease in organizational autonomy and the ability of individual organizations to plan for the future.

7. *Mutability (immutability)*: the extent to which the environment is open to manipulation and change by means of organizational activities. Examples: (1.) clients—personal characteristics of domain population that make them difficult to resocialize; (2.) organizations—extent to which the organization dealt with is constrained in its actions by virtue of links to other organizations or sponsors.

Most of the other dimensions carry the implication that the environment is doing something to the organization, whereas this dimension calls our attention to the fact that a great deal of organizational activity is directed toward changing certain aspects of the environment, or "doing something" to the environment. Perhaps mutability/immutability of the environment should not be introduced into the analysis until an investigator is able to reliably characterize the environment in terms of the six environmental dimensions previously introduced. I take this position because one could argue that whether the environment is stable, homogeneous, and so forth, will undoubtedly determine the degree to which it is open to organizational influence.

This dimension clearly has two sides to it, especially with reference to the manpower training system. On the one hand, we can talk in abstract terms of the vulnerability of the environment to organizational influence; but, on the other hand, we ultimately must specify "vulnerable to what?" The mutability of the environment basically depends upon what tactics or strategy the organization uses to attack it. This, in turn, is a function of the internal structure and resources of the organization. Predicting the potential for success in changing an aspect of the organization's environment requires an investigator to assess the adequacy and appropriateness of the techniques chosen vis-a-vis a specific environment. Thus, this dimension may not be separable from the previous six dimensions plus the characteristics of the organization itself.

DIMENSIONS OF INTERORGANIZATIONAL RELATIONS

The previous section dealt with the environment as a determinant of client-organization or organization-organization links, and by implication as an influence on internal organization structure. This section concerns the second part of this causal scheme, with interorganizational or client-organization links being treated as the dependent variable in a discussion of the dimensions of such relations.

In some cases I wish to talk about the relation of the organizations to other organizations, while in others I wish to talk about the organization's relations with elements in its environment that are not organizations, e.g., clients. This difference can be kept salient by following Warren's (1967) distinction between an analysis of an organization's position in its environment and an analysis of its relations with other organizations on a one-to-one basis. In examining organizational positions, one studies the relationship of the organization to sources of input, targets of output, clients, and so forth. This includes what Hall (1972) labels the "general environment." In examining specific links with other organizations, we narrow our focus to the study of particular interactional episodes or linkages. Phrased in this fashion, interorganizational analysis is a part of organization-environment analysis. This nesting of the two types of analyses pose difficulty for us only in those cases where the elements in the environment are not other organizations but are instead persons, institutions, or norms and values. The problem arises because we have not developed a very good vocabulary for describing such noninterorganizational relationships.

Since this study is mainly concerned with interorganizational relationships, all I will do at this point is indicate that the most general organization-environment relationship is a power relation (Emerson, 1962). Power, defined in organization-environment terms, is a property of social relations, not of individuals. Emerson points out that power resides implicitly in one actor's dependence upon another. Two propositions may be derived from this view of power. First, the dependence of A upon B is directly proportional to A's need for the resources controlled by B. Second, dependence is inversely proportional to the availability of these resources to A outside of the A-B relationship (Emerson, 1962). As noted by Blau (1964 : 124), there are four alternatives open to A if he wishes to avoid dependence on B: he can supply B with resources of equal value; he can attempt to obtain the resources elsewhere; he can take them by force; or he can do without. As the analysis progresses, I hope to develop a better conceptualization of nonorganizational linkages.

Properties of relations between organizations have received some attention in the literature. Marrett (1971) recently reviewed past studies of social welfare and social welfare agencies and derived a list of four dimensions of interorganizational relations. With minor variations, these four dimensions will serve as the initial dependent variables and later as building blocks in my analysis of relations between organizations in organization-sets and interorganizational fields. The dimensions and examples of each are as follows:

Formalization

This dimension is very similar to the concept of formalization as employed in intraorganizational analysis (Hage and Aiken, 1967), and can be disaggregated into two subdimensions:

A. Agreement formalization: the extent to which the transaction between two organizations or groups is given official recognition. Example: A relationship is "formal" if it is legislatively mandated, as is often the case with the State Employment Service. At one end of the continuum of agreement formalizations are the ad hoc arrangements made with other organizations on a temporary or intermittent basis, e.g., a chance referral from a local voluntary association to a manpower program. At the other end of the continuum is the explicit agreement entered into by institutional training centers under MDTA to refer all persons desiring placement in jobs through the State Employment Service.

B. Structural formalization: the extent to which an intermediary coordinates the relationship. Example: "Informal," if contact takes place solely through mutual clients rather than through an intermediary. No intermediary, in general, intervenes between the Neighborhood Youth Corps and the organizations to which it refers people, whereas the State Employment Service is responsible for processing and recording all transactions made between institutional training centers and private employers. Indeed, one of the more interesting features of the manpower training system is great variability across programs in the extent to which they are required to and/or actually do use the State Employment Service or some other organization as an intermediary in their relations with clients and organizations.

Intensity

This dimension concerns the degree of involvement between organizations and, hopefully, will assist us in quantifying the strength of a relation between organizations. This dimension is, in a sense, an operationalization of Mayhew's (1971 : 215) notion of the *investment* organizations have in their relations with others. Two subdimensions can be distinguished:

A. Size of the resource investment: the magnitude of an organization's resources committed to a relationship. Example: The number of services received from or provided to another organization. The manpower training system is interesting in this respect in that if a manpower organization is operating effectively, nearly all of its resources are committed to other organizations. I will use this dimension mainly in differentiating between organizations that commit their resources to only a small set of organizations versus those that spread their resources over a wide range of other types of organizations.

B. Frequency of interaction: the amount of contact between organizations, to be measured in relation to an organization's total contact with others. Example: How often during the year the requesting organization asks for referrals. Some manpower programs mandate a weekly contact between the local manpower organization and organizations to which clients are referred. Other programs leave the matter open, with the amount of contact dependent upon such things as "problem clients," seasonal demands for referrals, etc.

Reciprocity

Reciprocity refers to the symmetry of a relation between two or more organizations and ultimately has to do with what I described earlier as the degree of dependence in a relation. As Marrett (1971 :83–99) notes, the concept of dependence is difficult to work with and for the moment I will deal with only the following two subdimensions:

A. Resource reciprocity: the degree to which the resources in a transaction are mutually exchanged. Example: The balance between referrals sent to and those received from another organization. At one extreme are unilateral transactions where resources flow in only one direction. At the other extreme are reciprocal transactions where the flow in one direction is balanced by a flow in the other direction. Marrett notes a related type of transaction, where resources flow jointly from two or more organizations to a third party; but this type of relation is actually a composite of the two subdimensions and will concern us when we move beyond one-to-one relationships to an analysis at the organization-set or interorganizational field level.

The manpower training system is similar to other populations of public organizations in that there is no currency of exchange that functions as money does in the private sector. Transactions between organizations in the manpower training system quite often involve exchanges "in kind," rather than the flow of highly liquid and stable financial resources that characterize the private, profit-oriented sector. However, as noted earlier, the manpower training system is a mix of profit and nonprofit organizations, and the inducement for profit-oriented organizations to participate in a program often includes an exchange of funds (see White, Levine, and Vlasak 1973, for an excellent discussion of the difference between the profit and nonprofit sector). In the absence of a stable and liquid resource, achieving a balanced exchange in a transaction will always be problematic.

B. Definitional reciprocity: the extent to which the terms of the interaction are mutually reached. Example: Flexibility allowed the program by statutory guidelines in terms of setting entry and exit criteria. Some manpower organizations unilaterally set the conditions under which they will deal with others, usually because of policy constraints imposed by higher authorities. Other manpower organizations are able to exercise some discretion and to negotiate the terms of a transaction. Of course, the same situation applies in the case of nonmanpower organizations; some private or nonprofit organizations bargain over the conditions of their entry into a transaction, while others set conditions (generally threshold-type conditions) under which they will take part.

Standardization

Previous dimensions dealt with the background conditions and general terms of a relation between organizations, whereas the standardization dimension concerns the specific details of a transaction. As implied earlier, standardization is an especially difficult problem as far as nonprofit organizations are concerned. Two subdimensions may be noted:

A. Unit standardization: the fixedness of the units of exchange. Example: The heterogeneity of referrals received from or sent to another organization. This dimension subsumes some of my earlier discussion of the characteristics of resources required by organizations, including the notions of liquidity, stability, universality, and uniqueness. The underlying implication of this dimension is that the more unstandardized the units involved, the more problematic the transaction between organizations and the higher the probability of conflict.

B. Procedural standardization: the fixedness of the procedures for exchange. Example: Routine versus case-by-case basis for dealing with another organization. Even though an agreement may be formalized, the exact procedures for carrying out a transaction may remain ill defined and subject to case-by-case variation. Organizations in the manpower training system are people-processing institutions and since people are reactive objects, it is not surprising that the boundary-spanning components of manpower and associated organizations occasionally have to vary from set procedures (or not even establish them) to take into account the peculiarities of a case.

The four dimensions of interorganizational relations listed above guided the study design and the kinds of questions asked in interviews with informants. They are clearly relevant to a population of social service types of organizations; however, their applicability to other populations of organizations remains an open question. At the theoretical level, all four dimensions are perfectly general, but whether they can be operationalized and applied in other areas will be determined only when someone makes such an attempt.

Several propositions about the impact of environmental variables on interorganizational relations can be derived from the perspective described in previous sections. Two propositions are schematically portrayed in Figure 1 and will be described below.

Figure 1-A: Environmental stability leads to the development of formalized relations with other organizations by increasing the opportunities for and the predictability of contact between specific organizations. The concentration of resources attracts those organizations which seek to exploit the resources by entering into more frequent interaction with the organization holding the resources. A high frequency of interaction, in turn, leads to the development of more formalized relations as organizational learning takes place and each organization gives the transaction formal recognition. Formalized relations have a stabilizing effect on the environment and so a feedback loop is included in the figure.

Figure 1-B: Environmental heterogeneity and instability jointly lead organizations to adopt one or both of the following strategies. Either a lack of standardized procedures ensues, with the environment being dealt with

Figure 1

TWO PROPOSITIONS CONCERNING INTERORGANIZATIONAL RELATIONS

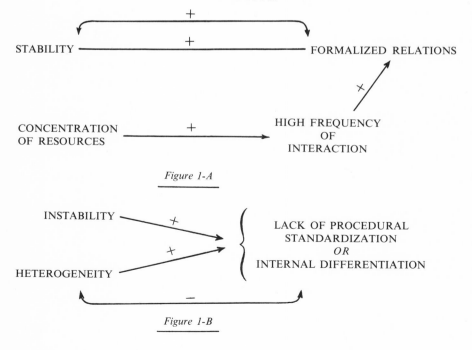

on a case-by-case basis, or internal differentiation takes place and the boundary personnel of the newly created subunits develop standardized procedures to deal with what is now a more homogeneous but perhaps unstable environment.

The implication of the second alternative is that the environment, from the organization's point of view, may seem less heterogeneous than before and thus a feedback loop is drawn into Figure 1-B.

Note that in both propositions I have made allowances for interaction over time between the organizations and their environments. These two propositions should give the reader the flavor of what this study attempts to accomplish.

SUMMARY AND CONCLUSIONS

The ultimate goal of this research is to be able to predict the state of relations in an organization-set or interorganizational field from a knowledge of the structure and technology of the organizations and the state of their environments. At present, predictions are limited to the state of interorganizational relations in one-to-one situations. As research techniques improve, we will move to making predictions about the state of sets of relations.

It is my contention that the organization-environment theory discussed in this paper has the potential for shedding new light on topics such as conflict between organizations and the impact of environments on organizations. Traditional approaches have been hampered by their focus on the internally stable characteristics of organizations and their failure to develop an adequate conceptualization of organizational environments. I have shown in a previous paper that it is possible to integrate the concepts of authority, membership, and organizational autonomy in the context of a theory treating organizations as goal-directed, boundary-maintaining, information-processing activity systems (Aldrich, 1971). This paper represents a modest attempt to extend that perspective into yet another area of concern to organizational theorists.

REFERENCES

Aiken, Michael, and Jerald Hage. "Organizational Interdependence and Intra-
1968   Organizational Structure." *American Sociological Review*, 33:912–29.
Aldrich, Howard. "Organizations in a Hostile Environment: A Panel Study of
1969   Small Businesses in Three Cities." Ann Arbor, Mich.: University of Michigan
        (unpublished Ph.D. dissertation).
———. "Organizational Boundaries and Interorganizational Conflict." *Human
1971   Relations*, 24:279–93.
Aldrich, Howard, and Albert J. Reiss, Jr. "Police Officers as Boundary Personnel."

1971   In Harlan Hahn (ed.), *The Police in Urban Society*. Beverly Hills, Calif.:
        Sage Publications.

Blau, Peter.   *Exchange and Power in Social Life*. New York: John Wiley and Sons.
1964

Buckley, Walter.   *Sociology and Modern Systems Theory*. Englewood Cliffs, N.J.:
1967   Prentice-Hall.

Crozier, Michael.   *The Bureaucratic Phenomenon*. Chicago: The University of Chicago
1964   Press.

Dalton, Melville.   *Men Who Change*. New York: John Wiley and Sons.
1959

Dill, William.   "Environment as an Influence on Managerial Autonomy." *Ad-*
1958   *ministrative Science Quarterly*, 2:409–43.

Durkheim, Emile.   *The Division of Labor*. Glencoe, Ill.: The Free Press.
1949

Emerson, Richard.   "Power-Dependence Relations." *American Sociological Review*
1962   27:31–40.

Emery, F. E., and E. L. Trist.   "The Causal Texture of Organizational Environments."
1965   *Human Relations*, 18:21–32.

Gouldner, Alvin.   "Reciprocity and Autonomy in Functional Theory." In Llewellyn
1959   Gross (ed.), *Symposium on Sociological Theory*. Evanston, Ill.: Row, Peterson,
        and Company.

Hage, Jerald, and Michael Aiken.   "Program Change and Organizational Properties:
1967   A Comparative Analysis." *American Journal of Sociology*, 72:503–19.

Hall, Richard.   *Organizations: Structure and Process*. Englewood Cliffs, N.J.:
1972   Prentice-Hall.

Hawley, Amos.   *Human Ecology*. New York: Ronald Press.
1950

Katz, Daniel, and Robert Kahn.   *The Social Psychology of Organizations*. New York:
1966   John Wiley and Sons.

Kerr, Clark, and Abraham Seigel.   "The Interindustry Propensity to Strike—An
1954   International Comparison." In Arthur Kornhauser, Robert Dubin, and
        Arthur Ross (eds.), *Industrial Conflict*. New York: McGraw-Hill.

Levine, Sol, and Paul White.   "Exchange as a Conceptual Framework for the Study
1961   of Interorganizational Relationships." *Administrative Science Quarterly*,
        5:583–601.

Litwak, Eugene, and Lydia Hylton.   "Interorganizational Analysis: A Hypothesis
1962   on Coordinating Agencies." *Administrative Science Quarterly*, 6:395–420.

Lovell, Malcolm.   "Politics of Manpower Planning." Paper presented to seminar
1972   of Manpower Research Program of NYSSILR, Cornell University, Ithaca,
        New York.

Marrett, Cora Bagley.   "On the Specification of Interorganizational Dimensions."
1971   *Sociology and Social Research*, 56:83–99.

Mayhew, Leon.   *Society: Institutions and Activity*. Glenview, Ill.: Scott, Foresman
1971   and Company.

Miller, Walter.   "Interinstitutional Conflict as a Major Impediment to Delinquency
1958   Prevention." *Human Organization*, 17:20–24.

70   INTERORGANIZATION THEORY

Olson, Mancur. *The Logic of Collective Action.* Cambridge, Mass.: Harvard Univer-
1965   sity Press.
Perrow, Charles. *Complex Organizations: A Critical Essay.* Glenview, Ill.: Scott,
1972   Foresman and Company.
————. "A Framework for the Comparative Analysis of Organizations." *American*
1967   *Sociological Review,* 32:104–208.
Ridgeway, Valentine. "Administration of Manufacturer-Dealer Systems." *Ad-*
1957   *ministrative Science Quarterly,* 1:464–83.
Sjoberg, Gideon. "Contradictory Functional Requirements and Social Systems."
1960   *Journal of Conflict Resolution,* 4:198–208.
Terreberry, Shirley. "The Evolution of Organizational Environments." *Adminis-*
1968   *trative Science Quarterly,* 12:590–613.
Thompson, James. *Organizations in Action.* New York: McGraw-Hill.
1967
Warren, Roland. "The Interorganizational Field as a Focus for Investigation."
1967   *Administrative Science Quarterly,* 12:396–419.
Warren, Roland, et al. "The Interactions of Community Decision Organizations:
1973   Some Conceptual Considerations and Empirical Findings." In Anant R.
        Negandhi (ed.), *Modern Organizational Theory:* 145–59. Kent, Ohio: Kent
        State University Press.
White, Paul, Sol Levine, and George Vlasak. "Exchange as a Conceptual Framework
1973   for Understanding Interorganizational Relationships: Application to Non-
        profit Organizations." In Anant R. Negandhi (ed.), *Modern Organizational
        Theory:* 174–88. Kent, Ohio: Kent State University Press.
Woodward, Joan. *Industrial Organization.* London: Oxford University Press.
1965
Yuchtman, Ephraim, and Stanley Seashore. "A System Resource Approach to Organi-
1967   zational Effectiveness." *American Sociological Review,* 33:891–903.

5

Mapping the Interorganizational Landscape: A Critical Appraisal

RAYMOND J. ADAMEK

After some eighteen years of increasing interest and empirical work in the field of interorganizational relations, students of complex organizations have begun to take stock of the underlying analytical paradigms which have guided their work. Marrett's (1971) early effort has been followed up by several others, two examples of which are the papers by Van de Ven, Emmett, and Koenig (Chapter 2), and Zeitz (Chapter 3), in this volume.

Undertaking intellectual mapping of this type is important. It helps us determine where we have been, how the various elements of the topography are related to one another, where the unexplored territory lies, and in which direction it might be best to proceed next. The task of the interorganizational cartographer is quite difficult, however. The territory is vast (over 150 articles and books have appeared in the past eighteen years), and the variety of the landscape seems endless (at least 130 variables thought to be relevant to interorganizational analysis have been identified, along with some seven major paradigms). It is not surprising, then, that while existing maps have given us a better idea of the lay of the land, none of them have given us a comprehensive, unified picture, nor generated agreement about the best way to "get from here to there."

Van de Ven, Emmett, and Koenig suggest that there are three major perspectives which have guided interorganizational research. These are viewing the environment first, as an external constraining phenomenon; second, as a collection of interacting organizations, groups, or persons; and third, as a social system. This categorization does help to orient the student of interorganizational relations, but it should not be taken too literally. That is, many studies contain elements of more than one of these orientations. Aldrich's contribution (Chapter 4), for example, falls primarily into the second category. But also, by virtue of its secondary emphasis on the interorganizational field, it belongs in category three. Determining the major perspective of a given study is important, however, for as Warren, Rose, and Burgunder (1974) have convincingly demonstrated, the paradigms guiding the academic investigator or action-oriented policy maker interested in interorganizational analysis definitely influence the conclusions reached.

Van de Ven and his colleagues' discussion of interorganizational collectivities (ICs) is helpful in that it lays bare the complexity of interorganizational relations. At the same time, it underscores the lack of agreement among investigators as to just what the basic unit of interorganizational analysis should be. Van de Ven, Emmett, and Koenig note that an IC is not an organization-set. They distinguish their concept from those of Evan (1966) and Caplow (1964), who themselves have quite different notions of what constitutes an organization-set.

Whether the concept of the IC will serve "as a basis for the systematic comparison and linking of social systems in a hierarchy of social orders," remains to be seen. Parsons' system-within-a-system-within-a-system approach is intellectually appealing, since it is a general theory which can be applied, at least at a surface level, to analyze the behavior of the individual actor, the family, the small group, the organization, the institution, and finally, the total society. His (1956a, 1956b) early treatise on organizations, however, although obviously applicable to interorganizational relations, has not generated much empirical work which directly applies his paradigm to the interorganizational field.

Like Van de Ven and his colleagues, Zeitz suggests that the relatively unexplored and perhaps most promising territory on the interorganizational map is the societal system, or the interorganizational field perspective. One may challenge him on the degree to which we have overlooked the forest for the trees by assuming and emphasizing organizational autonomy, but many of his objections regarding the shortcomings of the organizational level of analysis appear to be vindicated by the recent work of Warren, Rose, and Burgunder (1974). The latter authors demonstrate that utilizing an interorganizational field level of analysis provides a much different (and more accurate?) picture of the amount, nature, and consequences of interorganizational interaction than does the more frequently used organizational level paradigm.

Aldrich's paper differs from those by Zeitz and Van de Ven, Emmett, and Koenig in that it does not map the field of interorganizational analysis, but rather maps the "environment" of a given set of agencies to be studied empirically. It makes a valuable contribution by drawing together the work of several authors who describe various characteristics of organizational environments, and considering their impact on the dimensions of interorganizational relations specified by Marrett (1971). In any such listing, of course, one can think of additional variables which he feels should have been included (e.g., distribution of prestige among organizations).

As mentioned earlier, Aldrich's study illustrates the difficulty of pinpointing many studies at one and only one place on the interorganizational map. It not only spans Van de Ven, Emmett, and Koenig's second and third categories, but it also fails to conform exactly to any one of Zeitz's categorizations. To some extent it conforms with what Aldrich calls the "sociological tradition in which primarily government agencies have funded research projects trying to discover how best to achieve 'coordination' between a fragmented set of health or social service agencies," and thus carries with it certain ideological assumptions. At the same time, however, Aldrich attempts to employ the interorganizational field paradigm, which makes such assumptions explicit and thus "rises above" them. He suggests that this study is an attempt to replicate Warren's study of community decision organizations. The extent to which this effort is successful will depend largely upon how thoroughly the interorganizational field paradigm is employed, with both its theoretical and methodological implications (Warren, Rose, and Burgunder, 1974:159–67), and the extent to which it dominates the organizational level paradigm. Comparing the results of these two major studies will be of great interest to interorganizational scholars.

All of the authors under discussion suggest that we can ignore the larger perspective afforded by the social system or interorganizational field paradigms only at the expense of increased theoretical and practical understanding of interorganizational relations and society. At the same time, all would agree, I think, that we have hardly exhausted the potential of other (narrower?) paradigms, either theoretically or methodologically. While we may have sketched parts of the interorganizational landscape in broad outline, there remains much detailed exploring yet to be done in these areas, and much uncharted territory to cover.

REFERENCES

Caplow, Theodore. *Principles of Organization.* New York: Harcourt, Brace and
1964   World.
Evan, William M.   "The Organization-Set: Toward a Theory of Interorganizational
1966   Relations." In James D. Thompson (ed.), *Approaches to Organizational Design.* Pittsburgh: University of Pittsburgh Press.
Marrett, Cora Bagley.   "On the Specification of Interorganizational Dimensions."
1971   *Sociology and Social Research,* 56:83–99.
Parsons, Talcott.   "Suggestions for a Sociological Approach to the Theory of Organi-
1956a   zations—I." *Administrative Science Quarterly,* 1:63–85.
————.   "Suggestions for a Sociological Approach to the Theory of Organiza-
1956b   tions—II." *Administrative Science Quarterly,* 1:225–39.
Warren, Roland L., Stephen M. Rose, and Ann F. Burgunder.   *The Structure of*
1974   *Urban Reform.* Lexington, Mass.: D.C. Heath and Company.

PART II

Organization-Environment Interface

6

Environment, Organization, and the Individual

JAY W. LORSCH

INTRODUCTION

During the past ten years, there has been an increasing emphasis on contingency approaches to organization theory. The works of Burns and Stalker (1961), Thompson (1967), Udy (1970), and Woodward (1958), to name a few, have suggested that the internal structure and processes of an organization must be consistent with the requirements of the tasks that organization is performing. Our own work has pointed in the same direction (Lawrence and Lorsch, 1969). In essence, we have argued that there must be a fit between internal organizational characteristics and external environmental requirements if an organization is to perform effectively in dealing with its environment.

This fit between an organization and its environment, as we have examined it, has two related aspects. First, each functional unit (e.g., sales, production, and research) must have internal characteristics consistent with the demands of its particular sector of the total environment. Since the sectors of the total environment facing such functional units differ in the demands they place on that unit (e.g., certainty of information, time span of feedback of information, and dominant strategic variables), we have found that these units, to some extent, need to be different in their internal characteristics (formality of structure and members' time, goal, and interpersonal orientation). Further, Udy (1970) has suggested that this segmentation of organization and environment is not just a result of the logic of management about organizational design, but has developed because it helps to manage the inconsistencies among what he has labeled the social, production, and technological aspects of the environment. The second aspect of the organization-environment relationship which we found to be important is that the total organization must achieve, in spite of the differentiation among its units, the pattern of integration required by the total environment.

In developing these findings, this study, like most research studies,

raised some intriguing new questions. One question which we found particularly intriguing deals with the importance of differentiation (Lorsch and
Morse, 1974). Why is it that the fit between a functional unit's organizational
characteristics and its part of the environment, which creates the necessity
for differentiation, is related to effective performance? Does this match of
unit organization and environment simply meet the information-processing
requirements of the environment, thus leading to effective performance. or
does this consistency also have an effect on individual organization members
which motivates them toward more effective performance? This question
was particularly intriguing to us because it is in primary work units, such
as functional departments, that the individual, the organization, and the
environment interact.

Learning more about the interaction of these factors is important from
both a practical and a theoretical perspective. From the point of view of the
practitioner, the importance of motivating individual members to work
effectively toward organizational goals is obvious. Chances are, if you ask
any manager for a list of his ten most pressing organizational problems,
motivation of subordinates will be near the top of the list. Yet our understanding of the relationships among organization and task variables and
individuals' needs is still in a fairly primitive state. An important reason for
this seems to be the differing interests of organizational theorists and psychologists. Organizational theorists, who often are more sociologically bent,
focus on task (environment) and/or organizational factors, but tend either
to ignore the human variable or to treat it with simplifying assumptions
(March and Simon, 1958). Psychologists interested in organizational
phenomena, on the other hand, tend to focus on the individual and his
definition of the situation (Lawler and Porter, 1968). Thus, they have not
looked closely at the effect of variations in tasks or organization variables.
Instead, they have focused on the rewards an individual can expect to
receive from the work setting. Let me stress that I am not being critical of
either the organizational theorists or the psychologists for their limited
views. In fact, these narrow perspectives seem to be a natural consequence
of the current division of work among behavioral scientists studying
organizational phenomena. Yet the difficulty is that this differentiation
in approach has not led to an adequately integrated understanding of the
relationship between the organization, the individual, and the organization's environment. Thus, we are left with constructs like "inducement-
contributions" (March and Simon, 1958) and "reciprocation" (Levinson,
1968) which suggest an exchange relationship between individual goals and
organizational requirements, but which don't provide operational ways
of understanding the variations in human, task, and organizational variables
and the interaction among these factors (March and Simon, 1958). We need
to know more about the terms of the exchange relationship between organi-

zation and individual. What are the terms of the exchange? How do these terms vary for individuals who have different predispositions? How do variations in task requirements and organizational attributes affect this relationship?

By focusing on the relationship among organizational, individual, and environmental factors, we hope to build a bridge between the concerns of macroorganization theorists with organizational and environmental variables and the focus of psychologists on the individual as the unit of analysis. We are aware that such bridge building is a risky undertaking. It requires using a broader range of methodology and concepts than we have been accustomed to; thus it opens us to criticism from both flanks. Clearly, our conceptualization and our methods may lack the precision which satisfies either our sociologically or psychologically oriented colleagues. While we are not sanguine about this risk, we feel it is worth taking because, if the aspect of the territory we want to understand is man in organization, it is important to begin to explore all these variables simultaneously. To do this we need a conceptual model of the organization-environment interface. We also need a model of the individual which enables us to see how variations in environmental and organizational characteristics may impact on the individual's desire to perform the work required of him by the organization. In the balance of this paper, I want to elaborate on the concepts we are currently utilizing to explore this issue, and also very briefly discuss our preliminary results.

ORGANIZATION-ENVIRONMENT MODEL

Stemming from the prior work of Lawrence and Lorsch (1969), we conceive of the relationship between the organization of a functional unit and its environment as a contingent one. That is, the internal characteristics of an effective functional unit will be contingent on the characteristics of its immediate environment. In thinking about these internal characteristics, we have elaborated in a number of ways on the four dimensions of differentiation used by Lawrence and Lorsch. To begin with, in *Organization and Environment* (Lawrence and Lorsch, 1969), the formality of structure of a unit was found to be related to the relative certainty of its environment. But, in considering this further, we have realized that the formality of structure also may depend upon the degree of coordination within the unit required by the environment. While the extent to which formalized controls and procedures are utilized also will depend upon the degree to which the work can be preplanned or preprogrammed, the shape of the management hierarchy and the extent to which plans are utilized will also be a function of the amount of coordination required among unit members. Although it is possible that there may be a close correlation between the degree of coordination required by a unit's environment and the degree of certainty in the environment, we know of no evidence that suggests such covariance. Whether it does or does not exist is a matter for empirical testing in a wider sample of sites than is feasible for us. However, we can imagine highly uncertain environments requiring tight coordination (e.g., developing aerospace systems). Therefore, we have chosen to treat coordination required and certainty as independent variables, as they affect the formality of organization.

In thinking further about how formal structures and procedures need to be related to environmental requirements, we also have recognized that formal practices can vary not only in their formality, but also in the extent to which they emphasize various goal criteria and time horizons. For example, a unit operating in a part of the environment with a relatively short time span of feedback about results will require formal reports at more frequent intervals than a unit operating in a part of the environment with a longer time span of feedback. Similarly, unit formal practices must emphasize goals which are consistent with the strategic variables in its environment. That is, a production unit would require formal practices emphasizing cost, quality, and efficiency considerations, while a sales unit would need formal practices emphasizing market penetration and customer relations.

In *Organization and Environment* (Lawrence and Lorsch, 1969), the only measures of behavioral characteristics which were used to test a unit's fit with its environment were the members' goal, time, and interpersonal orientations. To study this issue in more depth, we decided to examine a broader range of variables measuring the behavior of unit members, including not only the work orientations they have, but also their influence over work activities and how work is coordinated within the unit. I should emphasize that the measures of behavioral characteristics we are using are perceptual measures of the member's own behavior or of behavior in the unit as a whole.

The work orientations with which we are concerned include the actual goal and time orientations of unit members. In effective units these would be expected to fit the environmental requirements in a pattern similar to that existing for formal practices. Influence over work activities includes: the members' perceptions of the autonomy or control of the formal organization; the influence over critical decisions that members believe to exist at various hierarchical levels of the unit; the total amount of influence which exists over these decisions in the unit as a whole; the influence members feel they have to decide on their own work and then to carry it out; and the supervisory style which is typically employed in the unit. We would predict that in effective units involved in more uncertain parts of the environment, members would perceive less structure, would feel that they have high influence over their own work, would perceive egalitarian influence distribution in general, and supervisory style would be seen as participative. The opposite set of conditions would fit a unit effectively dealing with a more certain environment.

With regard to coordination, we expect that effective units will achieve the degree of coordination of effort required by the environment. Following Lawrence and Lorsch (1969), we expected that achieving effective coordination within a unit would be accompanied by a greater reliance on the confrontation of conflicts within the unit, rather than handling conflicts by smoothing them over, or by one party forcing the other to comply to his desires.

These formal and behavioral attributes and the relationships they have to environmental requirements are summarized in Figure 1. As this diagram indicates, we are hypothesizing that in an effective unit there will be a fit between environmental requirements and both formal and behavioral characteristics. But, we also have schematically indicated our prediction that the formal characteristics will be one factor which influences the pattern of behavioral characteristics in the unit. While, as we shall discuss more fully below, members' behavior is influenced by their own personalities and their perceptions of the realities of the environment, it also will be affected by the signals they receive from the formal organization.

Figure 1
UNIT ORGANIZATION-ENVIRONMENT MODEL

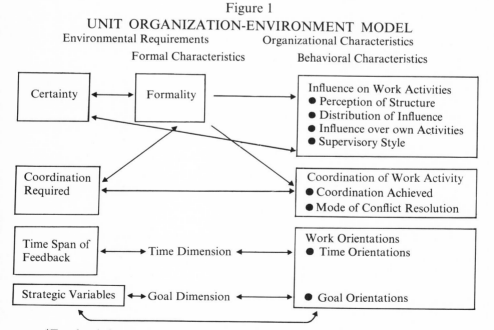

*Two headed arrows connote that the variables linked will be consistent with each other, if the unit is effective.

THE INDIVIDUAL AND THE ORGANIZATION

The development of the organization and environment model for a unit was largely an elaboration of earlier work (Lawrence and Lorsch, 1969) and did not represent a complicated conceptual problem. However, conceptualizing the individual's relationship to the organization and to its environment is much more complex. This complexity stems from the tangle of personality theories which are available. While it is well beyond the scope of this paper to try to make a summary of these theories, it is possible to provide a flavor of the alternative theories available by referring to Maddi's (1968) excellent comparative analysis. Maddi points to three competing models of individual personality: the conflict model, the fulfill-ment model, and the consistency model. The conflict model refers to the work of Freud and others who have argued that the behavior of individuals is a result of conflicting forces within man. According to this model, life "is necessarily a compromise, which at best involves a dynamic balance between the two forces (love and aggression) and at worst involves a fore-doomed attempt to deny the existence of one of them" (Maddi, 1968). While there are various permutations of this approach which differ as to the sources of these conflicting forces, the adherents of this model agree that man is inevitably caught in a conflict between them. He is motivated to behave in ways which reduce the tension caused by these conflicts. In the fulfillment model, there is an assumption that a single force toward growth and actualization shapes our behavior. In this model, conflict is seen as a possible occurrence, but one which represents an unfortunate failure. Here, tension is not associated with conflict that is to be reduced, but instead tension is actually sought because the greater the tension the more vigorous is the expression of the one great force. The consistency model in essence is not concerned with driving forces, but rather emphasizes the influence of feedback from the external world. If the feedback is consis-tent with prior expectations, the individual feels pleasure; but if there is inconsistency between feedback and expectations, the individual strives to decrease this uncomfortable state of affairs. Note that in its treatment of the relationship between tension and behavior the consistency model falls between the extremes of the other two. A little tension or a little incongruence is pleasant (as in the fulfillment model), but a lot of tension, that is, a large inconsistency between expectation and feedback, is uncomfortable and is to be reduced as in the conflict model.

This brief description may do a disservice to Maddi (1968) because of its oversimplification. But it is not intended to be thorough in any sense; rather, my intent is to illustrate the broad range of personality theories in existence. Even if one completely disagrees with Maddi's typology or where he places various theorists in these categories, his comprehensive analysis clearly points to the complex issues facing anyone who wants to link theories about individual motivation to organizational theory.

The organizational psychologists who have focused on the interface between the individual and the organization have adopted implicitly one of two strategies to deal with this complexity. One strategy has been to accept one theory as valid and to work from there. Thus McGregor (1960) developed his Theory Y assumptions about organization and management based on Maslow's version of the fulfillment model. The other strategy has been to develop an eclectic model which combines elements of several theoretical approaches. For example, Lawler and Porter (1968) slice motivation theory into drive—or what Maddi would call conflict—theory and expectancy theory; they recognize that it is also useful to build elements of drive theory into their model.

This eclectic approach is in essence the one which we have chosen to adopt because it provides us with what seems to be the most accurate map we can find for dealing with the territory of man's interface with his organizational work setting. In developing our eclectic model of the individual, we have tried to utilize those assumptions about human behavior which our reading of the literature indicates are widely shared. We recognize elements of the consistency, conflict, and fulfillment approaches in our model. We have also avoided, as far as possible, becoming involved in speculating about the internal structure and dynamics of personality systems. Recognizing that all we would be able to measure are individual feelings, interests, and attitudes, we have not gone very far in speculating about which are intrinsic and which are learned, or how one classifies them in terms of the structure of personality.

The assumptions about personality functioning which underlie our model of the individual in the organization are as follows:

1. In addition to the drives of affection and aggression identified by Freud and his disciples, a third source of energy exists—the individual's drive to feel competent or masterful in dealing with the external world (Erickson, 1960). White (1963) has labeled this energy source and the associated feelings as competence and the sense of competence, and we shall use his terminology.

2. The strength of these energy sources and the way they manifest themselves in behavior are shaped by the individual's biological makeup and his psycho-social development[1] (White, 1963).

---

[1] While we have drawn this conclusion from the work of Robert W. White (1963), it seems clear, as Maddi (1968) has pointed out, that there is a similarity between the concept of sense of competence and Maslow's notion of actualization.

Some behavior will result from the individual's desire to reduce internal tension and other behavior will be a result of the individual's desire to develop a sense of competence in dealing with the world around him.

3. Given the above, a person's current and future behavior will always have a consistent relationship not only to the rewards he expects now and in the future, but also to his past experiences and how they color his expectations about the rewards.

4. An important source of reward in the work setting is the opportunity to achieve a sense of competence. However, various individuals with different personalities will achieve a sense of competence in different ways. That is, they will prefer to act differently toward objects and other persons in their work setting. Similarly, individuals will differ in terms of their cognitive capacities to take in information, and this, too, can impact upon how they achieve feelings of competence (Driver, 1967).

These assumptions lead to a model of the individual in the organization which stresses that the psychological importance of the work and organizational setting for the individual depends upon the extent to which he gains feelings of competence from being in the organization and working on the task of dealing with the external environment. It is important to emphasize that when we speak of a sense of competence we are referring to feelings of fulfillment which the individual obtains from engaging with his environment and solving problems in it. In essence, the fulfillment comes from successfully performing a given task. Certainly, as I have suggested above, the work setting is an important locale for the individual to gain a sense of competence. We should also stress, as White (1963) has pointed out, that the feelings of competence can come from dealing with both objects and other persons.

Whether a person is to gain these important feelings of competence in a particular work situation would seem to depend upon the extent to which the organizational arrangements, both formally and in terms of the shared expectations of colleagues, are consistent with the environmental requirements so that he can in fact act competently in performing his task. Evidence that there is a connection between organizational arrangements and one's feelings of competence is provided by frequently heard complaints about excessive red tape or in other situations by statements such as "tomorrow we have to get organized." Such statements support our prediction that if a person is to feel competent he must be supported in acting competently by the organization. This provides an important argument as to why a fit between organization and environment is related to effective unit performance. When there is congruence between the organization and the environment, it enables individuals to work effectively. They gain feelings of competence which motivate them to continue working effectively, and this leads to effective unit performance. This hypothesized relationship is illustrated in Figure 2.

Figure 2
HYPOTHESIZED RELATIONSHIP

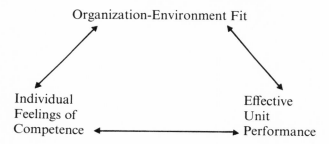

The double headed arrows in Figure 2 are intended to emphasize that the direction of causation can operate in two directions. Individual feelings of competence not only result from the organization-environment fit, they also lead to effective unit performance. However, the effective performance of the unit provides feedback to the individual about the worth of his individual performance and reinforces his feelings of competence. Further, the fact that the unit is performing effectively leads to a tendency on the part of individuals at all levels to maintain their current organizational practices and behavior patterns so these continue to fit the environment.

There is one important limitation of the model in the form outlined above. It does not take into account differences among individuals in terms of their predispositions. If a person is to feel competent in a particular organizational setting, as was suggested above, it would seem to follow that the organization should provide opportunities for him to relate to objects and persons in ways consistent with the behavioral and thought patterns stemming from his personality. In reviewing the organizational characteristics listed in Figure 1, we concluded that these four variables might describe the extent to which individuals were likely to get their psychological kicks from feeling competent in a particular organizational setting: the individual's cognitive structure, his tolerance for ambiguity, his attitude toward authority, and his attitude toward others. These factors, with the exception of cognitive structure, are simply tendencies to prefer acting in certain ways. We have avoided labeling them as needs or motives because of our desire not to become too involved in speculating about the internal structure and dynamics of personality.

Apropos to the cognitive structure of the individual, Driver (1967) found that individuals vary in the extent to which they are able to take in differentiated bits of information and to integrate them (Morse and Lorsch, 1970). This capacity has been labeled integrative complexity. We are hypothesizing that individuals who feel competent working in highly uncertain environments and in an organization with low formality would need to have greater integrative complexity than those who felt competent working on more certain tasks in a more highly formalized organization.

Similarly, we hypothesized that persons who would develop feelings of competence in working in different organization-environment settings might also vary in their tolerance for ambiguity. Persons working in an uncertain environment and an organization with low formality would need to have a greater tolerance for ambiguity than those working on more certain tasks in more formalized organizations. A person's tolerance for ambiguity also would be related to the rapidity with which the environment provides feedback. When feedback is frequent, persons would not require a high tolerance for ambiguity; but when feedback is less frequent, a higher tolerance for ambiguity would be important to the individual's achieving feelings of competence.

We also have predicted that persons feeling competent in different organizational settings might also vary in their customary ways of relating to authority. Individuals in a less formalized organization with more influence over decisions and working for a participatory leader would work more effectively if they preferred more autonomy and did not prefer strong authority relationships. Persons in more highly formalized organizations, where influence was more centralized and leadership more directive, would be more likely to feel competent only if they felt comfortable with more dependent authority relationships.

Finally, we predicted that different organization-environment settings would fit people who had different attitudes about working with others. In settings where little interdependence among unit members was required, persons who preferred being alone would tend to feel more competent. Persons who preferred spending time with others, those who were more group oriented rather than individually oriented, would be apt to feel more competent in units where more coordination was required by the environment.

In summary then, we are predicting that what is related to effective unit performance and feelings of competence is not only a congruence between the organization and the environment, but also between these two sets of factors and the individual (Figure 3). We should emphasize again that we are not implying any simple unidirectional cause and effect

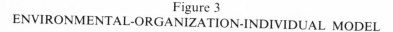

Figure 3
ENVIRONMENTAL-ORGANIZATION-INDIVIDUAL MODEL

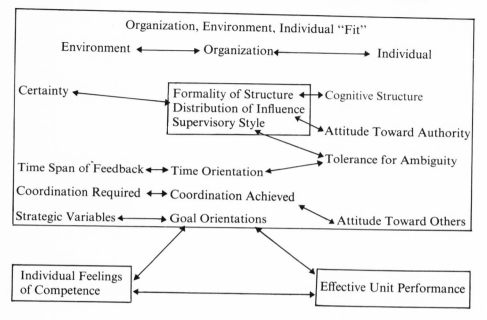

relation, but rather that we see these variables as a complex interactive system with several feedback loops. When this threeway fit is present, we are predicting that it will lead to both effective unit performance and feelings of competence for the individual. Thus there is an exchange between organization and individual goals, and the two undoubtedly interact.

STUDY DESIGN

To test this system of relationships, a study has been designed which examines these variables in two quite different environments (Lorsch and Morse, 1974). First, we have examined these variables in four production plants which are operating in relatively certain environments. Second, we have studied these variables in six research laboratories coping with a highly uncertain environment. In selecting sites of each type, we have obtained matched pairs of units in one company, so that one unit is highly effective and one less so, as judged by top management (Figure 4). Thus, we are in effect predicting that, based on unit performance, we can predict the other variables in the model.

Figure 4
RESEARCH DESIGN
ENVIRONMENT

	Uncertain			Certain	
Performance	Company I	Company II	Company III	Company IV	Company V
High	Lab I$_A$	Lab II$_A$	Lab III$_A$	Plant IV$_A$	Plant V$_A$
Low	Lab I$_B$	Lab II$_B$	Lab III$_B$	Plant IV$_B$	Plant V$_B$

PRELIMINARY RESULTS

The preliminary results of this work are reported elsewhere (Morse, 1970; Morse and Lorsch, 1970), and space does not allow a detailed treatment of our data here. I can report, however, that the data uniformly support the set of relationships which I have just outlined. We are now in the process of elaborating the model just described and have prepared a manuscript which reports the data and discusses its implications (Lorsch and Morse, 1974).

In closing, however, I cannot resist the temptation to focus on the major implication we feel this study holds for organization theory. To me, it is a further indication of the validity and value of a contingency approach to the study of organizational phenomena, even though the model I have described and our data which supports it still leave many questions unresolved. For example, we need to know more about cause and effect; we need to know how financial compensation would figure in the set of relationships. Further, the study only focuses on organization-environment settings at the extremes of certainty and uncertainty. Nevertheless, the results suggest that the contingency approach can help us to develop a clearer understanding of the complex relationship between man, organization, and the external environment of the organization. We now can understand more fully the nature of the exchange between the organization and the individual. We can see how task and organizational characteristics affect this relationship. While there is much to be done, and in spite of the fact that moving the development of organization theory in this contingency direction certainly involves us in more complex conceptual schemes and methods, the potential payout seems worth it.

REFERENCES

Burns, Thomas, and G. M. Stalker. *Management of Innovation*. London: Tavistock
1961 Publications.

Driver, Michael J. *Human Information Processing*. New York: Holt, Rinehart
1967 and Winston.

Erickson, Erik. "The Problem of Ego Identity." In M. R. Stein, A. J. Vidich, and
1960 David M. White (eds.), *Identity and Anxiety*. Glencoe, Ill.: The Free Press.

Lawler, Edward E., and Lyman W. Porter. *Managerial Attitudes and Performances*.
1968 Homewood, Ill.: Richard D. Irwin.

Lawrence, Paul R., and Jay W. Lorsch. *Organization and Environment*. Homewood,
1969 Ill.: Richard D. Irwin, Inc.

Levinson, Harry. *The Exceptional Executive*. Cambridge, Mass.: Harvard University
1968 Press.

Lorsch, Jay W., and John J. Morse. *Organizations and Their Members: A Contingency
1974 Approach*. New York: Harper and Row.

Maddi, Salvatore R. *Personality Theories, A Comparative Analysis*. Homewood,
1968 Ill.: The Dorsey Press.

March, James G., and Herbert A. Simon. *Organizations*. New York: John Wiley
1958 and Sons, Inc.

McGregor, Douglas. *The Human Side of Enterprise*. New York: McGraw-Hill.
1960

Morse, John J. "Organizational Characteristics and Individual Motivation." In
1970 Jay W. Lorsch and Paul R. Lawrence (eds.), *Studies in Organizational Design*.
Homewood, Ill.: Richard D. Irwin.

Morse, John J., and Jay W. Lorsch. "Beyond Theory Y." *Harvard Buiness Review*.
1970

Thompson, James. *Organization in Action*. New York: McGraw-Hill.
1967

Udy, Stanley. *Work in Traditional and Modern Society*. Englewood Cliffs, N.J.:
1970 Prentice-Hall.

White, Robert W. "Ego and Reality in Psychoanalytical Theory." *Psychological
1963 Issues*, 3:24–42.

Woodward, Joan. *Management and Technology*. London: Her Majesty's Printing
1958 Office.

7

A Contingency Theory of Organization Re-Examined in the Context of a Developing Country

ANANT R. NEGANDHI, BERNARD C. REIMANN

INTRODUCTION

In the current studies of complex organizations, one basic theoretical perspective is emerging: an organization's structure and functioning are dependent upon its interface with the external environment.

Research studies of Dill (1958:409–43), Woodward (1973), Burns and Stalker (1961), Chandler (1962), Lefton and Rosengren (1966: 802–10), Fouraker and Stopford (1968), and Lawrence and Lorsch (1969), to name a few, have particularly raised the question of environmental impact on organizational structure and functioning.

Dill (1958 : 409–43), for example, in his study of two Norwegian firms, indicated that executives operating in relatively dynamic environments had more autonomy (or at least perceived that they did) than those operating in relatively stable environments. Although not directly couched in environmental terms, Woodward (1973), in her study of industrial firms in South Essex, found a relationship between the number of levels in the hierarchy and the degree of predictability of production techniques. Burns and Stalker (1961) examined how the management patterns in some 20 industrial firms in the United Kingdom were related to certain aspects of their external environments. The specific environmental characteristics considered were the rates of change in the scientific techniques and markets of the selected industries. They found two distinctly different sets of management practices and procedures, which they classified as "mechanistic" and "organic." The "mechanistic" organizations consisted of highly centralized, bureaucratic structures, while the more flexible and decentralized "organic"

This article originally appeared in *The Academy of Management Journal*, Volume 15, Number 2 (June, 1972). The editor gratefully acknowledges permission to reprint the material in this volume.

organizations practiced many of the principles espoused by the proponents of the "human relations" movement (Roethlisberger and Dickson, 1939). Burns and Stalker's (1961) conclusion was that the "mechanistic" form of organization appeared to be the most appropriate under relatively stable environmental conditions, while the "organic" form seemed best suited to conditions of change.

Finally, the recent study of Lawrence and Lorsch (1969) indicated that the formality of the effective organization's structure was related to the degree of certainty and stability of its market and technological environments. Successful firms operating in relatively dynamic environments tended to be decentralized. On the basis of their results, Lawrence and Lorsch proposed a "contingency theory" of organization. This theory regards the "optimum" organization form as contingent on the demands of the organization's environment. These authors further propose that decentralization under stable environmental conditions and centralization under dynamic conditions may actually be dysfunctional. In other words, they argue that an organization must establish a "fit" between its internal structural arrangements and its external environmental demands.

PURPOSE OF THIS STUDY

The purpose of this study was to test the "contingency theory of organizations" proposed by the above researchers, and, particularly, the thesis advanced by Lawrence and Lorsch (1969), in the context of a developing country; namely, India.

The relevance of testing this theory in such a context becomes apparent when one examines the assertions made by many cross-cultural management researchers. For example, in the cross-cultural studies of Meade (1967), Meade and Whittaker (1967:3–7), Harbison and Myers (1959), and Haire, Ghiselli, and Porter (1966), to name a few, there seems to be an underlying theme that sociocultural variables exert considerable influence on the organization structure of industrial enterprises in developing countries. In particular, the consensus of these researchers is that decentralized structure is dysfunctional in terms of the effectiveness of industrial enterprises in those countries. Wright (1971), for one, recently made such an assertion with respect to American firms in Chile.

We make no claim that the simple testing of the contingency theory of organizations in a single developing country can provide the final answer to the suitability of decentralized structure in developing countries. Nevertheless, we hope our findings may throw some additional light on the impact of "other" environmental factors (other than sociocultural variables, which are exceedingly difficult to operationalize) on organization structure.

More specifically, we explored the impact of decentralization on organizational effectiveness of the firms under differing market conditions.

Sample

Data[1] for this study were collected from 30 manufacturing firms in India through personal interviews with various levels of personnel in each company and by consulting published materials. The companies studied represented various industrial categories, such as pharmaceutical, chemical, soft drinks, elevators, heavy machine tools, cosmetics, sewing machines, and typewriters.[2] Size, as measured by the total number of employees of these companies, varied from 120 employees to 6,500 employees.[3]

VARIABLES AND MEASURES

Degree of Market Competition

The following information was collected to determine the extent of market competition faced by a given firm:
(a.) The degree of price competition among manufacturers of similar products;
(b.) The degree of delay in securing a product;
(c.) The number of alternatives available to the consumer.
On the basis of this information, the following three descriptive categories were created to represent the different degrees of market competition in which the various firms in our sample were operating:
(1.) Highly competitive market;
(2.) Moderately competitive market;
(3.) Seller's market, or noncompetitive market.
Firms operating in a "highly competitive market" faced severe price competition from other manufacturers of similar products. At the same time, the consumer did not experience any delay in securing the needed product (the product could be picked from the shelves), and the number of alternatives available to the consumer varied from five to twenty. Firms

---

[1] This sample was drawn from a larger study undertaken in Argentina, Brazil, India, the Philippines, and Uruguay. See A. R. Negandhi and S. B. Prasad, *Comparative Management* (New York: Appleton-Century-Crofts, 1971).

[2] The firms in our sample were divided according to Woodward's technological classifications of process-, mass-, and unit-production. A comparison of decentralization indexes for these firms by the Kruskal-Wallis test showed no significant differences in decentralization among the three technological classifications.

[3] The effect of size was controlled in our analysis by the use of partial correlation (see analysis of data).

in this category manufactured pharmaceutical products, sewing machines, and soft drinks.

Firms operating in a "moderately competitive market" experienced little price competition, but there was no delay in securing the product, and the consumer had two to four substitutable products available in the same marketplace. Firms facing this market condition were manufacturing cosmetics, electric bulbs, and canned products.

Firms operating in a "seller's market" experienced no price competition; the consumer (in most cases industrial consumers) had to wait for six months to two years to secure the product, and there were no real alternatives available to him. Firms operating in this market condition were manufacturing automobiles, trucks, and heavy industrial machinery.

Decentralization in Decision Making

Nine factors were examined to evaluate the degree of decentralization in decision making observed in the companies studied. The factors examined were:

(1.) Layers of hierarchy—from top executive to blue-collar worker;
(2.) Locus of decision making with respect to major policies (e.g., mergers, major expansions or suspensions, major diversification decisions);
(3.) Locus of decision making with respect to sales policies;
(4.) Locus of decision making with respect to product mix;
(5.) Locus of decision making with respect to standard-setting in production;
(6.) Locus of decision making with respect to manpower policies;
(7.) Locus of decision making with respect to selection of executives;
(8.) The degree of participation in long-range planning;
(9.) The degree of information-sharing.

Decentralization Index

To arrive at a composite index for decentralization, we devised a three-point ranking scale for each of the factors evaluated. The final decentralization index for each company was computed by adding the points for each factor and dividing this total by the number of factors (i.e., 9). This gave us an index ranging from a minimum of 1.0 ("highly decentralized") to a maximum of 3.0 ("highly centralized").[4]

---

[4] For details on decentralization index and its relationship with task environment, see, A. R. Negandhi and B. C. Reimann, "Task Environment, Decentralization, and Organizational Effectiveness," *Human Relations*, Volume 26, Number 2 (January/February, 1973), 203–14).

Organizational Effectiveness

Organizational effectiveness was evaluated both in terms of behaviorally oriented measures and economic criteria. The factors examined were: (a.) ability to hire and retain high-level manpower; (b.) employee morale and satisfaction in work; (c.) turnover and absenteeism; (d.) interpersonal relationships; (e.) interdepartmental relationships; and (f.) utilization of high-level manpower. Economic or financial criteria examined were growth in sales and net profits during the past five years.

Three descriptive categories were created to evaluate the organizational effectiveness for each company studied, and a three-point ranking scale was devised. Two effectiveness indices were created, one for the behaviorally oriented measures and the other for the growth in sales and profits. These indices were obtained by dividing the total score by the number of factors. This gave us an index ranging from a minimum of 1.0 ("most effective") to a maximum of 3.0 ("least effective"). These data are presented in Table 1.

ANALYSIS OF RESULTS

To explore the impact of decentralization on organizational effectiveness of the firms under differing market conditions, we first classified the firms in our sample according to: (1.) the competitiveness of their markets, and (2.) their degrees of decentralization, resulting in the 3 × 3 matrix shown in Table 2. The effectiveness scores (both behavioral and economic) were then averaged for the firms in each of the nine resulting categories. These average scores are listed in the appropriate cells of the matrix, along with the number of firms used to compute them. As may be seen from this matrix, the relatively decentralized firms operating in highly competitive markets were relatively effective (average scores of 1.32 and 1.00 in behavioral and economic terms, respectively). On the other hand, the relatively centralized firms in highly competitive markets were considerably less effective (average scores of 2.60 and 2.25). Under these competitive conditions, firms with an intermediate degree of decentralization were in between the above two extremes on effectiveness (see Table 2). These results lend considerable support to the contention that, under relatively competitive market conditions, decentralized firms are likely to be more effective than centralized firms (Burns and Stalker, 1961; Lawrence and Lorsch, 1969).

However, contrary to our expectations, a similar pattern was found among the firms operating under noncompetitive market conditions. As may be seen from the third column of the matrix in Table 2, average organizational effectiveness (both behavioral and economic) was, again, greatest in decentralized firms. However, these differences in effectiveness between centralized and decentralized firms were noticeably smaller than under competitive market conditions.

Table 1

Firm No.	Market Conditions	Decentralization Index	Effectiveness Behavioral	Economic
1	Highly competitive	1.2	1.1	1.0
2		1.6	1.4	1.0
3		1.2	1.1	1.0
4		1.8	2.1	2.0
5		1.9	1.9	1.5
6		2.0	2.5	2.5
7		1.7	2.0	1.5
8		2.8	2.5	3.0
9		1.4	1.9	1.0
10		2.4	2.7	1.5
11		1.2	1.1	1.0
12		1.3	1.1	1.0
29		1.7	1.9	2.5
30		1.8	1.7	1.0
13	Moderately competitive	1.8	1.9	2.0
14		3.0	3.0	2.0
15		2.9	2.5	2.0
16		3.0	2.9	2.0
27		2.1	2.0	2.0
28		1.6	2.0	1.5
17	Noncompetitive	1.6	1.4	1.0
18		2.5	2.5	1.5
19		1.8	2.4	1.5
20		1.8	1.3	1.0
21		2.2	2.3	1.0
22		1.1	1.1	1.0
23		1.5	1.6	1.0
24		2.2	2.1	1.0
25		2.3	2.1	1.5
26		2.0	2.0	1.5

Table 2
ORGANIZATION EFFECTIVENESS (BEHAVIORAL AND ECONOMIC)

Degree of Decentralization	Market Conditions		
	Highly Competitive	Moderately Competitive	Noncompetitive
High (Index 1.0–1.6)	$E_b = 1.32$ $E_e = 1.00$ $(n = 6)$	$E_b = 2.00$ $E_e = 1.50$ $(n = 1)$	$E_b = 1.37$ $E_e = 1.00$ $(n = 3)$
Medium (Index 1.9–2.0)	$E_b = 2.13$ $E_e = 1.88$ $(n = 4)$	$E_b = 1.90$ $E_e = 2.00$ $(n = 1)$	$E_b = 1.80$ $E_e = 1.50$ $(n = 4)$
Low (Index 2.1–3.0)	$E_b = 2.60$ $E_e = 2.25$ $(n = 2)$	$E_b = 2.60$ $E_e = 2.00$ $(n = 4)$	$E_b = 2.25$ $E_e = 1.40$ $(n = 5)$

Note: E_b = Average of effectiveness scores on behavioral criteria.
 E_e = Average of effectiveness scores on economic criteria.

A similar increase of effectiveness accompanied increasing decentralization under moderately competitive conditions, although here this increase in effectiveness was rather slight (see second column of matrix in Table 2).

These results indicate that decentralization was also found to be functional in relatively noncompetitive markets.

The statistical significance of the observed differences in average organization effectiveness between the various cells of the matrix in Table 2 could not be tested because several of the nine categories contained only one or two firms. However, a reclassification of firms as operating in "moderately—to highly competitive," and "noncompetitive" markets, and as being relatively decentralized (below median index value) and relatively centralized (above median index value), permitted the use of the Kruskal-Wallis analysis of variance by ranks. This test indicated that the relatively decentralized firms were significantly more effective (at the 0.05 level) than the relatively centralized ones under both competitive and noncompetitive market conditions.

We should point out that our sample of firms, of necessity, was not randomly drawn from the population of all manufacturing firms, Indian or otherwise. Therefore, we cannot interpret this statistical significance in the usual sense to generalize from our findings. Strictly speaking, we can generalize only to manufacturing firms similar to the group in our sample. However, the sample of firms represents, in the judgment of the authors, a good cross-section of typical manufacturing firms in India, both locally and American-owned. Therefore, the nonparametric statistical tests have been used in our data mainly to determine which of the observed relationships between variables in our sample of manufacturing firms has a significantly low probability (less than 0.05) of occurring due to chance alone.

Influence of Market Competitiveness

As indicated earlier, the extent of the differences in effectiveness between relatively centralized and decentralized firms seemed to differ according to the competitiveness of the markets faced by these firms. To shed some further light on this observation, we calculated the correlations between effectiveness (behavioral and economic) and decentralization scores separately for each of the three levels of market competitiveness (Table 1). To control for any possible effects of organization size, Kendall's partial rank correlation was computed for this analysis to hold size statistically "constant."

The resultant values for Kendall's regular and partial correlation coefficients for the relationships between decentralization and effectiveness (behavioral and economic) are presented in Table 3. The relatively small differences between the regular and partial correlation coefficients indicated that organization size had little, if any, influence on the decentralization and effectiveness relationships.

While all but one of the correlation coefficients were significant, the relative strength for all correlations decreased substantially as the environmental conditions became more stable (Table 3). This finding indicated

Table 3
KENDALL'S CORRELATION COEFFICIENTS FOR DECENTRALIZATION
INDEX VS ORGANIZATION EFFECTIVENESS

Organization Effectiveness	Market Conditions		
	Highly Competitive	Moderately Competitive	Noncompetitive
(1) Behavioral criteria	0.80 (0.78)*	0.72 (0.69)	0.56 (0.56)
(2) Economic criteria	0.69 (0.66)	0.60** (0.52)***	0.44 (0.48)

*Coefficients in parentheses are Kendall's *partial* coefficients—organization size held constant.
**Not significant—all other correlations significant at 0.05 level (1-tail).
***No test of significance available for partial correlation coefficients.

that market conditions did at least influence the *relative importance* of decentralization to effectiveness of the firms. Therefore, the contingency theory appeared to be essentially valid in the environmental context of a developing country.

The results of our study provide further evidence in support of a contingency theory of organizations. Moreover, our results suggest that for this theory to hold in a developing country like India, it must be slightly modified. That is, we cannot say that organization effectiveness requires decentralization under dynamic or competitive market conditions, and centralization under stable, noncompetitive conditions. Rather, we would suggest that dynamic, competitive market conditions make decentralization *more important* to organizational effectiveness than do stable, noncompetitive conditions.

This finding actually was not at all surprising, considering the unique industrial climate prevailing in India. When their market environment was a relatively stable seller's market, the firms experienced little difficulty in being effective, regardless of organization structure. Under these stable conditions, therefore, the variations in effectiveness were associated only slightly with degree of decentralization. However, under more dynamic and competitive market conditions, the extent of decentralization may well have played a considerably more important role in influencing organizational effectiveness. Competition for consumers and various resources was more severe, and effectiveness was therefore more difficult to achieve. Consequently, the firm's organization structure became a more vital factor in satisfying consumers (economic effectiveness criteria) as well as organization members (behavioral effectiveness criteria).

Some of the differences between our results and those reported by researchers such as Burns and Stalker (1961) and Lawrence and Lorsch (1969) may therefore be explained by the considerable differences in cultural and industrial environments encountered in our studies. Moreover, it must be remembered that we considered only the variations in the competitiveness of the organization's market environment, while the above-mentioned researchers were able to examine differences in both market and technological (or scientific) environments.

Nevertheless, it should be encouraging to proponents of a contingency theory of organization that a slightly modified version of this theory still appeared to hold in a cultural setting very different indeed from industrially advanced nations like the United Kingdom and the United States. Certainly, this contingency theory affords a useful framework for studying organizations operating in various diverse environments.

REFERENCES

Burns, T., and G. M. Stalker. *The Management of Innovation.* London: Tavistock.
1961

Chandler, Alfred. *Strategy and Structure: Chapters in the History of Industrial*
1962   *Enterprise.* Cambridge, Mass.: The Massachusetts Institute of Technology
        Press.

Dill, William R.   "Environment as an Influence on Managerial Autonomy." *Adminis-*
1958   *trative Science Quarterly*, 11: 409–43.

Fouraker, L. L., and J. M. Stopford.   "Organization Structure and Multinational
1968   Strategy." *Administrative Science Quarterly*, 13:46–63.

Haire, M., D. E. Ghiselli, and L. W. Porter.   *Managerial Thinking: An International*
1966   *Study.* New York: John Wiley.

Harbison, F., and C. Myers.   *Management in the Industrial World.* New York:
1959   McGraw-Hill.

Lawrence, Paul R., and Jay W. Lorsch.   *Organization and Environment: Managing*
1969   *Differentiation and Integration.* Homewood, Ill.: Richard D. Irwin.

Lefton, Mark, and William R. Rosengren.   "Organizations and Clients: Lateral
1966   and Longitudinal Dimensions." *American Sociological Review*, 31:802–10.

Meade, R. D.   "An Experimental Study of Leadership in India." *Journal of Social*
1967   *Psychology*, 72:35–43.

Meade, R. D., and J. D. Whittaker.   "A Cross-Cultural Study of Authoritarianism."
1967   *Journal of Social Psychology*, 72:3–7.

Negandhi, A. R., and S. B. Prasad.   *Comparative Management.* New York: Appleton-
1971   Century-Crofts.

Negandhi, A. R., and B. C. Reimann.   "Task Environment, Decentralization, and
1973   Organizational Effectiveness." *Human Relations*, 26:203–14.

Roethlisberger, F. J., and W. J. Dickson.   *Management and the Worker.* Cambridge,
1939   Mass.: Harvard University Press.

Woodward, Joan. "Technology, Managerial Control, and Organizational Behavior."
1973   In A. R. Negandhi (ed.), *Modern Organizational Theory.* Kent, Ohio: Kent
        State University Press.

Wright, Richard W.   "Organizational Ambiente: Management and Environment
1971   in Chile." *Academy of Management Journal*, 14:65–74.

8

Organization-Environment Interface: A Critical Appraisal

Editor's Note

This brief chapter provides a critical evaluation of the papers by Professor Lorsch and Professors Negandhi and Reimann. Those commenting are Professors Arlyn Melcher (Kent State University), Winston Oberg (Michigan State University), Richard Viola (Temple University), and Raymond Adamek (Kent State University). Professor Lorsch chose to respond to some of the comments. His responses are included immediately following the critical appraisal of his presentation.

Comments on Lorsch's Paper

INADEQUATE CONCEPTUALIZATION OF KEY
VARIABLES—*Arlyn J. Melcher*

Of the papers presented in this section, Lorsch's paper is perhaps the most explicit on the nature of the model and the insights it offers on factors affecting the functioning of organizations. It has won wide attention as a useful and innovative effort. To a large extent, though, it has been accepted uncritically. While it clearly is a useful contribution, there are problems with the approach that confound its potential. The usefulness of Lorsch's approach turns on the adequacy of his model as an analytical and research tool. The logical and theoretical elements of the effort are critical.

A number of problems arise from the manner in which the variables of the model have been conceptualized and operationalized. Some of these problem-variables are elements of the environment, formal structure and practices, behavior, personality, certainty, time span of feedback, and coordination required. The problems with these are:

1. Certainty and feedback are not operationally distinguishable. Differing degrees of feedback are important factors affecting the degree of certainty.

2. Strategic variables are illustrated, but no analytical categories are provided; that is, the variable is not operationalized.

3. Coordination required within a unit apparently is operationally indistinguishable from work flow—clearly an internal variable. This can be conceptualized as an external variable, but it creates confusion on what is defined as internal and what is defined as external variables. Where one discusses an environment-organization interface, some minimal concern must be given to boundary definition, even if only in an implicit manner.

4. Certainty/uncertainty can be conceptualized either as an external variable or as an internal variable. Perrow (1972), for instance, calls this "technology" and considers it as an internal variable.

Logically, "formality of structure" and "behavior of members" should be distinct; but in this case they are interwoven. In most management textbooks, formal structure includes the degree of centralization/decentralization, number of levels, form of departmentation, use of committee, and elements of a control system. Here, we have included: (a.) "degree with which work can be (rather than *is*) programmed," which is operationally indistinguishable from degree of certainty—an element of external environment; (b.) "extent to which plans are utilized," hardly an element of formal structure (at least as usually conceived); (c.) "shape of management hierarchy," which presumably is number of levels; and (d.) an open-ended category of "extent formal controls and procedures are used." Most would contend there is no measure of centralization which is a major element of formal organizations. Instead, this is handled under behavior by asking individuals about the degree to which they perceive autonomy, or the degree of influence they have over decisions, and the discretion they exercise over their own work.

Lorsch, of course, can ignore traditional categories and conceptualize aspects of formal structure as behavioral measures if it contributes to our understanding of organizations. The logic of this approach, however, is not apparent. It appears to be a failure to critically examine the logical consistency of the model.

Similar problems are associated with the handling of goals and time. Goal and time critieria are defined as elements of formal practices. Illustrations are provided for both, but neither is operationalized. A statement such as: "Similarly, unit *formal practices* must emphasize *goals* which are consistent with the *strategic variables in its environment*" (emphasis added), has no meaning since the underlined terms have not been operationalized. If it is possible to abstract from the illustrations provided, the author has not done it. The problems are further confounded by suggesting that these aspects of formal practices are some of the factors that influence goal commitment and time orientation of members. The relationship cannot be explored usefully until the formal practices variable is operationalized independently of the behavior variables.

Supervisory style is considered as an aspect of behavior and viewed as a subdimension of "influence over work activities." The concern is only with the degree of participation used. One can focus upon this aspect of leadership only; but, again, it must pass the test of usefulness. This requires Lorsch to ignore other elements of leadership that have been considered important by other researchers.

Lorsch sees an "individual's feelings of competence" as a central variable in his model. He defines this factor as "feelings of fulfillment which the individual obtains from engaging with his environment and solving problems in it." This appears to be the same as "individual satisfaction," or the broader term "morale," that is frequently used by others. This could be classified reasonably as an element of behavior. It may be that he would like to make behavior the central element determining effectiveness, but this orientation is likely to be difficult to defend.

Personality is defined in terms of cognitive structure, tolerance for ambiguity, attitude toward authority, and attitude toward others. This seems a useful measure of personality.

In conclusion, Lorsch is concerned with identifying some of the factors influencing the effectiveness of organizations. There are conceptual, operational, and theoretical problems with his definitions of both independent and dependent variables. The approach parallels the efforts of others, but there is little building on their work. This is a problem for most specialists in this area, but it sharply reduces the degree of development.

REFERENCE

Perrow, Charles.   *Complex Organizations: A Critical Essay.* Glenview, Ill.: Scott,
1972   Foresman and Company.

BIG HEADWAY BUT LACKS THEORETICAL
UNDERPINNING—*Winston Oberg*

Lorsch's paper provides additional documentation for his and Lawrence's (1969) major contribution to organization theory, namely the contingency theory. Classical theorists sought universal principles or rules which would help organizations arrive at the one best way to organize for any purpose. Mary Parker Follett (Metcalf and Urwick, 1941) provided an early challenge to the classical school with her insistence that situations alter cases and that what is necessary is to discover the "law of the situation" and adapt the organization and management process to the needs of the particular situation. More recently, Lorsch with his contingency theory, and Shull (1965) and his associates with their matrix theory, are in the process of attempting to categorize situations and, in effect, to identify the "one best way" of organizing in a particular situation. For example, if the organization is operating in a turbulent environment—one requiring frequent and creative responses to the need for change—and if the work involves advanced technology requiring highly trained employees, then Lorsch suggests a participative, nonbureaucratic, "Theory Y" kind of organizational climate may be best; yet in a stable organizational climate, where tasks can be simplified, work can be de-skilled, and where competition is based on costs rather than creativity, the bureaucratic, centralized, hierarchical, authoritarian, "Theory X" kind of organizational climate may most effectively lead to organizational survival and growth.

I admit that this rather neat matching of sets of environment constraints and contingencies with sets of optimal organizational responses appeals to my sense of order, my instincts as a teacher, and my aspirations as an organizational scientist. But I think it may be too early to write off the somewhat opposing insight of Katz and Kahn (1966) which they subsume under the label of "equifinality." Equifinality implies that for any given organization in any given organizational environment there may be, and probably are, a number of equally appropriate ways to achieve a given end. Equifinality suggests that there may well be no one best way to organize even for a particular set of contingencies. The best contingency theory can do, if the idea of equifinality is accepted, is to identify a set of appropriate, but not necessarily optimal, organizational responses to a particular set of situational contingencies. There can be no single best way to organize to achieve any single objective in any particular situation.

I don't suppose Lorsch would disagree with this observation. Nowhere does he imply that he has arrived at, or expects to arrive at, any normative statements about "the one best way" to organize for any particular configuration of contingencies. But enthusiastic readers of his books and articles may be tempted to conclude that this is what he has in fact done. My comments are directed at such uncautious readers.

I have one additional comment on the Lorsch approach. His model is commendably eclectic. But, like all eclectic approaches, it is subject to criticism on esthetic and scientific grounds. Eclectic models tend to begin to look like Rube Goldberg inventions as they take on more and more concepts from more and more disciplines. Like the reputed product of a committee, they resemble a camel more than a horse. Occam's Razor may be needed to cut away the unesthetic and unessential. Unfortunately, without the guiding logic of a unifying theory it is difficult to know what is unessential.

Moreover, without the power of a general, underlying theoretical structure, eclectic models provide little guidance for future research. They do not imply hypotheses to be tested or conclusions to be looked for. My former mentor, Dale Yoder, once with tongue in cheek described the theoretical approach of the Minnesota Industrial Relations Section as "multiphasic macroeclecticism." As I see the development of the work of Lorsch and his associates, it seems to me this label increasingly applies to their model. Of course, the obvious response to criticism like mine is— why don't you develop something better? Unfortunately, I am better able to criticize than to create. And with its limitations, Lorsch's model and research on the environmental impact on unit organizations is still just about the best of its kind in this country. I use it, *and* teach it.

REFERENCES

Katz, D., and R. Kahn. *The Social Psychology of Organizations.* New York: John
1966   Wiley.
Lawrence, Paul R., and Jay W. Lorsch. *Organization and Environment.* Homewood,
1969   Ill.: Richard D. Irwin.
Metcalf, H. C., and L. Urwick (eds.) *Dynamic Administration: The Collected Papers*
1941   *of Mary Parker Follett.* New York: Harper and Row Publishers, Inc.
Schull, Fremont A. *Matrix Structure and Project Authority for Optimizing Organiza-*
1965   *tional Capacity.* Carbondale, Ill.: Business Research Bureau, Southern
        Illinois University.

IMPRECISE DEFINITIONS OF MAJOR VARIABLES,
RESEARCH DESIGN VAGUE—*Richard Viola*

Lorsch's model, based as it is upon the concept of contingency, is quite useful in conceptualizing the complex, interactive relationships between the environment, the organization, and the individual. Lorsch's paper, however, leaves one with a somewhat unsatisfactory feeling that there are important questions which have not been answered and others which should be raised. For example, what precisely does he mean by the term *environment?* At times, it would appear that Lorsch uses the terms *task* and *environment* synonymously. But one cannot be sure because he is not sufficiently clear on this point. If these terms do mean the same thing, then no consideration has been given to the varying complexity of organizational tasks, the differentiation of tasks in general, and the various hierarchical levels in the organization at which these tasks are performed.

Failure to consider this point has important implications for "individual feelings of competence"—a crucial factor in Lorsch's model. If he refers to a sense of competence as "feelings of fulfillment which the individual obtains from engaging with his environment and solving problems in it," then it is important to note that the level of complexity and difficulty of problems and tasks may be so low that an individual gets no sense of competence from solving or completing such problems and tasks. The further effects on unit performance are obvious. The nature of the work itself, together with the organizational levels at which it is performed, may be important variables that warrant consideration here.

A further point must be made regarding definitions. Lorsch has also failed to define what "effective unit performance" is or, in other words, what precisely constitutes an effective unit for his model. It would appear that any testing of his model would require this because some criterion for performance measurement is necessary. The necessity of this can be seen because of Lorsch's statement that "We are in effect predicting that, based on unit performance, we can predict the other variables in the model." He tells us in the section on study design that a unit is effective or "less so, as judged by top management." It would be interesting to know the criteria used to measure effectiveness, especially since the kinds of organizations dealt with (research labs and production oriented types) *would* have different criteria. With reference to the behavioral variables in Lorsch's model, he emphasizes that "The measures we are using of behavioral characteristics are perceptual measures of the member's own behavior or of the behavior of the unit as a whole." This use of an individual's perception as a measurement tool is at best risky. We know that since perception is based on such things as one's past experience, education, values, stimulus patterns that initiate perception, and one's prevailing motivation at the time, perceptual distortions may be all too frequent. Lorsch, for that matter, provides us with no measurement techniques for any of the variables in his model. Though his choice of environmental, organizational, and individual behavioral factors may be most realistic (except possibly for his failure to consider the informal group and its influence), the neglect of measurability makes it most difficult to see the model as one having a very high degree of predictability. Also, what are the relative weights of the variables? Are they operational? This is important, especially if one conceptually disagrees with Lorsch's thesis that an organization which has not made an accommodation to or enjoys a good "fit" with its environment probably will have a relatively small number of individuals who are fulfilled.

Finally, his study design is too vague; it does not tell us enough regarding methodology. In addition, his statement that "the data uniformly support the set of relationships which I have just outlined" is inadequate for a paper which presents a model that has "major implications for organization theory." Lorsch says, "It is a further indication of the validity ... of a contingency approach to the study of organizational phenomena." I trust Lorsch is not using the term *validity* in its strictest sense because there have not been the precision tools of analysis and measurement techniques present to provide enough adequate ways of empirically testing the complex relationships in his model. Until this is possible, a greater understanding of the mutually interactive effects of the variables in the model upon organizational behavior vis-a-vis environmental phenomena will have to wait. Conceptually, however, Lorsch's contingency approach to organization theory is most promising and hopefully will be a fruitful one. This is especially so because of its consideration of the environment—a crucial factor in any study of organization.

RESPONSES FROM PROFESSOR LORSCH

It seems to me that the best typology for dealing with the comments is the well established "sins of omission versus sins of commission." Viola is more concerned with errors of omission. He would have liked me to cover the methodology we used. I intentionally did not do so, because of the length of the job and the time and space I had available. But let me assure him we have measured the variables discussed in the paper. Whether he will be satisfied with our methods is something I will have to learn after he has seen our manuscript now in progress. Further, Viola is concerned because I have not mentioned anything about performance measurement. Again, I felt it was too complex an issue to deal with in the time allowed. But let me say that we felt, based on our own work and that of colleagues, that the simplest and perhaps only way to get any comparative data, given issues of confidentiality and the heterogeneity of environments facing the pair of units, was to rely on managers' perceptions. Finally, Viola complains that I have not presented more complete findings in the paper. My statement "the data uniformly support the set of relationships just outlined," was intended as a tantalizing postscript. Once we have finished the manuscript, Professor Viola and other listeners or readers can judge for themselves whether our data is in fact "a further indication of the validity of the contingency approach." I still think it is.

With regard to sins of commission, I first of all find myself in an interesting conflict. Oberg says I have violated Occam's razor by using too many concepts, while Viola finds the selection of variables is realistic. My own inclination is to agree with both of them. I have been concerned throughout this study that we have used too many variables, and this bothers me because as a teacher I have preached the virtue of Occam's principle. But in considering the matter I have concluded that when one is looking at individual, organizational, and environmental factors, one realistically needs this many variables, although we probably could have carved out one or two here or there.

Oberg also accuses me of multiphasic macroeclecticism. If I understand what that means, I am amused and horrified. Both adjectives are called for because to be a "multiphasic macroeclectic" violates all my principles as a researcher, and besides I don't think I am one. Although the number of variables and the complexity of the model may hide the fact, we actually started this study with the conceptual framework I outlined. It was not a product of a massive set of cross correlations.

Oberg's point on "equifinality" I take more seriously and I agree with him, if we accept the Katz and Kahn idea. What we need, however, is more research to determine whether or not the notion of equifinality applies to organizational systems. Our own work to date suggests that a certain overall pattern is necessary to meet a given set of environmental conditions, but there may be many different approaches to obtain this pattern.

Melcher's comments about definitions I find interesting, but my general response is that as long as we use systems concepts we will be caught up in many such definitional issues. Nevertheless, I shall use his comments as an impetus to more precisely state our definitions in the manuscript in progress, mainly because I feel a good deal of his confusion stems from the brevity of the paper and the fact that he has inferred complete definitions in the examples I chose to use.

Melcher's statement linking feelings of competence to satisfaction, morale, etc, is more worrisome, simply because while he treats it as an error of commission, I see it as an error of omission. What I should have stressed, but did not, is that feelings of competence, as we have measured them, are indicators of an individual's confidence in his own ability to solve problems— to master the environment. I think this is quite different from the more traditional views of satisfaction.

Having made these responses let me say that I have found all the comments provocative and timely. I am sure they will contribute to our thinking as we work further with these issues.

Comments on Negandhi and Reimann's Paper

CONCEPTUALLY TOO
NARROW — *Raymond Adamek*

The authors' explanation of the data presented in Tables 2 and 3 of this article are highly plausible and even intellectually compelling. However, their market-competitiveness measure, which is implicitly presented as an indicator of environmental stability, does not capture the full scope of the Lawrence and Lorsch (1967) concept of environmental stability. The latter authors deal with the relative stability (predictability) of three sectors of an industry's environment--the scientific knowledge-base, technical-economic factors, and market considerations. Since they found that the degree of uncertainty associated with these sectors varied independently of one another across industries, it is questionable whether the market sector alone can be taken as an adequate measure of environmental stability. Furthermore, Lawrence and Lorsch look at different dimensions of the market sector than do Negandhi and Reimann. They focus on the clarity of information executives have about the market, the certainty of causal relationships operative within the market, and the length of time it takes to get feedback about a particular product. Hence, the extent to which Negandhi and Reimann's measure of market competitiveness can be considered a valid indicator of Lawrence and Lorsch's notion of environmental stability is open to question. How one answers this question will obviously determine the extent to which he considers Negandhi and Reimann's effort a test of Lawrence and Lorsch's contingency theory.

Though the general tone of these comments may be critical, one must conclude after reading both of the Negandhi/Reimann papers in this volume that they do contribute to unravelling the complexities of organizational-environmental interaction, and point the way toward further understanding of these phenomena. Like the other paper, this article provides a good example of the difficulty and rewards of coming to grips with "the environment" in organizational research.

REFERENCE

Lawrence, Paul R., and Jay W. Lorsch.   *Organization and Environment: Managing*
    1967   *Differentiation and Integration.* Boston: Graduate School of Business Administration, Harvard University.

PART III

Conceptualization at the Organization-Set and Task Environment Levels

9

Problems in the Study of Interorganizational Relationships

RICHARD H. HALL, JOHN P. CLARK

The past few years have seen almost an explosion of concern and study about interorganizational relationships. The purpose of this paper is to examine some of the reasons for this interest and to point out some of the problems which have come about because of the way this area of research has developed. In addition, some of the problems associated with actual research on interorganizational relationships will be discussed. In this discussion, data from a current study will be used to illustrate some of the difficulties encountered in attempting to measure interorganizational relationships and relate them to the organizations and the environment of which they are a part.

This paper is not a review of the literature. Such reviews are available in many different sources (Aldrich, 1970; Mulford and Klonglan, 1973; and White and Vlasak, 1971). What we are concerned with is the state of the art at the present time. It is our overall impression that the state is low. Our intent is to point out why this is true and to suggest some means by which the state of the art can be improved.

INTEREST IN INTERORGANIZATIONAL RELATIONSHIPS

A majority of the research and literature on interorganizational relationships has developed from the broader field of organizational sociology. In the 1960s, sociologists and others concerned with organizations began to look outside the organization in the realization that much of what goes on in an organization is directly or indirectly affected by outside influences of various sorts. The recent upsurge of papers dealing with the role of technology and other environmental characteristics is indicative of this realization and indicates some attempts have been made to shift concern away from the internal workings of organizations. At approximately the same time, sociology became aware of and enamored with the systems approach to

This research was supported by NIMH Grant Number 17508–02.

organizations and its emphasis on the environment. The systems approach strongly implies that other significant factors in the environment play a crucial role in what happens to any particular organization as a system. The systems approach also opens up the possibility that groups of organizations could themselves be treated as a system. This possibility has not yet been fully developed.

Explicit statements regarding the systemic nature of organizations have been provided by Gouldner (1959), Thompson (1967), and Katz and Kahn (1966). From these statements the concepts of input, throughput, and output have become part of the standardized language of organizational analysts. Clearly, both input and output have immediate interorganizational implications for almost all organizations. Suppliers, customers, and clients are most likely to be "other organizations" for any particular single organization.

The field of organizations thus has a history of development which has led rather inexorably toward interorganizational concerns. In addition to this intellectual development, there are certain historical factors which should be mentioned to complete the picture of why we are where we are. The interest in interorganizational relationships experienced its greatest growth during a period when academic research was under great pressure to be "relevant." This demand for relevance came from the major research funding agencies of the United States government and, in a totally different form, from the field itself as it sought ways to bring about social change. Almost all of the research on interorganizational relationships is at least implicitly concerned with ameliorating social ills through improved delivery of services. Only a very small percentage of the work in the field seems to be concerned with more drastic changes in the delivery of services or alternative means by which human needs can be met. By our very determination to examine reality, there is little likelihood that much change in reality will be brought about as a result of our investigations. There is thus an inherent conservatism in the current concern with relevance. This is good or bad, depending on one's stance on the matter.

The subject matter in most research on interorganizational relationships is indicative of the interest in amelioration. Almost all of the work to date has been done in the area of human services. Thus we see examinations of health, mental health, social services, juvenile justice, manpower training programs, civil defense, and alcoholism programs. All of the research has the implicit goal of better delivery of services. This is a worthy goal to be sure. Unfortunately, however, research in these areas has led the field away from certain research areas which are of crucial theoretical and practical importance. There is virtually no work done on government agency-business, business-business, or government agency-government agency relationships. It would be very interesting to know, for example, the extent to which relationships between public utilities and government regulatory agencies, pollution control agencies, major suppliers, major consumers, and other public utilities impinge upon the operations of a local public utility. Similarly, the relationships between federal, state, and local departments of education or highways have not been examined from an interorganizational perspective. These are interesting areas of research from the standpoint of the distribution of power in society and the impact of interorganizational patterns on society. They also would be crucial tests for some of the notions which have been developed about interorganizational relationships in the areas of human services in local communities.

The intellectual and practical concerns traced above have thus affected development of the field of interorganizational relationships. The result is that our subject organizations and interorganizational networks have been skewed in terms of being any sort of representative sample of organizations. We can only hope that our conceptual development has not been similarly skewed because of the uniqueness of our subject matter.

Despite these problems, the analysis of interorganizational relationships remains a terribly important subject. This importance is based upon the fact that people, programs, organizations, and society itself are affected by the interorganizational relationships which are so important for society. This importance can be seen in several ways. In the delivery of human services, for example, the recipient of those services is clearly influenced by the nature of the system which delivers them. Is he passed from one organization to another? Is he fought over or avoided by organizations in the system? Is he overserved or underserved?

The more general public is also affected by the costs incurred in the delivery of human services. Here, the analysis of interorganizational relationships can make some major contributions in terms of answering at least some of the questions regarding costs and benefits. While lowering costs may not always be to the public good, it is almost always a public concern.

Of less concern, but probably of more importance, is the role of interorganizational relationships in the distribution of power in local communities and the society as a whole. With some notable exceptions, such as Perrucci and Pilisuk (1970), and Turk (1970), there has been very little attention devoted to this topic. Within the various organizational networks in a community or the society at large, there is a distribution of power. Similarly, these networks and the interrelationships among them are crucial in the power distribution.

Interorganizational relationships also have an impact on the participants. The participants in this case are the personnel involved and the organizations themselves. The evidence is quite clear that boundary personnel are subject to role conflict (Kahn, et al., 1964). Oddly, there have not been serious investigations regarding the different forms of interorganizational relationships which lead to different role conflict conditions. For example, do conflict situations between organizations contribute to more or less role conflict (using this concept in an undifferentiated manner) than cooperative situations? Casual observations would suggest that cooperation might lead to more role conflict.

Turning to the organizations involved, we have excellent discussions by Selznick (1948) and Thompson and McEwen (1958) regarding cooptation and other processes between organizations. There are few definitive studies, however, which examine the impact of interorganizational relationships on the organizational participants. Part of the problem here, of course, is the relative absence of longitudinal studies in the area. In the medical field, there have been several studies examining plans for hospital mergers; there are also studies of organizations which come together through the formation of super-agencies, as in the case of some private social service agencies. The more frequent occurrence would seem to be the continuation of relationships over time without merger or super-agencies, with the relationships among the parties continually changing, but with no distinct move toward merger or total disintegration of the relationships. It is in these situations that the effect on the organization itself should be examined.

This last point raises an additional issue in the analysis of interorganizational relationships. It is widely held that the analysis of interorganizational relationships should include three basic units—the organizations, the interorganizational relationships themselves, and the environment (see Aldrich, Chapter 4, for an excellent discussion of this point). While everyone would probably nod his head in agreement at this, a major problem remains in terms of ordering the relationships among these variables. The possibilities here are these:

Figure 1

ENVIRONMENT→ORGANIZATION→INTERORGANIZATION
ENVIRONMENT→INTERORGANIZATION→ORGANIZATION
ORGANIZATION→INTERORGANIZATION→ENVIRONMENT
ORGANIZATION→ENVIRONMENT→INTERORGANIZATION
INTERORGANIZATION→ORGANIZATION→ENVIRONMENT
INTERORGANIZATION→ENVIRONMENT→ORGANIZATION

Each of these is a reasonable possibility and also probably an actual fact. The relationships thus are probably better characterized as follows in Figure 2:

Figure 2
ENVIRONMENT

INTERORGANIZATION↔ORGANIZATION

While this is undoubtedly a quite accurate description, it is probably beyond our current methodological abilities to conduct research from this sort of framework. Determining the oneway relationship among these variables has taxed our abilities. Moving toward a reciprocal analysis is not yet within our grasp.

Before turning to some of the methodological problems, an additional point should be made in regard to conceptualizing interorganizational relationships. Analyses of interpersonal relationships have led to the conclusion that the nature of the ongoing relationships affects subsequent relationships (Homans, 1950). This should be equally true among organizations. At a simple level, frequent contacts among organizations would be hypothesized to be related to higher levels of coordination which should increase over time. Later in this paper we will present some data pertinent to this issue. We raise this point because none of the units depicted in Figure 2 can be taken as simply influenced by the other units. Each has its own dynamics.

SOME METHODOLOGICAL PROBLEMS

We turn now to some of the methodological problems which emerged as we conducted research on interorganizational relationships. The research is concerned with organizations which deal with problem youth. These involve the juvenile court, juvenile probation, detention halls, school pupil personnel services (particularly school social workers), child protection or children services units of welfare departments, juvenile police, mental health clinics, and occasionally detached worker programs and other programs designed to divert youths from the juvenile justice system. The research is being conducted in 12 large cities across the United States; however, the data to be discussed are based only on the study of the first city, which is in the upper midwestern section of the country.

The first methodological problem was, on the face of it, very simple. We had to decide who was in and who was out of this network of organizations. We began the research in the major public agencies with observations and unstructured interviews, moving later to more structured interviews and questionnaires. The early observations and interviews revealed that a vast number of organizations in this city were concerned in one way or another with problem youth. It soon became apparent that it would be impossible to include all of them in our study. This led to the distribution of a questionnaire which, among other things, asked:

... (In thinking about these things) you were undoubtedly reminded of the
fact that there are other organizations in the community which are also concerned
with problem youth. In fact, your organization and the others might be thought
of as a "network" or "system" of organizations which in one way or another
comes into contact with problem youth.

In the spaces below, please list these other organizations. Where appropriate,
please indicate the specific section or unit concerned with problem youth. The
list should include all of the organizations which the people in your own organization would probably think of as part of this "network" or "system" which
handles problem youth.

This questionnaire was distributed to all of the professional personnel
in the original (eight) organizations. The returned questionnaires permitted
us to develop a set of "orgio-grams" for each organization. Figure 3 depicts
the major characteristics of these results, without reflecting the specific

Figure 3

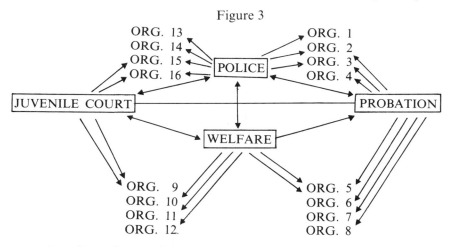

number of mentions each organization received; this figure is not the complete set of orgio-grams, but is symbolic of the results.

The major impact of the findings from this facet of the research was
that we had, indeed, isolated the core agencies from the outset. The results
also informed us that one of the agencies we thought was central to the
core set was not, and that an organization we had only briefly considered
should be included in the study. These results are in no way startling;
however, they are somewhat bothersome. Results such as these simply
indicate the gross number of times an organization gets mentioned, without
any indication of the frequency, intensity, or importance of the contacts.
It is totally reputational and may deviate from reality to an unknown degree
when other criteria are used.

At the same time, the results also led to a critical decision-making point in the research: which organizations to include and which to exclude. There was no rule of thumb for the number of mentions an organization must receive in order to be included in a network of organizations. Each of our focal organizations had its own "set" of organizations. This set includes the other core agencies which we have included in our study, which is fortunate for the purposes and the results of the study. The set also includes many other organizations. These have not been included in our study, but must be viewed as crucial in the operation of any particular organization. Our focus is on those organizations involved in direct service to youth.

The conclusion which must be reached in a study such as this is that an examination of any particular set, network, or system of organizations almost by definition excludes other important organizations for any of the members of the set. For example, the state department of welfare is crucial for a county welfare department; but it does not show up as part of our network of organizations. Each organization in the network thus has other networks in which it operates. Tactical decisions must thus be made in any interorganizational research about which organizations to include and which to exclude. The inclusion of all organizations and each of their major contacts would result in ever-increasing circles of organizations which would not stop until *all* organizations are included. At the same time, the tactical decision to include a particular set of organizations must be recognized for what it is—a compromise between the ideal of a complete picture and the reality of the actual conduct of research. Of course, the administrators and workers in any organization do not use the full range of interorganizational contacts as they work and make decisions. This, also, is a selective thing. Different sets of organizations are selected for different purposes. It remains a distortion of reality, however, to settle on a particular network of organizations as *the* network of organizations.

Recognizing all of this, we proceeded with our research plan. This involved asking the organizations identified as the core network of organizations concerned with problem youth more detailed questions about the nature of their interorganizational relationships. (These questions are only part of the total research project.) All of the professional personnel in each organization were presented with a "map" of the other organizations in the network. This map is depicted in Figure 4.

These detailed questions (listed in Table 1) represent an attempt to quantify the quality of the relationship within each organization. Each respondent was asked to indicate the frequency, importance, etc. of his organization's contacts with *each* of the other organizations in the network. We thus were able to derive scores for each organization in regard to its contacts with each of the other organizations. We are ignoring the very serious problem of the use of a single question for each variable. The limita-

Figure 4

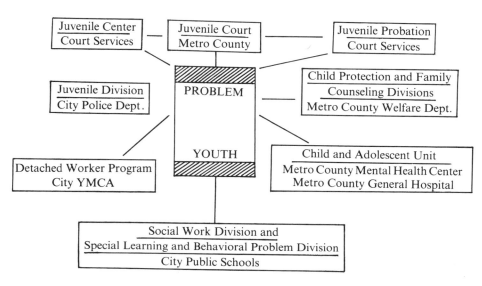

tions of space on the questionnaire precluded (from the outset of the research) any scaling for each of the variables.

It is here that additional serious methodological problems emerge. The first is a relatively simple one, that of organizational size. Some of these organizations are very small—as few as five members. By standard criteria, a mean score cannot be used in such situations. At the same time, we wanted to depict the organization and had no recourse but to use the mean. This problem would not arise if there were objective measures independent of individual responses which could be used to determine the level of coordination or conflict. This is not the case, and we were forced to use the mean. Fortunately, through the use of the coefficient of variation for each mean, we were able to determine that the means are representative scores for each organization.

Having determined that we could use the mean scores, we were faced with a more serious problem, one that appears in all interorganizational research when the organization is used as a starting point. For example, in describing something as simple as the frequency of contact between the police and the schools, we have scores from the schools in regard to their frequency of contact with the police, and vice versa. We do not, however, have a true measure of frequency standardized for all interorganizational relationships. It makes no sense to combine the means in the example of the police and the schools, since what may be listed as frequent contact for one organization may be much less for the other organization because of the one way nature of some contacts. The average score here has the potential for great distortion.

We resolved this problem by taking each organization's score on each question as a unit of data. In this particular case, there were eight organizations. Each organization had relationships with each of the other seven organizations. Thus for each variable measured we have 56 (8 × 7) scores. This is sufficient for our analysis.

This resolution contains its own problems, however. The major one is that it is now impossible to relate organizational characteristics to interorganizational scores which are used in this fashion. Each organization has seven scores on each variable. We have not yet determined how we can relate an organizational characteristic, such as the extent of conflict within the organization or the level of bureaucratization, to such things as communications with other organizations. As we get more data in from other cities, perhaps a solution to this dilemma can be achieved.

SOME PROBLEMATIC FINDINGS

In this section some of the very preliminary findings will be presented. They are very preliminary because they represent the data from only one of the 12 cities which comprise the total study. They are also preliminary because they are merely zero-order correlation coefficients. We are presently utilizing various multiple regression techniques to try to make more sense out of this first set of data. Some questions have also been recoded from discrete to continuous categories (questions 2, 3, 4, 9, and 11).

Table 1 presents these correlation coefficients, along with the questions which were asked in regard to each variable. These findings contain a few surprises. For example, conflict between organizations is positively related to good communications, as is frequency of interaction. It appears that communication patterns can be of good quality, be used frequently, and be based around conflict situations. On the other hand, as one would expect, coordination of efforts is rather strongly associated with such factors as the availability of personnel, the importance of the contacts, compatible operating philosophies, the assessment of good performance on the part of the other agencies, and the assessment that the other organizations have competent personnel. Coordination is also positively associated with good communications, suggesting that communications can perhaps play a dual role in leading to coordination and being part of conflict situations. The use of multiple regression techniques should help straighten out some of these patterns.

It is interesting to note that power differences between organizations do not make much difference on any variable; perhaps the questions asked were not strong enough. There is an additional indicator of power differences

Table 1
INTERCORRELATION OF INTERORGANIZATIONAL PHENOMENA

	Frequency	Personalization	Immediacy	Voluntary Legitimation	Availability	Importance	Coordination	Conflict	Individual-Domain Conflict	Conflict Resolution	Formalization of Conflict Resolution	Compatibility	Performance	Communications	Competence	Power
1. How often are contacts made between your agency and each of the following ones? 1 = a few times a year 6 = continually		.523	.506	−.638	−.552	−.711	−.425	−.336	−.013	−.154	−.310	−.011	−.177	−.462	−.091	.002
2. How are most of the contacts made: (Personalization) 1 = letter or memo 2 = person to person			.569	−.301	−.414	−.300	−.305	.084	.094	−.098	.149	−.111	−.266	−.509	.012	−.086
3. What are the reasons for the contacts? (Immediacy) 1 = to pass information 3 = coordinate, plan				−.122	−.215	−.344	−.121	.041	.018	.151	.179	−.043	−.148	−.464	.012	−.083
4. What are the bases of the contacts with each agency? (Voluntary Legitimation) 1 = required by law 3 = formal agreement between agencies					.592	.482	.380	.143	.062	−.101	−.490	.054	.201	.305	.230	−.105

Table 1 (*cont.*)

	Frequency	Personalization	Immediacy	Voluntary Legitimation	Availability	Importance	Coordination	Conflict	Individual-Domain Conflict	Conflict Resolution	Formalization of Conflict Resolution	Compatibility	Performance	Communications	Competence	Power
5. Are the appropriate personnel of the other organization generally *available* when members of your organization need them? (Availability) 1 = Always 4 = Never						.574	.617	−.087	.205	.136	−.197	.221	.399	.492	.314	−.137
6. How *important* are the contacts with each of these organizations to the work of your own organization? (Importance) 1 = Very Important 4 = Not at all important							.663	.196	.368	.068	.175	.255	.366	.312	.324	.192
7. How well are the activities of your organization and each of the other organizations *coordinated?* (Coordination) 1 = All very well 5 = All very poorly								.297	.526	.601	.021	.696	.817	.269	.739	.078

Table 1 (cont.)

	Frequency	Personalization	Immediacy	Voluntary Legitimation	Availability	Importance	Coordination	Conflict	Individual-Domain Conflict	Conflict Resolution	Formalization of Conflict Resolution	Compatibility	Performance	Communications	Competence	Power
8. To what extent do *disagreements* or *disputes* characterize the relations between your organization and each of the others? (Conflict) 1 = To a great extent 4 = Never									−.249	−.618	−.126	−.517	−.503	−.239	−.421	−.151
9. What is the *basis* of the disagreements or disputes between your organization and each of the others? (Individual-Domain Conflict) 1 = Specific cases or personality differences 3 = Duplication of services and inefficiency										.519	.224	.643	.548	−.142	.566	.142
10. How well are any differences between your organization and the others *worked out*? (Conflict Resolution) 1 = Very well 5 = Very poorly											.177	.734	.801	.158	.627	.390

Table 1 (cont.)

	Frequency	Personalization	Immediacy	Voluntary Legitimation	Availability	Importance	Coordination	Conflict	Individual-Domain Conflict	Conflict Resolution	Formalization of Conflict Resolution	Compatibility	Performance	Communications	Competence	Power
11. In *what way* are these differences between your organization and each of the others handled? (Formalization of Conflict Resolution) 1 = Discussion by individuals 3 = By formally established committees												.183	.024	−.434	.006	−.052
12. How compatible is your organization's *operating philosophy* with that of each of the other organizations? (Compatibility) 1 = Very compatible 3 = Not compatible													.816	.054	.774	.252
13. How *well* does each of the other agencies perform its tasks in regard to problem youth? (Performance) 1 = Very well 5 = Very poorly														.198	.821	.394

Table 1 (cont.)

	...	Competence	Power
14. How would you characterize the quality of *communication* between your organization and each of the other organizations? (Communications) 1 = Very good communication 3 = Very poor communication		-.061	.023
15. How would you describe the *competence* of the personnel in each of the other organizations? (Competence) 1 = All are competent 5 = None are competent			.232
16. If we define *power* as the extent to which one organization affects another organization, how would you characterize the power relationship between your organization and each of the others in regard to the handling of problem youth? (Power) 1 = My organization is much more powerful 7 = My organization is much less powerful			

Column headers (rotated): Frequency, Personalization, Immediacy, Voluntary, Legitimation, Availability, Importance, Coordination, Conflict, Individual-Domain Conflict, Conflict Resolution, Formalization of Conflict Resolution, Compatibility, Performance, Communications, Competence, Power in the network of organizations which has not yet been brought into the analysis. Another moderate anomaly is the fact that frequency of interaction is positively related to coordination, communication, and conflict (note that the correlation coefficients are negative because of the scoring direction of the items). In this case, frequency of interaction does seem to lead to better, more coordinated efforts; at the same time it also leads to conflict. These results must be taken as very tentative; however, they reemphasize one of the points made earlier in this paper.

Interorganizational interactions per se are related to each other. Quite clearly, the only way to specify the dynamics of how ongoing interactions help structure future interactions is through a longitudinal study. The cross sectional design which we have employed can only suggest what some of these dynamics are. It would be unwise to extrapolate from interpersonal interactions to the interorganizational level and assume that some of the dynamics from this type of situation also operate at the interorganizational level. Individuals are the media through which organizations interact, to be sure; but organizations in almost all spheres of life have their own goals and pursue their own activities. They also operate in a complex legal environment which, in many cases, sets limits on the amount and quality of interactions. This same legal environment can force organizations to interact.

Another apparent difference between interorganizational and interpersonal interactions is the fact that the actors can and frequently do change on the interorganizational level. Normal turnover and personnel reassignments lead to new boundary personnel. Each succeeding generation of personnel is affected by the lore of the past—remembering the good old days when the other organization was not so high and mighty, or remembering grievous injuries of the past. The organization provides its actors with at least partial role expectations. The organization also has its particular role to play in terms of its and the environment's expectations of where it fits into the society's division of labor.

CONCLUDING REMARKS

In this paper we have examined some of the problems that arise when interorganizational relationships are studied. Like most researchers, we have raised more issues than we have resolved. There has truly been an explosion of interest in the interorganizational phenomenon. Our own project has already generated over 50 requests for our conceptual model and instrumentation. As can be seen from this paper, the conceptual model is not all that well developed. One of our major concerns is that by taking the approach used in this study, or any of the relatively few other empirical studies in the field, there will be a grossly underdeveloped set of concepts and methods in the field. Our personal experience with some scales for bureaucracy and professionalism is that there is a tendency for investigators to adopt techniques and conceptualizations prematurely and uncritically. Certainly, it is good to accumulate knowledge through common approaches in different situations. At the same time, however, the remarks here should not lead to the conclusion that we are ready to begin this sort of accumulation.

The present study has not solved the issue of how to bring the more general environment surrounding the organizations and interorganizational network into the analysis through sound measurement. It appears that organizational analysts are really not yet ready to comment with clarity about the general environment. Aldrich's work in this volume is a step in the right direction; but this only specifies the organizational environment and fails to provide a basis for comparing the environments of different organizations.

There also remains much to be done on the nature of personnel in the organizations. Most studies of interorganizational interactions have dealt with organizations which have a high concentration of professional staff. If the professional staff share a common background, as in the case of Aiken and Hage's (1968) study, one could expect that cooperation and increased interorganizational interactions would probably ensue. When the organizations are staffed with people having different professional backgrounds, the opposite might be true. This will be tested out in future months.

As noted earlier, the ordering of environmental-organizational-interorganizational interactions must be examined with great care. Right now it is our impression that we do not have measurements or longitudinal studies of sufficient depth and power to say much about this issue. It certainly appears that this important set of relationships must be placed in a system's perspective. The placement of the components of the system, however, is still in doubt.

The analysis of interorganizational relationships must be informed by what we know from analyses of interpersonal relationships and organizations themselves. Most students of interorganizational phenomena have come from the field of organizations. We can only hope that this will lead to greater understanding of interorganizational interactions, as well as the completion of our conceptual models of organizations.

REFERENCES

Aiken, Michael, and Jerald Hage. "Interorganizational Interdependence and Intra-
1968   Organizational Structure." *American Sociological Review*, 33:912–30.
Aldrich, Brian. "Relations between Organizations: A Critical Review of the Litera-
1970   ture." Minneapolis: University of Minnesota (unpublished paper).

found in the hospital emergency room) to a broad interest in the client as a person, as a product of and participant in society (as in the case of a psychiatric out-patient clinic). Longitudinality, on the other hand, is a time dimension referring to the fact that organizational interest in a client may vary from a truncated span of time (again, as the emergency room) to an almost indeterminate span of time (as in chronic illness hospitals or nursing homes). Our argument is that these interests may vary independently of one another and the four logically different kinds of arrangements which emerge will have significantly different impacts on the internal structures, interpersonal processes, and external relationships of organizations. The four biographical variants are depicted in Table 1.

Table 1
THE FOUR BIOGRAPHICAL VARIANTS

| | Biographical Interest | |
Empirical Examples	*Lateral* (*Social Space*)	*Longitudinal* (*Social Time*)
Acute General Hospital	—	—
TB Hospital, Rehabilitation Hospital, Public Health Department, Medical School	—	+
Short-Term Therapeutic Psychiatric Hospital	+	—
Long-Term Therapeutic Hospital, Liberal Arts College	+	+

The logic of this typological system suggests that certain similarities ought to be found between those organizations manifesting a similar lateral interest in their clients, even though they may differ sharply in the extent of their longitudinal concern. Thus, for example, one would expect to find some structural similarities between a general hospital and a TB hospital, in spite of the fact that the latter has an extended longitudinal concern in the client, while the former does not. That is, the orientation of both institutions toward their clients, i.e., patients, is highly specific, focusing as each does upon relatively well-defined disease entities. Thus, although each organization may take account of such lateral life-space factors as occupation, family life, age, and sex, the relevance of these to the defined client problem is minimal. Conversely, those institutions which have a similar stake in the longitudinal careers of their clients should share some features in common despite possible marked differences along the lateral dimension.

Thus, a long-term psychiatric hospital, for example, should logically resemble in some respects a TB hospital, even though the former has a broad lateral interest in the client, while the latter does not. And similarly, each of the four types should, we argued, reflect some organizational characteristics which distinguish them.

Assuming the logical validity of the typology and, more important, the reasonableness of the way organizational interest in the clients was conceptualized, we then attempted to show how organizations with similar and/or logically dissimilar interests in clients manifest systematic similarities and/or differences in a number of structural and functional patterns. For our purposes in this paper, the most significant of these patterns deals with interorganizational collaboration, although it should be noted (and will be discussed later) that matters relevant to the internal dimensions of organizational processes are critically related to this special concern. For the moment, however, let me describe the initial effort to relate the client biography model to problems of interorganizational relations.

Two considerations are basic to this effort. The first has to do with designating what is meant by interorganizational collaboration; the second involves showing how and in what ways organizational laterality and longitudinality relate to different organizational propensities for collaboration.

With respect to the first of these considerations, it seems useful to make the distinction between collaboration at the policy-administrative level and at the operating-implementing level. While both may be desirable and perhaps essential, they do not necessarily take place together; for example, separate hospitals may indeed engage in collaborative efforts on general fiscal matters, channeling of information concerning plans for long-range development, and other administrative matters which serve essentially to insure, in a relative sense, maintaining the status quo. But they may not collaborate at all at the operational level (the point of contact with the patient) through joint utilization of scarce professional personnel or by sharing newly acquired treatment knowledge, and the like. The reverse may occur, though it is likely that administrative collaboration takes place more often than joint operational participation.

It is of further use to make the distinction between formal and informal interorganizational collaboration. By *formal* is meant those processes by which members of two or more organizations engage in relationships with one another in their capacities as members of their organizations. By *informal* is meant those strategies of interorganizational contact in which the collaborators act in some capacity other than as organizational members. Hence, it is the substance of the interaction between organizations not necessarily its structural form which forms the distinction.

Let us discuss the second major consideration—namely, in what particular ways are these modes of interorganizational collaboration related to the nature of the organizations' interests in their clientele groups? We will examine the two extreme types depicted by the laterality-longitudinality paradigm and address these matters in terms of the medical arena, particularly the realm of interhospital relations.

Given the assumption that all organizations, to a greater or lesser extent, take account of other organizations in coming to decisions about their clients, it is our hypothesis that those organizations characterized by greater degrees of lateral and longitudinal interest in their clients will manifest greater readiness for interorganizational collaboration (and would be more successful at it) than those having specific and short-term interests in their clients. The attempt to prove at the least the heuristic value of such a hypothesis is better characterized as description, not demonstration.

We argued, for example, that the specific and short-term focused institution—the community general hospital—typically has little propensity for formal and direct collaboration with other hospitals at either the administrative or the operative levels. The specificity of its interest in the patient and its concern with finely discriminated strategies of care tend to make such hospitals isolated professional islands in the community (Elling, 1963 : 73–112; Hall, 1946 : 30–44). They may, however, be thrust into dialogue with one another through intermediary organizations—e.g., the local medical society or the local hospital planning councils. Nonetheless, the interstitial character of such bridging organizations makes them fertile grounds for introducing themes in interhospital dialogue not directly addressed to patient care per se. These themes can range from ethnic and racial differences to the firmly encrusted barriers between public and private sponsorship, to even more subtle manifestations of local community power cliques and spheres of influence. Perhaps even more important, it is in the highly focused acute hospital that a major avenue of operational collaboration is *least* likely to occur, i.e., the joint appointment of medical personnel to two or more medical establishments. Indeed, the competitive character of the typical general hospital mitigates against utilizing this promising mode of strategies to follow their departed clients. "Checking" on patients requires the development of administrative mechanisms for getting information from other organizations which may later be responsible for the welfare of the patient.

All of this appears true only at the formal level. Hospitals such as these are usually caught up in a complex network of informal relationships which may include the local medical society and health insurance programs in the community, and the major institutional establishments via the members of its boards of trustees, as well as the local community power structures. We do not mean to imply that the specifically focused and short-term hospital does not engage in contact or dialogue with other hospitals; we mean merely that control over the kind and extent of collaborative activities has been given over to *extra* hospital persons and agencies.

On the other hand, the more broadly oriented and long-term hospital stands in marked contrast. The elite psychiatric hospital, for example, is customarily involved in a massive and sometimes conflicting set of operative and administrative linkages at both the formal and informal levels. The wide range of professional personnel it utilizes tends to extend their professional contacts into other similarly organized institutions. Further, the fact of a longitudinal interest in the client's future biography means that the organization must devise ways of establishing working relationships with other organizations which may ultimately be held responsible for the later career of the patient (client). Thus one is likely to find that the nonlateral/nonlongitudinal organization (hospital or not) has no established linkages with the juvenile court, nursing home, family welfare agencies, and so forth, while the administrative personnel of the longitudinal institution are often intimately tied in with a wide range of their interested institutions (Levine and White, 1961 :583–601; Litwak and Hylton, 1962:395–402; Saunders, 1960 :229–32; Thompson, 1962 : 309–24).

As brief as this discussion has been, it does serve to underscore a major underlying proposition—that hospitals (and service organizations in general) have different capacities for effective and meaningful collaboration at both the operational and administrative levels. Further, that these capacities derive ultimately from the ways and extent to which such organizations choose to intervene in the lives of their clients (patients).

THE SALIENCY OF CLIENT CHARACTERISTICS

Admittedly, the discussion thus far has been at a rather high level of abstraction and quite speculative. This is not to say that we regard it lightly. On the contrary, we feel that the concerns and directions suggested by the client biography paradigm are of major sociological relevance and, even more to the point, provide an analytic departure point that links a series of seemingly disparate issues and problems confronting our major service networks. With this statement, I think that it is important to backtrack somewhat and address two major problems associated with the originally formulated client biography scheme. These problems are closely related but nevertheless analytically separate. The first of these deals with the analytic status of the focal constructs, laterality and longitudinality. More specifically, by depicting them as "sensitizing" ideas we avoided (and in a sense justifiably so) the question of whether they are to be considered as independent or dependent variables—if indeed they refer to empirically demonstrable variations as implied. The second dilemma stems from the former—namely, our tacit assumption that it is a relatively simple matter to delineate both the range and saliency of selected client characteristics that inform a given organization's orientation toward its clients.

The remainder of this paper is devoted to considering these issues. It is hoped that by so doing, still another, and perhaps more empirically useful, departure point for relating client characteristics to matters of interorganizational relations will emerge. In the first place, let us reverse the strategy used in the original formulation of the client biography model. That is, rather than regarding laterality-longitudinality as given or easily identifiable modes of organizational interest in clients, I think it equally appropriate to regard these constructs as referring to sets or dependent variables; in other words, rather than merely showing that lateral and longitudinal interests are related to the structural and functional patterns of organizations, I now choose to regard such interests not as departure points, but as organizational outcomes involving the dynamic interplay between and among the following ingredients: (1.) the existing structural and functional patterns that obtain in a given organization; (2.) the predominant normative directives that indicate the objectives an organization has for its clients; and (3.) the client himself as a reacting or potentially reactive factor to what an organization is doing to or for him.

This alternative approach to laterality-longitudinality was prompted in part by a nagging thought that although the original formulation focused on client characteristics as "integral factors influencing the structure and functioning of such systems," the model set forth made no provision for showing how the client, implicitly or explicitly, plays an active role in actually influencing the orientation the organization has with respect to him or with respect to the service it renders. In a word, my social-psychological self took issue with my more purely sociological side.

These particular concerns were heightened as the result of a study conducted by one of my graduate students which pointed to the problems inherent in designating the saliency of client characteristics (Gersuny, 1968). The study involved three sheltered workshops where it was supposed that since such organizations deal with handicapped persons, the diagnosed disability would be a paramount client characteristic. However, it appeared from discussions with agency personnel and an examination of workshop publications that the client's diagnosed disability was not defined as a relevant criterion. Rather, clients were evaluated primarily on the basis of their productive capacity. Furthermore, the minimal importance attributed to diagnosed disability as a salient client characteristic for such organizations was made explicit by responses to the question: "If the clients in this agency had different handicaps, would the evaluation of the agency's goals change?" The vast majority of the personnel working in the organizations studied indicated that their orientation toward their clients would be the same even though they had different disabilities.

This is not to say that the nature of a client's diagnosed handicap was completely ruled out as having some influence on staff evaluations. The findings do, however, suggest that what appears obvious and specific may be manifested in indirect and in more general forms. For example, while evaluations may be the same regardless of specific handicaps, distinctions were found in terms of characterizing clients along a continuum ranging from "regular worker" at one extreme, to "patient or ward" at the other. While there were no significant differences in the way clients were defined between the agencies studied, there were marked differences among staff components within those agencies. Specifically, production supervisors are least likely to consider the client as resembling a "real worker" while administrative personnel are most inclined to so characterize him. Professional staff workers fell somewhere between the extremes.

While such findings are tentative, they do strengthen several important inferences concerning the relationship between client characteristics and the structure and functioning of service organizations. Of special interest is the notion that the saliency of client characteristics involves not only the relevance of specific attributes at a given moment in time (e.g., what the agency considers as appropriate service once the person becomes a client of that organization), but also directs attention to the fact that any given client attribute may function episodically. For example, what may operate as the salient feature for the purposes of admission may no longer be regarded as critical in the later stages of service delivery, or in decisions having to do with stopping such service.

In addition, what may be a significant client attribute for one part of an organization may not be so considered by another· therefore, what eventually emerges as a dominant view of the client may be as much a function of intraorganizational cooperation or conflict, or both. On the other hand, it may well be the case that what gets to be considered a "modal" view of the client is in reality "a many splintered thing"—a variety of orientations packaged under a common rubric for purposes of public relations but which is not reflective of actual organizational operations.

Such considerations lead to another—namely, that if we grant the proposition that the selection of salient client characteristics by an organization is a process involving the give and take between and among its component parts, then it also seems reasonable to suppose that the client himself, by virtue of the numerous attributes he carries with him to any given organization, is as much a part of the selection process as are the parts of the organization which ultimately provide services to him. That is to say, selection involves a declaration of what is relevant from what is irrelevant, and the combination and array of attributes presented by a client becomes as much a factor in this process as are the mechanisms which exist to assess, diagnose, or whatever it takes to ready the client for the work of the organization.

In an earlier paper, I tried to come to grips with the problems alluded to above (Rosengren and Lefton, 1970:17–36). The critical conceptual device for that attempt involved redefining *laterality* in order to force attention to the proposition that organizational interests in their clients is as much a resultant as it is steady state. Laterality II (and by implication longitudinality, although this discussion primarily concerns laterality), therefore, was defined as referring to the extent to which an organization is responsive to the reaction or reaction-potential of its clients in determining formal procedures in the delivery of service. Plus-laterality, thus, indicates a high degree of organizational responsiveness to client reactions (and inputs) demonstrated in official operations. Minus-lateral organizations, conversely, make little or no effort to permit client reactions to influence formal operations. These definitions may seem merely to call attention to the fact that some organizations adhere to rigid bureaucratic methods, while others are more flexible and adapt to changing pressures. The concern is not with discussing alternative ways of defining bureaucratic types of organization. The interest is in explaining why organizations, especially hospitals, differ in their responsiveness to client reactivity. The redefinition of laterality was designed to permit inquiry into the logic of certain organizational structures for specific service activities, and the factors which seem to sustain, negate, or otherwise affect such structures. By suggesting that the client and his characteristics are involved in the determination of formal structures, I was seeking to underscore the proposition that whether a hospital will be more or less lateral is problematic and, therefore, better characterized as an empirical question than a taken for granted fact or presupposition.

Focussing on the TB hospital as a reference illustration, I tried to show just how formal medical organizations respond and ultimately select from a variety of patient attributes those it chooses to regard as salient for its functional pursuits and, likewise, just how such institutions manage to de-emphasize other features of their clients. It was my contention that specific organizational interests in patients will significantly influence the organizational patterns of a given hospital when these are assumed to be potentially relevant to patients at admission rather than being emergent conditions which develop during the course of an illness and its treatment. In other words, of special interest in understanding hospital dynamics is whether patient exigencies are either (1.) "cooled out" in the sense of being managed without being allowed to affect ongoing structure, or (2.) are viewed as an intrinsic part of the medical problem so that these factors become intricately interwoven with the structural apparatus of the hospital. A "universalistic" as opposed to a "particularistic" stance regarding extra disease factors implies that they are intrinsic to the medical problem at the point of admission. It means also that the organizational apparatus designed to provide the relevant services shall be commensurate with the magnitude and scope of its task in terms of adequate staff, equipment, and space, and appropriate status and decision-making influence. Implied also is that the operations of such "departments" are considered to be functionally effective and professionally competent by virtue of specialized training, and that such operations will be permitted to apply the standards and criteria intrinsic to the discipline involved. In short, the capability of extra-disease considerations (concerning personal attributes of the patient) to force an organizational response is directly related to the degree to which such factors are permitted expression through specific structural mechanisms characterized by "universalism" and functional autonomy.

In more general terms, the suggestion here is that laterality II is structurally conditioned in that the organizational arrangements of the hospital are designed to anticipate extra-disease contingencies. It is of special importance that patient characteristics are differentially evaluated at the point of admission. The extent to which they operate as feedback variables into the larger system depends not on their intrinsic significance but on organizational readiness to accept their relevance by expanding problem definitions and providing structural means for their expression and management. The choice of general categories among which degrees of laterality II are differentiated might be expected to vary from one hospital to another and to have far-reaching and distinctive implications for the organization in such basic matters as staffing patterns, ranking of positions, and the nature of interorganizational linkages.

IMPLICATIONS FOR INTERORGANIZATIONAL ANALYSIS: A TALE OF TWO THEMES

Now to the matter of interorganizational analysis and the relevance of the two themes described in this paper. In the first section, I summarized an approach to interorganizational relations that although somewhat innovative is nevertheless orthodox in that its major objective was to lend to an understanding of how organizations *qua* organizations relate to other organizations *qua* organizations. To say that this avenue is conventional is not to imply that all the returns are in, or that a field of study has been crystallized (to the extent that formal organizations is a field of study). I mean that to talk about administrative or financial encounters, formal or informal linkages, and the structural ingredients of given organizations that give rise to assumed propensities for interorganization collaboration, is to draw attention to those factors that describe the ways organizations take other organizations into account in their operations as entities (Litwak and Rothman, 1970:137–86). It seems to me that this concern with describing the external manifestations that apparently bind or in one way or another relate one organization to others presumes that a rational system composed of several organizations does, indeed, empirically exist, and that observable linkage in the form of communication, exchange, or notions of interchange is a viable representation of that fact. Whether such is the case remains to be empirically demonstrated, and I am not denigrating such efforts. I have myself been involved in such analyses and will continue to be involved in them. The point I am trying to make is that the first theme reflects a view of the field of interorganizational relations characterized by a high level of abstraction and which operates in accord with a logic and integrity *sui generis*. Although we may agree that there is much to be gained analytically from such a perspective, there is indeed a price to be paid. It seems to me that an overemphasis on the shape of networks, complexes, systems, or however else the relations between and among organizations are characterized, almost always implies that the relations depicted occur among more or less analytically equivalent units. This stress on the commonalities of interacting social units, although appropriate for certain analytic tasks, does tend to draw attention away from a concern with matters of *intra*organizational dynamics which have a bearing on our focal concern and which are unnecessarily and inadvisably de-emphasized in the wake of efforts to operate at a higher level of integration.

I submit that the second theme considered in this paper (i.e., the discussion of laterality II) affords an alternative view of how interorganizational relations may be analyzed and is one which is based on firmer empirical supports than its predecessor. This is so on two counts: first, an operational definition of *laterality* is offered whereas previously it was registered as a "sensitizing" idea; and second, the critical ingredients involved in the dynamics leading to more or less laterality are specifically designated and easily identified (the client, professional staff, administrative personnel, ancillary staff, and so on). In short, the new version of laterality more clearly regards the interactions between clients, on the one hand, and the organization, on the other, as dynamic and problematic. It prompts the proposition that organizational interest in their clients is more appropriately regarded as an outcome rather than an assumed given. Laterality II, then, represents a view of formal organizations that preserves its essential qualities as a series of ongoing processes occurring in the context of an empirically efficacious and readily identifiable social unit.

I submit further that laterality II, although focusing attention on intra-organizational matters, has clear relevance for the analysis of interorganizational relations. In what follows I would like to briefly sketch just how I think this relevance is accomplished. In the arenas of health and welfare, attention to clients (on the part of the functionaries and operatives of service organizations) usually considers as potentially pertinent characteristics those attributes classified under the rubric of "client-as-person." That is, the pool of characteristics from which the salient ones are somehow abstracted for the work of the organization are generally associated with his socio-economic status, his psychological profile, and/or his physiological well-being—the ingredients that ostensibly define the client as a complete person. Given the traditional pathways into the medical and health care delivery system, this is not surprising—i.e., it is persons with particular problems that present themselves to service organizations, and the view of the client in individualistic terms is commensurate with how he got there in the first place. To the extent, however, that the pathways into our service organizations become increasingly motivated and sponsored by organizational entities (Blue Cross, H.I.P., welfare departments, city health departments, OEO-supported inner-city clinics, community mental health associations, etc.), a new look at what is to be regarded as a salient client characteristic may be necessary. The suggestion is that increasingly the client-as-a-person frame of reference will include as a very fundamental attribute one or more formal organizational identities.

The experience which prompted these thoughts was a transcript of an interview conducted by a graduate student with a social case worker assigned to a county welfare agency in this state. In her description of how a specific client was managed by her agency, no fewer than ten separate organizational entities were involved in addition to the client's family and personal physician (the county general hospital, a chronic illness referral agency, an extended care facility, two nursing homes, the state welfare department, the city health department, the Visting Nurses Association, the U.S. government via Medicare, and a well-elderly clinic attached to a senior citizens housing project). These organizational inputs were in addition to the particular set of socio-psychological-physical problems exhibited by this one specific client.

The crucial issue as I see it is *not* how these ten (or more) agencies and associations relate to each other but how the social case worker and her organization respond to the fact that the client is a many-sided social being requiring immediate response and handling. This is, of course, not to say that the particular agency at issue does not have working agreements with the other organizations, nor that an identifiable network between and among them does not exist. This is to say rather that these working agreements or whatever else may define operations at a higher level of analysis are operational inputs to be somehow managed at the point of contact between client and agency. It is not the fact that the ten agencies are bound together by virtue of all manifesting some sort of interest in a given client that I see as the overriding concern giving rise to an interest in the larger interorganizational network. Rather, it is that individual organizations must react to these factors in a way that balances structural and functional arrangements that characterize the organization, operational goals, normative objectives, and the pool of potentially salient client characteristics including his organizational identities. Put more succinctly, I am suggesting that, given the dynamic interplay involved in relating client characteristics to organizational interests, it is equally as appropriate (and perhaps more heuristic) to study interorganizational relations from the vantage point of a single organization confronting other organizations through its clients, rather than to deal with the relations between and among the organizations per se.[1]

Admittedly, the illustration prompting these thoughts may be somewhat extreme but its message is fairly clear. In the health fields particularly, the relevance of organizational identities as salient components of the client's profile is bound to become much more important than heretofore.[2] Consider, if you will, the push for health maintenance organizations, nationalized health insurance programs, the growing demand for comprehensive care, and last, but most certainly not least, the legitimate incorporation of well-being as a national responsibility in addition to the declared right to proper care and treatment when sick. In this light, it seems reasonable to argue that the pathways into the medical system, as well as the meandering that takes place once inside, will increasingly be formalized and bounded by one's organizational memberships and affiliations. This is not to say that all such identities are equally important nor do they overrule legitimate medical concerns, but that the factors of organizational life are as much a feature of responsiveness to clients as are their physical or psychic complaints.

Just how we begin to ascertain the validity of these notions is an open question in my mind. It also may be that what I have described is merely a case of "old wine in new bottles," and that what I am calling for is a step backward from more fruitful approaches to interorganizational relations. However, what I am suggesting is clearly worth the risk. In matters where

---

[1] I must emphasize that my suggestion is for an additional perspective: I do not mean to imply that the single organization framework herein espoused is to substitute for more direct approaches to the field of study.

[2] In discussing these ideas with a colleague, he reacted by flashing his Kaiser Community Health Foundation card and indicated that whenever and wherever he or members of his family confronted the medical delivery system, he would produce the card in an effort to make known this rather salient client characteristic.

even the problems for investigation are uncertain, the case for considering alternative analytic approaches is patently obvious.

REFERENCES

Blau, R. P., and W. R. Scott. *Formal Organizations:*77. San Francisco: Chandler
1962   Publishing Company.
Elling, Ray. "The Hospital Support Game in Urban Center." In E. Friedson (ed.),
1963   *Hospital in Modern Society:* 73–112. Glencoe, Ill.: The Free Press.
Etzioni, A. *Modern Organizations*: 94. Englewood Cliffs, N.J.: Prentice-Hall.
1964
Gersuny, C. "Sheltered Workshops and Differential Client Characteristics." Cleve-
1968   land: Case Western Reserve University (unpublished Ph.D. dissertation).
Hall, O. "The Informal Organization of the Medical Profession." *Canadian Journal*
1946   *of Economics and Political Science*, 12:30–44.
Lefton, M., and W. R. Rosengren. "Organizations and Clients: Lateral and Longi-
1966   tudinal Dimensions." *American Sociological Review*, 31:802–10.
Levine, Sol, and P. White. "Exchange as a Conceptual Framework for the Study of
1961   Interorganizational Relationships." *Administrative Science Quarterly*, 5:
          583–601.
Litwak, Eugene, and L. Hylton. "Interorganizational Analysis." *Administrative*
1962   *Science Quarterly*, 6:395–402.
Litwak, Eugene, and J. Rothman. "Towards the Theory and Practice of Coordination
1970   Between Formal Organizations." In W. R. Rosengren and M. Lefton (eds.),
          Organizations and Clients: Essays in the Sociology of Service: 137–86.
          Columbus, Ohio: Charles Merrill Publishing Company.
Parsons, T. "Suggestions for a Sociological Approach to the Theory of Organiza-
1961   tions." In A. Etzioni (ed.), *Complex Organizations: A Sociological Reader:*
          39–40. New York: Holt, Rinehart and Winston.
Rosengren, W. R., and M. Lefton. *Hospitals and Patients.* New York: Atherton
1968   Press.
————. "Client Characteristics and Structural Outcomes: Toward the Specification
1970   of Linkages." In W. R. Rosengren and M. Lefton (eds.), *Organizations and
          Clients: Essays in the Sociology of Service:* 17–36. Columbus, Ohio:
          Charles Merrill Publishing Company.
Saunders, J. V. D. "Characteristics of Hospitals and of Hospital Administrators
1960   Associated with Hospital-Community Relations in Mississippi." *Rural
          Sociology*, 25:229–32.
Thompson, James D. "Organizations and Output Transactions." *American Journal
1962   of Sociology*, 68:309–24.

11

Task Environment, Decentralization, and Organizational Effectiveness

ANANT R. NEGANDHI, BERNARD C. REIMANN

INTRODUCTION

The importance of environment and its relation to all aspects of human endeavor has become a matter of increasing concern to both social and physical scientists. In recent years, a growing number of organization theorists have focused their attention on the environment and its impact on organizational functioning. This trend is illustrated by the conceptual schemes and empirical research efforts recently published by such writers as Emery and Trist (1965), Dill (1958), Thompson (1967), Burns and Stalker (1961), Lawrence and Lorsch (1969), Lefton and Rosengren (1966), and Thorelli (1967).

However, as Thompson has remarked, "the notion of environment turns out to be a residual one, it refers to 'everything else.'" To simplify the analysis, Dill, Thompson, and Thorelli are among those who have advanced the concept of task environment. Dill, in his study of two Norwegian firms, defined task environment as "that part of the total environment of management which was potentially relevant to goal setting and goal attainment." He identified the following as relevant task agents: customers, suppliers, employees, competitors, and regulatory groups. Dill explored the relationships between the task environment and the autonomy of managerial personnel. His study indicated that the executives operating in more dynamic environments had greater degrees of autonomy (or perceived that they had more autonomy) than those operating in stable environments.

Thorelli and Thompson also defined the task environment in a similar fashion and argued for its relevance to organization structure. Similarly, Burns and Stalker found that firms operating in stable technological and

---

This article originally appeared in *Human Relations*, Volume 26, Number 2 (January/February, 1973). The editor gratefully acknowledges permission to reprint the material in this volume.

market conditions were more structured than those facing dynamic conditions.

In the same vein, Lawrence and Lorsch studied the impact of two environmental variables on organizational functioning and structural arrangements. These were (a.) rate of technological change in both products and processes; and (b.) market conditions. They studied twelve industrial firms operating in varied environmental conditions. Briefly, the results of their study indicated that the formality of a unit's structure was related to the relative certainty of that unit's environment. Organizations or organizational units operating in dynamic environmental conditions tended to be decentralized, while those facing stable environments were relatively centralized.

Working primarily in the contexts of health and welfare organizations, such scholars as Etzioni (1964), Perrow (1965), Eisenstadt (1964), Glaser and Strauss (1965), and Lefton and Rosengren (1966) have attempted to explore the relationships between clients and organizations as critical determinants in the structure and functioning of formal organizations. Lefton and Rosengren (1966), for example, postulated that organizations with high longitudinal and lateral concern for clients tend to have decentralized structures, while those with low longitudinal and lateral concern may have relatively centralized structures.

Perception as a Mediating Variable

All the above research, with the possible exception of Dill's (1958) study, has emphasized the importance of actual environment conditions rather than the perception of those conditions formed by the decision makers. However, various sociological and behavioral researchers (March and Simon, 1963; Likert, 1967) have demonstrated that the "individual's reaction within a situation is a function of his perception of the situation rather than his interaction with a solitary combination of 'real' stimuli and constraints" (Graham, 1968 : 292).

We, too, contend that the impact of the "true" task environment on organizational functioning and structure may not be direct; rather, it may be mediated through the perception of decision makers.

As we shall see below, this particularly seemed to be the case in our study of business firms in India. The Indian industrial environment can best be classified as stable; both technological and market changes are more predictable and controllable than those found in an industrially developed country such as the United States. Yet the different enterprises in India did not necessarily view their environmental conditions in a similar manner. Particularly, their concern toward task environmental agents (i.e., clientage groups, such as consumers, suppliers) represented many different dimensions. Some viewed them in long-term perspectives, while others viewed them in short-term perspectives.

Purpose of This Paper

In this paper, two sets of relationships are being explored:

1. Organizational concern toward task environmental agents and the degree of decentralization in decision making; and
2. The degree of decentralization and organizational effectiveness.

Figure 1 shows the nature of relationships investigated in this study. The straight arrows between variables indicate the assumed direction of the relationships to be investigated. While we do not deny that these relationships may be in the reverse direction (wavy arrows), we feel that it is more logical to expect that the degree of concern toward task agents influences the way in which the organization's activities are structured rather than vice versa. Also, we would anticipate that organization structure would be more likely to influence a firm's effectiveness than vice versa.

Sample

Data for this study were collected from 30 manufacturing firms in India. Data were collected through personal interviews with various levels of personnel in each company, and by consulting published materials. The companies studied represented various industrial categories, such as pharmaceutical, chemical, soft drinks, elevators, heavy machine tools, cosmetics, sewing machines, and typewriters.[1]

VARIABLES AND MEASURES

Scope of Concern

The organizational concern toward task environmental agents variable was labelled "Scope of Concern." Of course, in business management literature this type of variable has been termed alternately as "Management Policy," "Management Philosophy," "Management Creed," etc. (Litzinger

---

[1]The firms in our sample were divided according to Woodward's (1965) technological classifications of process-, mass-, and unit-production. A comparison of decentralization indexes for these firms by the Kruskal-Wallis test showed no significant differences in decentralization among three technological classifications. The firms selected for our sample were generally representative of Indian manufacturing firms.

144

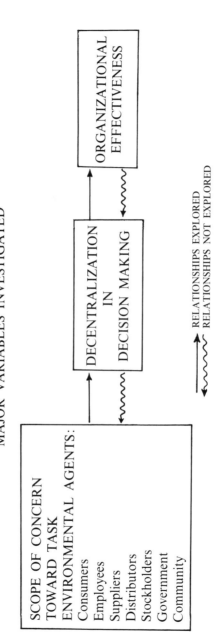

Figure 1
MAJOR VARIABLES INVESTIGATED

and Schaefer, 1966). We, also, have used such descriptive labels elsewhere to identify this variable (Negandhi and Estafen, 1965; Negandhi and Prasad, 1971). However, the recent conceptual analysis of the relationship between an organization and its clients offered by Lefton and Rosengren (1966) indicates that "Scope of Concern" may be somewhat more appropriate to describe the specific variables we have in mind.

The task environmental agents identified in this study were similar to those suggested by Dill (1958), Thompson (1967), and Thorelli (1967). These were: consumers, employees, suppliers, distributors, community, government, and stockholders.

To examine the organizational concern towards these task agents, we interviewed top-level executives of these companies. On the average, we interviewed 15–20 executives in each firm, taking from one to three full working days for each interview. Group interviews were held in the preliminary sessions, followed by an intensive personal interview with each executive. Persons interviewed held the following positions: (a.) chairman or president; (b.) board director; (c.) general manager; (d.) director of marketing, sales, production, finance, and personnel; (e.) chief accountant or comptroller.

Organizational concern for task agents was evaluated in terms of the degree of longitudinal and lateral interest in task agents evidenced by decision makers in each organization. Scores were derived from the intensity of concern shown, and three descriptive categories were created to rank the companies' "Scope of Concern." This is shown in Appendix A.

Both people involved in interviewing independently evaluated the information collected to rank each firm's concern toward its task groups. The differences between the two interviewers did not exceed eight points out of a possible one hundred.

Decentralization in Decision Making

Nine factors were examined to evaluate the degree of decentralization in decision making observed in the companies studied:

1. Layers of hierarchy—from top executive to the blue collar worker.
2. Locus of decision making with respect to major policies (e.g., mergers, major expansions or suspensions, major diversification decisions).
3. Locus of decision making with respect to sales policies.
4. Locus of decision making with respect to product mix.
5. Locus of decision making with respect to standard-setting in production.
6. Locus of decision making with respect to manpower policies.

7. Locus of decision making with respect to selection of executives.
8. The degree of participation in long-range planning.
9. The degree of information-sharing.

Decentralization Index

To arrive at a composite index for decentralization, we devised a three-point ranking scale for each of the factors evaluated. Details of this scaling are presented in Appendix B. The final decentralization index for each company was computed by adding the points for each factor and dividing this total by the number of factors (i.e., 9). This gave us an index ranging from a minimum of 1.0 (highly decentralized) to a maximum of 3.0 (highly centralized).

Organizational Effectiveness

Organizational effectiveness was evaluated both in terms of behaviorally oriented measures and economic criteria. The factors examined were: (a.) ability to hire and retain high-level manpower; (b.) employee morale and satisfaction in work; (c.) turnover and absenteeism; (d.) interpersonal relationships; (e.) interdepartmental relationships; (f.) utilization of high-level manpower. The economic or financial criteria examined were growth in sales and net profits during the past five years.

Three descriptive categories were created to evaluate the organizational effectiveness for each company studied, and a three-point ranking scale was devised. Two effectiveness indices were created, one for the behaviorally oriented measures and the other for the growth in sales and profits. These indices were obtained by dividing the total score by the number of factors. This gave us an index ranging from a minimum of 1.0 (most effective) to a maximum of 3.0 (least effective). The details of this scaling are shown in Appendix C.

RESEARCH FINDINGS

Scope of Concern and Decentralization

To examine the relationships between organizational concern ("Scope of Concern") toward task environmental agents and the degree of decentralization in decision making, Spearman's rank correlation coefficient was computed. The correlation coefficient between these two variables was 0.81. Detailed data concerning these relationships are presented in Table 1.

To explore the relationships between organizational concern toward individual task agents and decentralization, the Kruskal-Wallis Test was administered. As shown in Table 2, significant relationships were observed between organizational concern toward each of the task agents and the degree of decentralization. These relationships were found relatively stronger in cases of organizational concern toward employees, consumers, and suppliers.

Decentralization and Organizational Effectiveness

Spearman's rank correlation was also used to examine the relationships between the decentralization and organizational effectiveness indices. The correlation coefficient between decentralization and the behavioral measures of effectiveness was 0.89; between decentralization and economic criteria for effectiveness, it was 0.62. The lesser degree of relationship between decentralization and economic effectiveness reflects the seller's market conditions in India. Under such market conditions it is relatively easier to expand sales and generate profits in a desired manner. In spite of such market conditions, it still shows that the decentralized firms were more effective in generating higher sales and profits than the centralized enterprises. The detailed results on these relationships are shown in Table 1.

DISCUSSION AND IMPLICATIONS

Translated into actual managerial practices, our findings suggest that firms having greater concern for task environmental agents (i.e., firms viewing their task agents in long-term perspectives) are likely to have fewer layers of hierarchy in their organizational structures. They opt for the consultative type of decision making regarding major policies, sales, product mix, production, standard-setting, manpower policies, executive selection, and long-range planning. On the other hand, firms viewing their task environment in short-term perspectives are likely to have more layers of hierarchy and the chief executive or owner is probably making all decisions regarding functional areas and major policies. The results also show that the decentralized firms are more effective in both behavioral and economic terms.

These findings are somewhat in contrast to the earlier studies, particularly those reported by Lawrence and Lorsch (1969) and Lorsch (1973). They have argued that organizations, in order to be effective, must establish a fit between their internal structures and external environments. In essence, their studies suggest that centralized structures in stable environmental conditions and decentralized structures in dynamic conditions will be associated with a high degree of organizational effectiveness, while decentralized operations in stable environments and centralized operations in dynamic conditions may be dysfunctional.

Table 1
SUMMARY OF RESULTS

Firm number	Scope of concern score	Decentralization index	Effectiveness index Behavioral	Economic
1	100	1.2	1.1	1.0
2	95	1.6	1.4	1.0
3	100	1.2	1.1	1.0
4	59	1.8	2.1	2.0
5	71	1.9	1.9	1.5
6	42	2.0	2.5	2.5
7	54	1.7	2.0	1.5
8	22	2.8	2.5	3.0
9	59	1.4	1.9	1.0
10	46	2.4	2.7	1.5
11	100	1.2	1.1	1.0
12	100	1.3	1.3	1.0
13	49	1.8	1.9	2.0
14	22	3.0	3.0	2.0
15	25	2.9	2.5	2.0
16	22	3.0	2.9	2.0
17	51	1.6	1.4	1.0
18	25	2.5	2.5	1.5
19	46	1.8	2.4	1.5
20	90	1.8	1.3	1.0
21	46	2.2	2.3	1.0
22	100	1.1	1.1	1.0
23	59	1.5	1.6	1.0
24	69	2.2	2.1	1.0
25	43	2.3	2.1	1.5
26	54	2.0	2.0	1.5
27	46	2.1	2.0	2.0
28	51	1.6	2.0	1.5
29	40	1.7	1.9	2.5
30	72	1.8	1.7	1.0

Spearman rank correlation results:
  (1) Scope of Concern vs Decentralization: 0.81
  (2) Decentralization vs Effectiveness—Behavioral: 0.89
                                        —Economic: 0.62
(all significant at $p < .0001$)

However, we found a positive relationship between decentralization and organizational effectiveness despite the relatively stable task environment in India. Findings in this study thus underscore the importance of perception

Table 2
SCOPE OF CONCERN TOWARD EACH TASK ENVIRONMENTAL AGENT AND THE DEGREE OF DECENTRALIZATION (KRUSKAL-WALLIS TESTS)

Task environmental agents	H value	Level of significance (1-tail)
Employee	19.7	.0005
Consumer	16.8	.0005
Community	12.5	.001
Government	10.2	.005
Supplier	19.1	.0005
Distributor	15.9	.0005
Stockholder	10.4	.005
Total score	19.0	.0005

of decision makers and show how it acts as a link between environmental stimuli and decision maker's overt responses. Our results are in agreement with Dill's (1958:443) contention that "the autonomy of managerial personnel is a function of task environment structure, the accessibility of information about the task environment, and the managerial perception of the meaning of environmental information."

We thus agreed with Dill that in examining the impact of external environment on the internal functioning of organizations one needs to put "explicit emphasis on the cognitive activities of organizational participants as a link between environmental stimuli and the participants' overt responses."

REFERENCES

Burns, T., and G. M. Stalker. *The Management of Innovation.* London: Tavistock
1961   Publications.

Dill, William R.   "Environment as an Influence on Managerial Autonomy." *Adminis-*
1958   *trative Science Quarterly,* 2:409–43.

Eisenstadt, S. H.   "Bureaucracy, Bureaucratization, and Debureaucratization." In
1964   Amitai Etzioni (ed.), *Complex Organization: A Sociological Reader:* 276.
New York: Holt, Rinehart and Winston.

Emery, F. E., and E. L. Trist. "The Causal Texture of Organizational Environment."
1965   *Human Relations,* 28:21–31.

Etzioni, Amitai. *Modern Organizations.* Englewood Cliffs, N.J.: Prentice-Hall.
1964

Glaser, Barney, and Anselm Strauss. *Awareness of Dying.* Chicago: Aldine Press.
1965

Graham, Gerald H.   "Correlates of Perceived Importance of Organizational Ob-
1968   jectives." *Academy of Management Journal,* 11:292.

Lawrence, Paul R., and Jay W. Lorsch. *Organization and Environment: Managing*
1969   *Differentiation and Integration.* Homewood, Ill.: Richard D. Irwin, Inc.

Lefton, Mark, and William R. Rosengren. "Organizations and Clients: Lateral
1966   and Longitudinal Dimensions." *American Sociological Review*, 31:802–10.

Likert, Rensis. *The Human Organization: Its Management and Value.* New York:
1967   McGraw-Hill Book Company.

Litzinger, W. D., and Thomas E. Schaefer. "Management Philosophy Enigma."
1966   *Academy of Management Journal*, 9:337–43.

Lorsch, Jay W. "Environment, Organization and the Individual." In Anant R.
1973   Negandhi (ed.), *Modern Organizational Theory*: 132–44. Kent, Ohio: Kent
        State University Press.

March, James G., and Herbert A. Simon. *Organizations.* New York: John Wiley
1963   and Sons, Inc.

Negandhi, Anant R., and B. D. Estafen. "A Research Model to Determine the
1965   Applicability of American Management Know-How in Differing Cultures
        and/or Environments." *Academy of Management Journal*, 8:319–23.

Negandhi, Anant R., and S. B. Prasad. *Comparative Management.* New York:
1971   Appleton-Century-Crofts.

Perrow, Charles. "Hospitals: Technology, Structure, and Goals." In James March
1965   (ed.), *Handbook of Organizations*: 650–77. Chicago: Rand-McNally.

Thompson, James D. *Organization in Action*: 30–38. New York: McGraw-Hill
1967   Book Company.

Thorelli, Hans B. "Organizational Theory: An Ecological View." *Proceedings of*
1967   *the Academy of Management Conference*: 66–84.

Woodward, Joan. *Industrial Organization.* London: Oxford University Press.
1965

Appendix A

RANKING SCALE FOR THE FIRM'S CONCERN TOWARD TASK AGENTS

	Much or very much concern	Mild concern	Little or no concern
Employee	20	10	0

	Consumer, the king	Consumer, a necessary agent	Consumer, passive agent
Consumer	20	10	0

	Much or very much concern	Some concern	Little or no concern
Community	10	5	0

	Good partner	A necessary evil	Government, be damned
Government	10	5	0

	Good relationship absolutely necessary	Good relationship helpful	Relationship a necessary evil
Supplier	15	7.5	0

	Good relationship absolutely necessary	Good relationship helpful	Relationship a necessary evil
Distributor	15	7.5	0

	Owners, masters, good public relation personnel	Owners, masters only	Profit-eaters
Stockholder	10	5	0

Appendix B

RANKING SCALE FOR THE FACTORS EVALUATED FOR
DECENTRALIZATION INDEX

Factors	Points
1. Layers of Hierarchy (top executive to blue-collar worker)	
(a) 3 to 6 layers	1
(b) 7 to 10 layers	2
(c) 11 and more layers	3
2. Locus of Decision Making (major policies)	
(a) broad representation of executives and stockholders	1
(b) top level executive committee	2
(c) chief executive or owner only	3
3. Locus of Decision Making (sales policies)	
(a) executive committee with representation of all functional areas	1
(b) chief executive with the help of sales manager	2
(c) top executive/owner only	3
4. Locus of Decision Making (product mix)	
(a) executive committee with representation of all functional areas	1
(b) chief executive with the help of production/ marketing manager	2
(c) chief executive/owner only	3
5. Locus of Decision Making (standard-settings in production)	
(a) executive committee with representation of all functional areas	1
(b) chief executive with production manager— production manager only	2
(c) chief executive only	3

Appendix B (*Contd.*)

Factors	*Points*
6. Locus of Decision Making (manpower policies)	
(a) executive committee with representation of all functional areas	1
(b) chief executive with personnel manager	2
(c) chief executive only	3
7. Locus of Decision Making (selection of executive personnel)	
(a) executive committee with representation of all functional areas	1
(b) chief executive with personnel manager	2
(c) chief executive only	3
8. The Degree of Participation in Long-Range Planning	
(a) all levels of executives—top, middle and lower	1
(b) top level with some representation of middle level executives	2
(c) chief executive/owner only	3
9. The Degree of Information-Sharing	
(a) considerable—general memos on all major aspects of company's operation	1
(b) fair—special reports on company's affairs distributed to only top level and middle level executives	2
(c) little—all information kept secret from everybody except few top level executives	3

Appendix C

RANKING SCALES FOR THE FACTORS EVALUATED FOR ORGANIZATIONAL EFFECTIVENESS INDICES

Factors	Points
Behavioral Measures	
1. Ability to Attract and Retain High-Level Manpower	
(a) able to attract and retain highly trained personnel	1
(b) able to attract and retain moderately trained personnel	2
(c) not able to attract and retain even moderately trained personnel	3
2. Employee Morale and Satisfaction in Work	
(a) excellent morale and highly satisfied	1
(b) average morale and somewhat satisfied	2
(c) poor morale and highly dissatisfied	3
3. Employee Turnover and Absenteeism	
(a) 0–5 percent	1
(b) 6–11 percent	2
(c) 12 percent and more	3
4. Interpersonal Relationships in Organizational Settings	
(a) very cooperative	1
(b) somewhat cooperative	2
(c) poor cooperation	3
5. Departmental Relationships (subsystem relationship)	
(a) very cooperative	1
(b) somewhat cooperative	2
(c) poor cooperation	3
6. Utilization of High-Level Manpower (what executives did)	
(a) policy-making and future planning	1
(b) coordination with other departments	2
(c) routine work, day-to-day work and excessive supervision with subordinate's duties	3
Economic Criteria	
7. Sales Growth (average of the past five years)	
(a) phenomenal growth (50 to 100 percent)	1
(b) moderate growth (25 to 49 percent)	2
(c) declining or stagnant	3
8. Net Profits on Invested Capital (average of the past five years)	
(a) 25 percent and more	1
(b) 15 to 24 percent	2
(c) less than 15 percent	3

12

Conceptualization at the Organization-Set and Task Environment Levels: A Critical Appraisal

Editor's Note

This chapter critically evaluates the contributions presented by Professors Hall and Clark, Lefton, and Negandhi and Reimann. Commentators are Professors Raymond Adamek, Arlyn Melcher, and Anant Negandhi, all of Kent State University.

Comments on the paper by Professors Hall and Clark were taken directly from transcripts of the conference made during the discussion session. The transcripts were organized in question form by Professors Melcher and Negandhi and fed back to the authors for responses. These questions and responses are reproduced here first; comments on the other papers follow. The other authors in this section chose not to provide responses.

Comments on Hall and Clark's Paper

QUESTION:

By reading your paper and listening to your presentation, we thought you were going to provide us with some methodological insights. For example, you seem to use the systems concept and systems terminology, but you do not provide any clue as to what are the inputs, throughputs, and outputs in your study; nor do you explore reciprocal relationships between your variables.

RESPONSE:

I think the most important point you raised is the question of reciprocity. How do you measure it? How do you do anything with it? Frankly, I'd like to know myself! It's really a tough issue, and I think it comes down to a question of the very bases of relationships. The real problem is determining how something (including reciprocal relationships) enters an organization. Where does it come in? Where does it have an effect? Where does it go out of an organization in relation to where it entered? The best I can do is attempt to conceptualize it for you because I've not seen anything in the literature that covers it.

Take, for example, this whole thing on technology in organizations. There has been considerable emphasis on technology in the literature, but we just do not know where technological issues enter the organization. Who decides where they come in? Who determines the effect technology has on the organization when it enters? I guess we are just not very good at determining that, so my answer to your question can only be, "why don't you know?" Why don't any of us know?

I am not even sure systems terminology is very useful in resolving this problem. For example, in our research we have our "set of organizations"; very early in our research we established this term. Well, essentially this "set" is a system of organizations; yet, on the other hand, it is not a system. It is a network of organizations. In very few ways does it have characteristics of a social system or any other system by anyone's terminology. It is simply a set of organizations that happens to be there or happens to interact with other units or sets. I frankly think it would be absurd to call it a system, at least based on my understanding of what a social system is. I know everyone defines it differently, but I think it is rather dangerous to call everything a social system. I simply do not think it is there.

In my paper, I tried to give you a very brief description of the delivery system as to what its inputs and outputs were. Perhaps it is not clear. For me, the inputs are really the other organizations that provide homes, services, plans, etc. They provide customers and staffs. They provide money. The input is actually those organizations which provide services. The output, and this is an important part of the paper, are the services provided to the youths and the multiple relationships with the other organizations. We don't want to slide over that fact. We tried to measure some of the problems of the systems approach, but we have not necessarily been successful. This might not be a satisfactory answer, but this is the best I can do at this time.

Now, so far as our approach is concerned, let us begin with the theory of interorganizational relationships. In the first place, there is no theory of interorganizational relationships. There are elements of a theory, but there is no *actual* theory. And in terms of the presentation given here, I'd say we are about half way ... no, only a third of the way through the data analysis. And I hope I don't sound too apologetic. It's rather difficult to analyze and present data which is not yet on cards.

QUESTION:

Your analysis of input and output suggests that you would have some type of conceptualization about the significant core organization-set in your research. Yet rather than taking this more conceptualized approach, you instead asked participants in the study to identify their own organization-set. Then, instead of eliminating or isolating these after some sort of interrogation period, you throw it right into the research design and let it become your interorganization-set. I'm not sure where you got the questions you used, but there doesn't appear to be any particular rationality in their selection. Yet when you deal with them, you talk about some type of statistical correlation. Isn't this empiricism?

RESPONSE:

I think the selection of questions represented some essential elements of the major aspects of the theory of interorganizational relationships. For example, what is the basis of the relationship? Is it an exchange relationship? Is it over issues?

In terms of the questions themselves, we included things that are, in the main, central to interorganization theory. Unfortunately, there was not time nor space to review all of the questions and sort these things out. I felt that the level of interorganizational relations, and the study of them, is such that we have to begin with organizational theory (or nontheory) and see if elements of this approach work. Then I think we have to throw in some other things that appear to be related to interorganizational relationships. For example, not included in the paper presented here is the point that certain organizational characteristics lead to certain qualities in interorganizational relationships. We have the data on this, but it has not as yet been analyzed.

I know that nearly everyone says most of these interorganizational relationships are based on exchange; take White, Levine, and Vlasak, for example, as stated in this volume. But you see, they have only minimal amounts of data, and from only one organization-set. I think that we, in a sense, are trying to explore further. In the first place, I do not think that exchange is really all that important in terms of reasons and consequences for interorganizational relationships. I just do not think it is all that critical an issue because some things are just not exchanged.

My desire is to go out into the field and say, "what seems to be here." Not that I disregard the literature; however, the literature in this area is fairly new and I think this can mislead us more than lead us. I guess, in this sense, I accept the accusation of being an empiricist.

QUESTION:

What are the implications of taking the organization as the focus of analysis, as is done by yourself and most sociologists following the Weberian concept, or taking subunits as a focus of analysis, such as is done by Lawrence and Lorsch (1969)?

RESPONSE:

I don't think that it makes too much difference, conceptually or methodologically. Certainly intraorganizational variations have been well documented.

QUESTION:

We have an example of nearly pure empiricism in this study. Measures are developed on 16 activities, processes, and relationships, with scales varying from dichotomized answers to seven-point scales. No theoretical model is presented that would explain the relevance of any of the questions posed. One can unravel the implicit model, but you do not even order the questions so that an implicit model can emerge. No attempt is made to conceptualize variables and relate the operational questions to the variables. No attempt is made to conceptualize the direction of the expected relationships in terms of independent, mediating, and dependent relationships. Rather, your thrust is to intercorrelate each question with simple and later multiple correlations. These correlation coefficients are supposed to provide some meaningful insights into the character and determinants of interoganizational relationships; however, this procedure raises several questions: Can such research procedure ever be justified and, if so, how and under what conditions? If this procedure is used in other studies, in what way can these studies be additive, particularly where the organizations studied are different and the questions are modified? And, even if the whole procedure can be justified, how can meaningful relationships be developed where the scales vary from dichotomyzing the data to a seven-point scale?

RESPONSE:

The basic perspective or theory is given in my book. *Organizations: Structure and Process* (Hall, 1972). The section on interorganizational relationships contained therein presents the framework around which the research was based. This section is intentionally eclectic, since I still maintain that while there are appropriate theoretical perspectives, no single one captures the essence of interorganizational relationships.

The question of additivity is puzzling, since there are very few other studies to begin with. Mulford and Klonglan (1973) find only seven studies which combine methodological and empirical emphasis. Ours is one of these. This is a sorry state of affairs.

QUESTION:

Since interorganizational analysis is concerned with the interactions and relationships of two or more organizations, what implict and explict definitions are being used to define the organizations and their boundaries in your research? Are clients part of organizations (i.e., students in universities, patients in hospitals)? Are supplies part of organizations (i.e., service units providing inputs into a hospital) ?Are franchised units part of organizations (i.e., car dealers)? What problems are created by not explicitly defining organization boundaries in your study or in other studies?

RESPONSE:

In our more extensive report we spell out these issues in detail. Briefly, we took those organizations or their units which dealt directly with problem youth.

QUESTION:

Why do interorganizational researchers ignore the contribution of economics which is centrally concerned with interorganizational relationships that are mediated completely by the market mechanisms (pure competition), partially by market mechanisms (monopolistic competition or oligopoly), or by public bodies (monopoly)? Work by Alfred Kuhn (1963) concerning the "unified society" would seem central to conceptualizing interorganizational relationships.

RESPONSE:

I agree with the point. My guess is that sociologists in general are too ignorant of economics and also rather too narrowly discipline-oriented to bring in the economic factors in meaningful way.

REFERENCES

Hall, Richard H.   *Organizations: Structure and Process.* Englewood Cliffs, N.J.:
1972   Prentice-Hall.
Kuhn, Alfred.   *The Study of Society: A Unified Approach.* Homewood, Ill.: Richard
1963   D. Irwin, Inc., Dorsey Press.

Lawrence, Paul R., and Jay W. Lorsch. *Organization and Environment.* Homewood,
1969   Ill.: Richard D. Irwin, Inc.
Mulford, Charles L., and Gerald Klonglan. "An Assessment of Interorganizational
1973   Research: The Need for Synthesis and Integration." Ames, Iowa: Depart-
        ment of Sociology, Iowa State University (unpublished report).

Comments on Lefton's Paper

TOO LIMITED VIEW OF ORGANIZATION—
Arlyn J. Melcher and Raymond J. Adamek

Lefton and Rosengren introduced a typology in organizational analysis
which they found fruitful in terms of generating hypotheses on organizational structure, client-organization relations, and interorganizational collaboration. This typology is also useful in calling attention to the manner in
which organizational structure and client characteristics interact with one
another, and to the potential power clients wield over organizations.
Lefton's dicussion of the tuberculosis hospital is particularly illuminating.
At least some clients, consumers, and customers of other types of organizations are also becoming increasingly sensitive to the approach such organizations take to them, and to their potential role in changing organizational
structure and policy.

The present paper by Lefton highlights the significance of the client.
However, where organizations and their clients have conflicting interests,
his and Rosengren's overall analyses suggest that, with the exception of
some OEO agencies, organizations are still firmly in command. Rosengren
(1970:117–35) suggests that an organization's initial and subsequent
lateral/longitudinal orientation toward its clients is determined more by
concerns of early survival, system maintenance, and firm entrenchment in
an organizational set than by client demands or needs for special services.
Similarly, even in his discussion of laterality II, which he defines as the
"extent to which a given hospital is responsive to the reactions or reaction
potential of its clientele, and the effects on hospital procedures and structural
outcomes," Lefton notes that it is the organization's perception of client
characteristics which is a major determinant of its structure and functioning,
and not client characteristics per se.

While the Lefton-Rosengren typology sensitizes us to the dynamics
of client-organizational interaction, it adds few new insights to our understanding of interorganizational relations. It suggests that if one is interested
in which organizations are likely to engage in collaboration (formal or
informal) at different levels (administrative or operative), one should
take into account organizational goals, the means utilized to achieve these
goals, organizational structure, and the characteristics of organizational

staffs and clients. While most agree with this, the Levine and White schema is more comprehensive and explicit in treating the variables affecting interorganizational collaboration. Further, even if, as Lefton suggests, clients increasingly carry organizational identities into service organizations, this does not necessarily tell us which organizations will collaborate, or for what purposes and in what ways. To learn this, we must still look to organizational and environmental characteristics and measure contacts as they occur between and among organizations. The Lefton-Rosengren analysis suggests that the organization still determines the relevance of client characteristics for itself and its relations with other organizations. Moreover, they note that contacts between organizations are also initiated by staff members and other nonclients outside the organization-set. Lefton's paper seems to depict somewhat passive organizations being spurred to action and interaction by client characteristics. Thompson's (1967) treatment of "organizations in action" seems more accurate.

REFERENCES

Rosengren, W. R. "The Careers of Clients in Organizations." In W. R. Rosengren
1970   and Mark Lefton (eds.), *Organizations and Clients*: 117–35. Columbus, Ohio: Charles E. Merrill.
Thompson, James D. *Organizations in Action.* New York: McGraw-Hill.
1967

Comments on Negandhi and Reimann's Paper

METHODOLOGICAL PROBLEMS — *Raymond J. Adamek*

It is gratifying to see the operational indicators of the major variables published as appendices to this paper. Too often these are omitted from professional publications, thus "saving space" but hindering the critical and cumulative development of the discipline. Such candor does, of course, subject the authors to what some might consider nitpicking methodological critique. At the same time, however, it permits the refinement of theoretical concepts and their operational measures for future use.

As is often the case, being able to scrutinize the operational indicators of a variable in detail raises as many questions as it answers. Why, for example, were "competitors" omitted from the "concern for task agents" measure? Surely competitors are an important part of the task environment, as noted in the literature cited. How were the weights assigned to the various agent-components of the "concern" index determined—intuitively or empirically? To what extent are those interested in using this measure to be guided by the verbal description of the points on the task agent continua? They do not appear to be unidimensional but rather convey notions of good/bad, and much/little, in addition to the longitudinal/ lateral dimension mentioned in the text. Apparently the authors themselves were able to resolve these ambiguities, as they report high inter-rater agreement.

While additional criticisms might be made of the other indices, the major point here is that publishing these data not only permits critical analysis (thus sharpening further research efforts and facilitating replication), but also sensitizes the researcher to the difficulty of attempting to construct measures of complex variables.

Turning to more substantive matters, few would argue with Negandhi and Reimann's contention that the impact of task environment on organizational functioning and structure is influenced by the decision makers' perceptions of the environment. This is not to say, of course, that the failure of decision makers to take note of certain aspects of the environment render those aspects irrelevant for the organization's functioning. Indeed, the data on economic effectiveness suggest that decision makers who are not attentive to the task environment hinder the organization's growth and profitability. (The data on behavioral effectiveness and decentralization do not relate directly to the environment, but indicate that workers and managers are more attracted to and effective in relatively decentralized organizations.) Furthermore, although it may be true that an organization will not behave on the basis of information of which it is ignorant, Emery and Trist's (1965) discussion of turbulent fields suggests that we will not be able to account for all that happens to an organization if we conceive of its environment as consisting only of information which becomes available to it. That is, not all of the environment's impacts on an organization will necessarily be "mediated through the perception of decision makers."

Few would argue also with the authors' decision to focus on the causal direction of relationships as outlined in Figure 1 of their paper. At the same time, however, in ongoing organizational-environmental systems, mutual causality among the variables under consideration seems quite likely. Dill (1962), for example, notes that how an organization is structured (e.g., highly centralized or decentralized) may well determine which environmental factors will be perceived and recorded, which will be interpreted as tasks for the organization, and which tasks will be acted upon. Or, in the terminology of Negandhi and Reimann, how decentralized decision making is in an organization may well influence the scope of concern toward environmental agents. The chief executive of a highly centralized firm obviously has less time, energy, and capacity to attend to the organization's task agents, and the environment in general, than does a staff of task-agent specialists within the organization. This may help to explain the finding that decentralization is positively related to economic effectiveness even in relatively stable (noncompetitive) environments.

Finally, it should be pointed out that the authors contradict themselves in the treatment of the environment in this paper as compared with the paper presented earlier in this volume. Here, they characterize the environment in India as uniformly stable and note that in spite of this uniform stability, "the different enterprises ... did not necessarily view their environmental conditions in a similar manner." This contention is used to underscore the role which decision makers' perceptions of the environment play in organizational structuring and functioning. In the earlier paper, however, their analysis of market competitiveness is used to argue that the environment of different types of Indian firms does, in fact, vary in stability.

REFERENCES

Dill, William R.   "The Impact of Environment on Organizational Development."
1962   In Sidney Mailick and Edward H. Van Ness (eds.), *Concepts and Issues in Administrative Behavior*: 94–109. Englewood Cliffs, N.J.: Prentice-Hall.
Emery, F. E., and E. L. Trist.   "The Causal Texture of Organizational Environments."
1965   *Human Relations*, 18:21–32.

PART IV

Conceptualization at the
Organizational Field Level

13

The Interaction of Community Decision Organizations: Some Conceptual Considerations and Empirical Findings

ROLAND L. WARREN, ANN F. BURGUNDER,
J. WAYNE NEWTON, STEPHEN M. ROSE

INTRODUCTION

The Interorganizational Study Project at Brandeis University has two principal objectives—to develop some systematic knowledge about community decision organizations and to contribute to the field of interorganizational behavior.

Community decision organizations are defined as organizations which are legitimated at the community level to make decisions on behalf of the community. Six types of community decision organizations have been studied in nine cities. The six types are: public school administration, health and welfare planning council, antipoverty community action agency, mental health planning agency, urban renewal agency, and the Model Cities agency. This sample was deliberately chosen to assure some variation on such dimensions as the ratio of program activities to planning activities, governmental status (whether a governmental agency or nongovernmental), and certain other variables assumed to be important in organizational interaction.

The interaction of these organizations in each of nine cities was studied within the setting of the Model Cities program, in which each city participated.

In connection with the first objective, systematic knowledge about different types of community decision organizations, it was necessary to be selective. The study placed stress on three major dependent variables:

The research project on which this paper is based was supported by a grant from the National Institute of Mental Health.

responsiveness, innovation, and the dimension of cooperation/contest.

Though carefully conceptualized and rigorously executed, a study of this nature must necessarily be largely descriptive. Nevertheless, so that the data gathered would be comparable and comprise indicators of variables which were considered important, extensive preliminary work was done in conceptualizing the variables and in constructing propositions—we use the word *hypotheses*, but modestly—which would necessitate a sharpening of the research design. These hypotheses not only arose deductively from the work of others, but also speculatively as we agreed that certain variables probably were important and speculated how and why these might be related to each other. Numerous hypotheses thus served the purpose of guiding our inquiry. It was not expected that we could test them once and for all in any definitive fashion. Yet, it is gratifying that we were able to test more of them, in a formal sense, than was originally expected.

There are three levels or orders of organizational phenomena that transcend the purely intraorganizational, or, to put it another way, that treat the relationship between the organization and its environment. For purposes of the subsequent discourse we will include an intraorganizational level, making four levels in all:

1. *Intraorganizational level*—concerns the relationship of intra-organizational variables to each other.

2. *Organizational position*—concerns the relationship of the organization to its environment, including its input, output, and generalized position in the interorganizational field.

3. *Specific organizational interaction*—concerns interactional episodes where a focal organization interacts with one or more others in a specific interactional framework.

4. *Interorganizational field*—concerns the properties of an aggregate of interacting organizations as distinguished from the properties of the individual organizations themselves.

The fourth level, that of the interorganizational field, may appear somewhat perplexing. This level is most readily described by saying that one can describe and analyze as a single system of interaction any group of organizations whose properties may differ from those of the interacting organizations themselves and cannot be reduced to properties of these individual organizations. This theoretical possibility was in our awareness at the outset of the study and was mentioned briefly in one of our earlier papers; but at that time we were unable to formulate hypotheses suitable for testing.

The hypotheses for the study all deal with one or another of the first three levels. Yet, as the study progressed, the findings were such as to support the importance of this fourth level and indeed to make the findings from levels two and three understandable only in terms of the fourth level. Putting this more simply, it became apparent that the interaction between specific community decision organizations can be adequately understood or accounted for only in reference to the characteristics of the interorganizational field within which such specific interaction takes place. Since this statement is highly important, if true, we will return to it later in this paper.

At the present it is not possible to give more than a sampling of the study's findings since intermediate analyses, though nearly completed, are still underway. Further, the study is complex and ambitious, thus a brief report can include only part of the findings. Hence, we present here merely a selection of illustrative findings, and examine some of their possible implications (for detailed findings, see Warren, Rose, and Burgunder, 1974).

First, a brief word about the three major dependent variables. The first dependent variable is *responsiveness*. Although this variable is pertinent for community decision organizations and certain other types of formal organizations, no claim is made regarding its usefulness as a general analytic concept. It concerns the extent to which a community decision organization is sensitive to and adaptive to the expressed needs and wishes of a disadvantaged clientele.

We have approached this concept through the twin concepts of input constituency and output constituency. Input constituency is that group of actors which an organization acknowledges to have a legitimate role in determining its policy. Output constituency is that group of actors which an organization acknowledges an obligation to serve. The sample CDOs differ in the extent to which a disadvantaged clientele is an explicit part of their output or service constituency. For example, the antipoverty organization and the Model Cities organization are much more explicitly designed to serve a disadvantaged clientele than is the urban renewal agency. Likewise, CDOs differ in the extent to which representatives of the poor are part of their input constituencies, being allotted a formal decision-making role in policy formation. The antipoverty agency, for example, must have representatives of the poor comprise at least one third of its governing board, and the Model Cities agency has analogous though somewhat different requirements; but this is not the case with any of the others.

In operationalizing this variable, it was found useful to distinguish between formal structures for citizen input into decisions and informal interaction episodes, including petitions, confrontations, requests, and the rest, which occur independently of the regularized organizational channels for citizen input. Our data are both from narrative accounts of developments and from a formal schedule of questions administered to three levels of participants for each CDO: the CDO executive level, the level of the citizen head of the Model Neighborhood Board of the Model Cities program, and the level of leadership of active ethnic organizations. The process of blending these data into judgments and ratings is complex, as everyone knows. It is not yet completed for this variable, but we have already completed a similarly complex process for rating the cooperation/contest variable—with gratifyingly high interjudge reliability—and have some preliminary findings to report.

On the variable of *innovation*, the data come almost exclusively from a lengthy innovation schedule which is designed to record changes in each organization's functions and programs, structure and administration, relationships with other organizations, and a "miscellaneous" category.

Four different measures of innovation were employed, each being successively more refined and demanding. The first is simply a gross counting of changes in all the above categories, after careful editing. The second is a select group of categories which we believe are more likely to have some possible impact on the lives of a disadvantaged clientele. The third category is a still more selective list of changes relating much more directly to the impact of the CDO's output on a disadvantaged clientele (i.e., in its hiring patterns or in a change from a punitive approach to a therapeutic approach to a particular social problem). The fourth category, extremely demanding, is what we call change of paradigm; it involves a shift from programs based on an individual deficiency diagnosis of urban social problems (paradigm I) to a diagnosis based on defective social structure (paradigm II). Roughly, programs based on paradigm I consist of improved social services to help disadvantaged people; programs based on paradigm II are addressed to changing the social structure in terms of major resource or power redistribution, political organization of the poor, and so on. We found only one such major change out of the 52 organizations included in this particular analysis. We are at present relaxing this fourth most demanding category of innovation so as to make it more inclusive for purposes of testing certain hypotheses.

Under the present scoring system, 28 or slightly more than half of these CDOs have undertaken one or more innovations at level 3, a level which is judged to have direct relevance to the agency's impact on a disadvantaged clientele.

The Model Cities program was intended to stimulate innovations in such organizations as these. Pending the final analysis, our impressionistic conclusions are that the innovation in structure or program attendant upon the Model Cities program was extremely modest. Our subjective interpretation is that such innovations are highly inadequate for effectively addressing the problems of the inner cities, casting doubt on the feasibility of a Model City's type approach to bring about changes of sufficient magnitude to make a major impact on the problems it addresses.

Our third dependent variable is *cooperation/contest*. Most suggested definitions of cooperation, though plausible in conceptualization, were found difficult if not impossible to operationalize. After an arduous process, *cooperation* was defined as an interaction process under which the actors seek to achieve a similar issue outcome, and *contest* as an interaction process under which the actors seek to achieve different issue outcomes. Two organizations might be represented on the same ad hoc committee, but that does not necessarily mean they are cooperating. They might be working for mutually incompatible objectives. We found that once the interaction process was related to a desired issue outcome level, and once the system level was specified, it was possible to make consistent judgments. We used the broad term *contest*, incidentally, to include various types of opposition.

LEVEL 1 — INTRAORGANIZATIONAL VARIABLES

Turning to the four levels of analysis mentioned earlier, it may seem strange for the project to be dealing with the first, intraorganizational level, at all. Yet, it was assumed that certain organizational characteristics might affect behavior toward other organizations, or might affect an organizational output such as innovation. This might, in turn, affect interorganizational relations.

For example, we developed a classification system for the leadership style of the chief executive. Various studies show the importance of the chief executive's interorganizational role. Previous interviewing had suggested the usefulness of a typology which comes from Max Weber, with much adaptation: bureaucratic, charismatic, and collegial leadership. We hypothesized *that organizations with charismatic leaders would be the most innovative, with collegial less, and bureaucratic still less.* This hypothesis was not substantiated by the data for innovation 1, 2, and 3. It has not yet been tested for innovation 4.

We also attempted to tease out the effect, if any, of organizational structure on certain other variables. Following a distinction made earlier (Warren, 1967), it was hypothesized *that unitary organizations would produce more innovations than would federative organizations.* This hypothesis was not supported since no significant relationship was found.

We also assumed that organizations charged with maintaining extensive program activities might differ in other respects from organizations almost exclusively devoted to planning. We therefore devised a rough measure

of the percentage of each organization's activities which was devoted
to operating programs. We hypothesized *that the higher the ratio of regular
program to planning, the lower would be the innovation.* This hypothesis
was rejected at all innovation levels except in the single case of innovation
level 4. We will comment on this later.

We hypothesized and found a significant *positive association between
percentage of program activities and the unitary form of organization.* But
two other hypothesized relationships were unsupported, namely, between
leadership style and organizational structure.

LEVEL 2—ORGANIZATIONAL POSITION IN ENVIRONMENT

Let us proceed to the second level, that of the position of the organization within its environment. As a preface to this level, let us observe that
ever since the noteworthy contribution of our colleagues, Levine and White
(1961), there has been a tendency in interorganizational analysis to subsume all interorganizational relations under the concept of transactions
and exchange. Yet it is obvious that, helpful as the concept of exchange
may be, it does not exhaust or even usefully treat many pertinent aspects
of the relations of organizations to their environment. For example, the
excellent analysis by Emery and Trist (1965) of "The Causal Texture of
Organizational Environments" and the extension of this analysis by Terreberry (1968) are highly important but do not readily fit into the rubric of
exchange between specific organizations.

So far, we have only been able to test a single hypothesis which deals
with the generalized position of the organization within its interorganizational environment. It was hypothesized *that innovation is inversely related
to dependence of CDOs on local community organizations for input resources.*
This hypothesis was not found to be substantiated for innovation 1 and
innovation 2, but was significant for innovation 3. On the fourth level, the
single case also conforms to it.

LEVEL 3—SPECIFIC ORGANIZATIONAL INTERACTION

In regard to specific interaction, the study developed ratings on a co-
operation/contest scale for each pair of CDOs, city by city. Some of the
hypotheses relate the nature of this interaction (called "paired interaction")
to certain other variables concerning the relationship of the specific organizations involved in the pair. From the paired interaction data, summary
ratings for each organization were developed using a seven-point scale
from high cooperation to high contest. In this way ratings were obtained
not only about pairs of organizations, but also about any given organization's interactional style as it was classified on this scale. A lengthy process

of abstracting from both narrative and schedule data were involved, and then judgments were made by three judges acting independently and blindly but following specified criteria. Their judgments were highly consistent and in the few cases where they differed, a rating was negotiated. Two other variables also were obtained through this process: frequency of interaction, by pairs and for single organizations; and initiative in cooperation, where it could be fairly definitely established that the initiative in a cooperative interaction was taken by a given organization.

On the most general level, it is interesting to note the distribution of specific pairs of CDOs from the nine cities on the seven-point cooperation/

Table 1

NUMBER OF CDO PAIRS RECEIVING EACH RATING ON COOPERATION/CONTEST

Rating	Number of CDO Pairs
High cooperation	1
Moderate cooperation	17
Low cooperation	46
Equal admixture	19
Low contest	8
Moderate contest	5
High contest	2
no data	27
insufficient data	10

contest scale. As can be seen in Table 1, the model rating of pairs of interacting CDOs was that of low cooperation.

For purely descriptive purposes, it is interesting to compare the CDO types on the cooperation/contest scale. Actually, there are some hypotheses about who cooperates or contests the most; but these are related to discrete variables rather than the empirical types, such as a community action agency or urban renewal agency. Analyses will be made holding the empirical types constant while measuring the variation attributable to certain variables singly and in combination. The degree of cooperation/contest, by summated CDO type, is given in Table 2.

Which CDOs interacted most frequently with any of the other CDOs? Table 3 gives the order of frequency and the actual frequency score for each organizational type.

In the paired interaction, as might be expected, the Model Cities Agency, the Community Action Agency, and the Public School Administration showed the highest frequency of paired interaction with each other across the cities. On a more general level, it had been hypothesized that *the closer*

Table 2
DEGREE OF COOPERATION/CONTEST
BY CDO TYPE
*(The higher the numbers, the higher the component or proportion
of contest behavior.)*

Public School Administration	3.55
Model Cities Agency	3.50
Health & Welfare Council	3.43
Community Action Agency	3.33
Urban Renewal Agency	3.00
Mental Health Planning Agency	3.00

Table 3
CDO FREQUENCY OF INTERACTION WITH OTHER SAMPLE
CDOs

Model Cities Agency	207*
Community Action Agency	187
Public School Administration	169
Health & Welfare Council	119
Urban Renewal Agency	98
Mental Health Planning Agency	84

*Since the Model Cities Agencies had only a "half-life" during the study period, these figures suggest a much higher frequency than that indicated here.

the interest field of two or more organizations, the more frequent would be their interaction. This hypothesis was tested somewhat indirectly. It was supported strongly by the data.

An interesting question on the cooperation/contest scale concerns the relationship between frequency in interaction and type of interaction. For example, one might ask whether the degree of contest, as opposed to cooperation, goes up or down as their frequency of interaction varies. There appears, by inspection, to be a significant and substantial positive correlation between frequency of interaction and contest. Putting this another way, across these nine cities, the pairs of CDOs which interact the most show a higher proportion of contest than those which interact less.

Numerous questions can be raised about the theoretical implications of these findings, but it is premature to draw firm conclusions since all the hypotheses are interrelated theoretically, and not all of them have as yet been tested. But we will make a few brief comments regarding the initial theoretical framework, the manner in which it shifted during the study, and the way we now anticipate it may be taking shape.

From a certain line of theoretical reasoning, we had hypothesized that *unitary organizations take less initiative in cooperation than federative organizations.* This hypothesis was supported by the data. Putting this another way, the unitary organizations tend to go their own way, while the federative organizations tend to seek out opportunities for cooperation. We have not made a special analysis of initiative in contest.

We had also hypothesized that *organizations with charismatic leaders would take the least initiative toward cooperation, while those with collegial leaders would take the most.* This hypothesis was not supported.

We had hypothesized *a direct relationship between organizational innovation and interorganizational contest.* We had assumed both that contest would be more conducive to innovation than cooperation, and that innovation would more likely increase contest rather than cooperation. At mid-point in our study, we became aware that it might not be innovation in general, but the impact of the innovation in terms of disturbing the interorganizational consensus that might be positively associated with contest. Hence, the successive measures of innovation are more refined in their potential impact on the interorganizational consensus, with level 4 (paradigm change) having the greatest potential impact. We came to expect that the hypothesis would not hold up at innovation levels 1 and 2, but would perhaps hold up at level 3 and would be still stronger at level 4. The relationship at innovation levels 1 and 2 is not significant. At level 3 there is a slight but insignificant distribution in the opposite direction from the hypothesis. Our single case of level 4 innovation rates extremely high on the contest scale, supporting the hypothesis; but generalization from this case is, of course, dangerous.

The analysis so far has been in terms of bivariate hypotheses, but the intention is to employ multivariate analysis and attempt to tease out some of the configurations of variation. Meantime, some preliminary findings are available from a more intensive analysis of interaction episodes.

From a special substudy of 150 instances of specific organizational interaction for which comparable data were obtained on a number of important outline variables, there has emerged a series of observations which lead us to elaborate further the concept of cooptation in a way which it is hoped will constitute a new facet of interorganizational analysis. In this substudy, it was noted that certain types of CDOs were able to handle episodes of potential or actual contest in ways which were much more routinized than was the case with other CDOs. Such organizations, as they approached a potential contest, seemed able to contain it with a minimum of difficulty. It seemed as though they were able to get the contest played out on their own home field, as it were, with their own ground rules. It was found that the organizations best able to do this were those with a determinate rationality, such as the school system administration and the urban renewal agency, as distinguished from organizations with a less determinate rationality, such as the community action agencies and the Model Cities agencies.

Further analysis of the data led to an expanded conception of cooptation and its employment to include organizations as objects of cooptation rather than only individuals. Organizational cooptation, as distinguished from Selznick's (1949) concept of cooptation which we call "personnel cooptation," is defined as "the process of convincing one party (in a contest situation) to accept another's organizational rationality as manifested in its technical, administrative or institutional aspects, and to act accordingly." Once the issue in contest has been defined in accordance with the organization's rationality, the problem can be routinized, and the organization can be assured that whatever the outcome, it will not threaten the organization's continued viability.

Organizational rationality is seen as comprised of technical, administrative, and institutional components. These components correspond approximately to Parsons' (1959:5–6) three levels of the hierarchical structure of organizations: technical, managerial, and institutional.

An organization's *technical rationale* is the most frequent source of interorganizational contest because the technical rationale concerns itself with how activities should be carried on and who within the organization should perform them, usually a matter of professional expertise and always a matter of jobs and of budgets. An organization's technical rationale enables it to insist that it has the knowledge, the skill, and even the ethical base from which programs should be operated. Some organizations, such as the public school system and the urban renewal agency, for example, possess highly determinate technical rationales compared with the indeterminateness of the technical rationales of the poverty agency and the Model Cities agency. As a result, *technical cooptation* may occur, for example, when a CDO of indeterminate technical rationale accepts the definition of the appropriate technology to be used in dealing with a problem which is espoused by a CDO with a determinate technical rationale, and, by so doing, removes itself from contention for operation of a program.

An organization's *administrative rationale* is concerned on the one hand with those activities which mediate between the environment and the technological tasks, and on the other hand with essential maintenance activities. The administrative rationale deals not only with internal and external support for task and maintenance activities, but also with acceptance of those routines and procedures deemed necessary to sustain them. *Administrative cooptation* takes place when a focal organization succeeds in getting another organization to define a contested issue in terms of the focal organization's administrative rationale.

The institutional component of organizational rationality, or the *institutional rationale*, relates, first of all, to its legitimacy, its right to exist, based upon greater or lesser support in the community for the functions it performs. Another aspect of an organization's institutional rationale is its domain, its locus in the interorganizational network. Domain includes an organization's manifest goals, its channels of access to resources, its service field and type of program, its service population, and its geographic area. *Institutional cooptation* occurs when a focal organization succeeds in getting another organization to define a contested issue in terms of the focal organization's own institutional rationale and thus to acknowledge the focal organization's primary rights to the domain.[1]

Note that there is a difference between defining an issue in terms of the organization's legitimated domain (then letting the resolution of the issue develop whichever way it will) and engaging in a dispute over whose definition of the domain question will prevail. Once the focal organization gets the domain issue defined in terms of its own institutional rational, the actual resolution of the dispute (still to be determined) will more likely be acceptable to the focal organization. Cooptation relates to defining the issue, not to its resolution.

It appears that organizations with more determinate rationalities are at an advantage in contest situations since they can muster claims to expertness and "generally accepted" principles to support their positions. For example, the school superintendent in a dispute over curriculum can point to a whole shelf of technical books on curriculum construction. If the dispute regards administration, he can likewise point to a whole shelf of books describing his administrative rationale. The community action agency has no such shelf of books to point to, nor does the Model Cities agency. The situation regarding institutional rationale is analogous.

The result seems to be that organizations with determinate rationales are able to employ these types of organizational cooptation more readily than organizations with less determinate rationales.

In such analyses, quantitative tables are somewhat premature. Yet it is interesting, and probably no coincidence, that in the 150 action episodes, the relationship of determinate rationality organizations to indeterminate rationality organizations was as follows. The most frequent cases were instances of indeterminate rationality cooptation by an organization of determinate rationality. By contrast, the case of an organization with determinate rationality coopting another organization with determinate rationality was much less frequent, as was the case where an organization of indeterminate rationality was able to coopt another organization of indeterminate rationality. The fourth possibility, that of an

---

[1]The above three paragraphs are taken from an earlier paper, J. Wayne Newton, "Cooptation Among Community Decision Organizations," Brandeis University (mimeographed report), 1970.

organization of indeterminate rationality coopting an organization of determinate rationality, did not occur at all.

As a consequence, organizations with indeterminate rationalities require other methods of handling contest situations, and a systematic analysis of these 150 action episodes is now being made in order to determine what alternative strategies were used by such organizations and with what results. Of course, it is not assumed that organizations with determinate rationalities employ only cooptation in interaction episodes.

We have been extremely brief in presenting these interesting findings and interpretations, but the paper by Newton (1970) treats them at greater length.

LEVEL 4—THE INTERORGANIZATIONAL FIELD

Turning now to the fourth level, that of the interorganizational field, it will be noted that the study's hypotheses—and we have mentioned only those which have been tested to date—are at the first three levels. None of them address the interorganizational field within which specific organizations behave and interact with each other. Most of the hypotheses are at level 3, that of interaction between or among specific organizations. A large part of the study has been exploratory and on a descriptive level. From both sources, we begin to realize that the basic assumptions about the interorganizational field (on which the study was based) are in need of major revision. In this brief paper they can be indicated only in large, impressionistic strokes.

It was assumed that all of these community decision organizations faced great uncertainties, both from the input of federal funds and programs on the one hand, and from citizen residents of disadvantaged neighborhoods on the other. They were to face great threats and great opportunities (in the form of federal funding) through the Model Cities program. Since their domains overlapped, it was anticipated that there would be a high rate of interaction, and because of the combination of uncertainty, threats, and opportunities, it was assumed that the interaction would be for comparatively high stakes and hence be intense. With these organizations pitted against each other in a competitive struggle for scarce resources, it was anticipated that major impacts would be made on the relative positions of these organizations. Such competition was expected to generate innovation, and innovation, in turn, was expected to feed back into contest, since it was assumed that innovation would disturb the organizational consensus—the existing ecology of organizations—in a way which would be threatening and disruptive. Likewise, it was expected that as one or another organization became more responsive to the wishes and needs of a disadvantaged clientele, it would be brought out of the existing ecological balance and thus create a strain on relationships with other organizations.

Yet what has been the experience? Innovations have been extremely minor and have not seemed to make much difference. Leadership style, and many of the other variables do not seem to have affected the interaction very much. Mild cooperation continues to be the modal form. Few major changes have taken place in either agency structure or programs. These agencies have been able to accommodate the major impacts of federal dollars and program direction and citizen participation with a surprising degree of individual stability, and with an unexpected degree of mutual forbearance. Such contest as occurs happens only at the margins and does not usually threaten organizational viability. The same can be said for innovation and for responsiveness in the form of citizen participation. Domain contest, especially, has been at a much lower rate and intensity than anticipated.

What we now believe we had overlooked, or failed to understand, at the outset was the manner in which the interactional field—the aggregate system of interaction among these organizations—serves to reduce uncertainty to controllable dimensions, to minimize contest, to resist change, and to assure organizational viability. This interorganizational field we have described in a preliminary formulation as an institutionalized thought structure characterized by a high degree of consensus and by a process of competitive mutual adjustment at the margins where issues arise. We use the expression *institutionalized thought structure* in order to include not only structural and procedural relationships, but also the ideological and technological underpinning of the interaction. We see this thought structure as based on a general consensus regarding the diagnosis of urban social problems and on the type of intervention strategy such diagnosis calls for. We see these in turn supported by a belief-value system from the larger American society. This institutionalized thought structure is reflected in the technological and administrative rationales of the community decision organizations, in the source of their legitimation and their relation to the power configuration of the cities involved, and in the relation of their technical rationales to social research and evaluation.

We cannot expound on this complex phenomenon now. A lengthy paper is already available, entitled "The Sociology of Knowledge and the Problems of the Inner Cities" (Warren, 1971). So, in a highly fragmented way, we will only indicate the approach which that paper takes by saying that the prevalent diagnostic paradigm for the problems of the inner cities is that of individual deficiency, and that from this is derived a strategy of attack on problems based on improved services to help people cope with their deficiencies. Where these services are found ineffective in addressing the problems, the solution is not to turn to an alternative paradigm which might explain inner city social problems in terms of the American social structure rather than individual deficiency, but rather to attribute the ineffectiveness of the services to lack of coordination. Hence the contemporary emphasis on systems analysis, program budgeting, and the rest.

At the same time, organizational domains have been mutually worked out over a period of time, based on consensus in the overall approach within which division of labor provides for different approaches and different technologies. Contest between such different organizations is a contest within a larger framework of cooperation. We use the analogy of two friends playing a game of chess on a rainy afternoon. They may throw considerable effort into who wins the particular chess game, but that is less important than that they are both playing the same game, with the same set of rules. On this more inclusive level—the interorganizational field level—there is great stability based on consensus around the desirability of the game and the inviolability of the rules. To lose a game may be a disappointment, but hardly a disaster. The contestants each win a considerable share of the games.

To apply the analogy, our interaction episodes are such games. The contestants are the community decision organizations. They all agree on the desirability of the game—the prevalent diagnostic strategy for attacking social problems—and on the rules for settling individual contests. Here we must leave the analogy, for among the CDOs there is a division of labor and hence mutual dependence. The areas of competion are more limited than one might expect. Contests occur, therefore, only at the margins. Contests seldom threaten organizational viability, and particularly where organizational cooptation is possible, the organizations can adjust to whatever outcome results. It is interesting that essentially the same group of CDOs is present in all cities of a given size. The system is surprisingly stable and can absorb change impacts within the framework of the institutional thought structure. Vigorous contest occurs only at the margins. Uncertainty is routinized because the individual organizations exist in this relatively benign environment.

This being the case, we can understand that innovation within the institutionalized thought structure need not lead to contest. We can understand that large measures of citizen participation need not disturb an organization's viability, so long as the participation is based on an acceptance of the diagnostic paradigm and an acceptance of the ground rules for how one conducts himself in contest situations. If this assessment is valid, then one would expect innovations which challenge the paradigm, ones which are not readily compatible with the institutionalized thought structure, to be resisted with great intensity. Likewise, we can expect a type of contest strategy going against the accepted rules of the game for contest resolution to create intense resistance, and this we have also found.

In sum, we find an impressive stability of community decision organizations despite their own relatively indeterminate organizational rationales, and despite their uncertain environment and threatening impacts both from federal program sources and from organized disadvantaged neighborhoods. This surprising stability and relative impermeability to change is difficult to explain on the basis of individual organizations acting according to their respective requirements for viability, but only as one considers the nature of the field within which such interaction takes place.

Our analysis is far from complete. This paper should be taken as a report of work in progress rather than as a definitive statement either of our findings or of our conclusions.

REFERENCES

Emery, F. E., and E. L. Trist. "The Causal Texture of Organizational Environments."
1965   *Human Relations*, 18:21–32.
Levine, Sol, and Paul White.   "Exchange as a Conceptual Framework for the Study
1961   of Interorganizational Relationships." *Administrative Science Quarterly*,
5:583–601.
Newton, J. Wayne. "Cooptation Among Community Decision Organizations."
1970   Waltham, Mass.: Brandeis University (mimeographed report).
Parsons, Talcott. "General Theory in Sociology." In Robert K. Merton, et al.,
1959   *Sociology Today: Problems and Prospects*: 5–6. New York: Basic Books.
Selznick, Philip.   *TVA and the Grass Roots*. Berkeley, Calif.: University of California
1949   Press.
Terreberry, Shirley. "The Evolution of Organizational Environments." *Adminis-*
1968   *trative Science Quarterly*, 12:590–613.
Warren, Roland L. "The Interorganizational Field as a Focus for Investigation."
1967   *Administrative Science Quarterly*, 12:396–419.
————. "The Sociology of Knowledge and the Problems of the Inner Cities."
1971   *Social Science Quarterly*, 52.
Warren, Roland L., Stephen M. Rose, and Ann F. Burgunder. *The Structure of*
1974   *Urban Reform*. Lexington, Mass.: D. C. Heath and Company.

14

Exchange as a Conceptual Framework for Understanding Interorganizational Relationships: Application to Nonprofit Organizations

PAUL E. WHITE, SOL LEVINE,
GEORGE J. VLASAK

INTRODUCTION

The peculiar set of conditions common to nonprofit health organizations has challenged a number of investigators to search for factors which might explain their interaction. Historically, such organizations have been supported largely either by philanthropy or by public funds. The predominant activities of nonprofit health organizations have been predicated upon a belief in the sanctity of life and in the importance of preserving life. Payment by one nonprofit health organization to another for goods and services received has been infrequent. Yet, apparent nonreciprocal—i.e., not "in kind"—transfers of resources have, in fact, occurred among them. The problem is to explain the bases of these transfers. At the time of our original article on exchange (Levine and White, 1961), industrial and commercial organizations had received much more study than health organizations. Transfers of resources among these profit-making organizations are mediated by money, the most liquid means of exchange, and their behavior appeared to be more amenable to explanation in terms of economic theory and market behavior. Pricing, utility, demand, and similar concepts seemed to "account" for much of the interaction among these organizations. However, these economic concepts did not appear suitable for explaining interaction among nonprofit health organizations.

Policy makers and civic leaders, too, have been interested in understanding the relations among nonprofit health organizations and have been actively involved in trying to induce a "rational" transfer of goods and services among these relatively autonomous organizations. Attempts to introduce "rationality" into the health system were premised on a set of assumptions about the "motivation" of principal decision makers in health organizations. The theme underlying these early efforts was one of a prevailing altruism and a spirit of cooperation. This belief in altruism and in an inherent tendency to cooperate probably has its origins in the philanthropic and humanitarian foundations of health-related activities. In these early explanatory efforts, the focus on implicit, natural inter-organizational cooperation was combined with an epidemiological frame of reference: health organizations would, presumably, coordinate their respective goods and services as soon as the extent of health problems and "community needs" became known.

And yet, when even the knowledge of community needs, brought about by various surveys, failed to produce a rational system (and, on the contrary, brought to light some striking cases of noncooperation), belief in the inherent, "invisible-hand" altruism *cum* rationality of health organizations was not abandoned by those analyzing the health and welfare scene. Instead, the problem was rephrased to assume the existence of systemic barriers to cooperation itself. At least two phases can be identified in this particular formulation of the problem. First, lack of mutual knowledge among the organizations was alleged to be the main barrier; the solution, therefore, called for mechanisms to encourage communication among the organizations regarding their respective needs and resources. Sensitization of each organization in the given community to the problems of each of the other organizations was the proposed vehicle, and mutual understanding the anticipated solution.

The second, and so far the latest, phase is typified by attempts to create a "rational system" by some form of extraneous control and rationing of resources: allocation of varying amounts of resources to organizations whose current activities are deemed important in terms of some system of "rationally derived" priorities or inducing, or bribing, organizations to modify their activities to accord with that system of priorities. Thus, the first phase assumed that some more rational order would emerge more or less automatically if only barriers to (natural, spontaneous) cooperation were removed. The second phase, still with us, similarly assumes that some central body can reach consensus on priorities, manage to retain its "centrality," and (have enough of the appropriate kinds of power to) induce conformity.

The first phase relied upon inherent, naturally dominant altruism as motivation for cooperation. The latter phase takes initial cognizance of self-interest, but fails to anticipate strategies organizations employ in *preserving* their self-interest, strategies which often defeat attempts to rationalize transfers of resources among health organizations.

The concept of exchange provided a basis for understanding the impetus for the movement of resources among health organizations. Our original paradigm (Levine and White, 1961 : 583–601), it will be recalled, tried:

> ...to explain relationships among community health and welfare agencies by viewing them as being involved in an exchange system. Organizational exchange is defined as any voluntary activity between two organizations which has consequences, actual or anticipated, for the realization of their respective goals or objectives. Organizations have need for three main elements: (1) clients, (2) labor services, and (3) resources other than labor services. Theoretically, were all the essential elements in infinite supply there would be little need for organizational interaction and for subscription to cooperation as an ideal for health agencies. Under conditions of scarcity, however, interorganizational exchanges are essential to goal attainment. The interdependence of the agencies is contingent upon three related factors: (1) the accessibility of each organization to necessary elements from outside the health system, (2) the objectives of the organization and particular functions to which it allocated the elements it controls, and (3) the degree to which domain consensus exists among the various organizations.

In the sense in which we employed it, the concept had its origin in the seminal article by Marcel Mauss (1955). Mauss proposed an explanation for the seemingly one-way transfer of resources when he pointed out that the receipt of the gift created an obligation in the recipient. The gift, therefore was frequently based not on altruism, but in the expectation of a deferred repayment in some form—goods, services, or other favors and values. The gift, therefore, represented part of an exchange based upon rational self-interest. Later repayment in some form could be expected. "Repayment" could also be immediate or simultaneous with the act of giving, such as gratitude on the part of the recipient, or at one end of a continuum, the satisfaction of giving, fulfilling the goals of the giver.

Applied to exchanges in general, the concept implies, and stresses, the fact that no goods or services are ever transferred without reciprocity of some kind being involved. In organizations, as among individuals, the reciprocal aspect of a "one-way transfer" of resources may be intangible, i.e., fulfillment of its own goals. The exchange concept, then, provides a framework which accounts for seemingly nonreciprocal or apparently one-way transfers of resources. It presumably could account for one-way transfers of resources in terms of organizational needs and rational self-interest instead of in terms of altruism. By considering the goals of organizations, the making of a "gift" could be viewed as rewarding in itself. This aspect of the concept is also emphasized by Homans (1958 : 597–606).

There were several advantages, then, in using the exchange concept. It focused attention on the factors determining the need for resources and special services as distinguished from behavior antecedent to exchanges or behavior which postponed exchange. (With cooperation an avowed value in the health system, it is often necessary for organizations to behave as if they were cooperating but without actually exchanging resources.) It also focused attention on exchanges between dyads as dependent variables, with open-system variables as independent ones.

PROBLEMS IN THE SEARCH OF SYSTEM INTEGRATION

Goals, Organizational Structure, and Survival

Assuming that the exchange concept provides an understanding of the motivation for transfer of resources in terms of rational self-interest, a central problem is to determine the basis of this self-interest. The question may be stated most simply as follows: What variables predict exchange relationships between *given dyads of organizations?* Litwak and Hylton (1962 : 129) have alluded to organizational interdependence as a predictor of interaction. A crucial problem, however, is that of defining when, in fact, interdependence exists. What are the characteristics of organizations and of their task environments that produce interdependence?

Our first formulation of this problem was expressed in terms of organizational goals. The goals of the organization, in view of the general condition of scarcity of resources, are expressed in particular purposive activities which we call organizational functions. Two factors, then, could lead to a propensity to exchange: the need for resources to carry out ongoing functions, and the fact that an organization cannot always realize its goals or even carry out its more limited specific functions without relying upon other organizations. This latter point is related to Lefton and Rosengren's (1966 : 802–10) concept of longitudinal and lateral orientations. Organizations vary in the degree to which they rely on other agencies to provide the services necessary to accomplish their own goals.

There are several problems related to the concept of organizational goals, however. As several writers have noted, it is difficult to predict an organization's functions from statements regarding its goals. Moreover, different actors in the organization may perceive its goals differently.

These problems in definition and delineation may be solved largely by considering goals in relation to various decision-making processes within the organization. We may view the hierarchy of an organization in terms of increasing constraints on the decision-making prerogatives related to procuring and committing organizational resources. Under the constraints of the organizational constitution or agreements of affiliation, the trustees or the board of directors make long-term commitments by delineating the specific functions of the organization and the resources to be devoted to them. Within these limits, the executive, head administrator, or manager formulates his decisions regarding resource allocation; on the staff level, day to day decisions are made within a narrower framework. In their concern for the continual flow of resources over the long run, those near the apex of the hierarchy are more oriented to the problem of organizational survival, even to the point of changing the organization's functions or redefining its goals, depending on the nature of the dangers of demise. At the same time, it is only when a crisis in the procurement of resources becomes evident that those at the base of the hierarchy become oriented to aspects of organizational survival. Thus, the degree to which the problem of survival is important to different organization personnel depends on their respective statuses in the organizational hierarchy, as well as on the actual probability that resources will continue to be available. This formulation may, to a degree, clarify the controversy over whether organizations "exist to survive" or "exist to pursue their goals." It also diminishes the tendency to anthropomorphize the organization.[1]

Goals, Domain, and Conflict Resolution

Although stated goals may not permit the analyst to predict the specific functions to which an organization allocates its resources, nor identify the other organizations with which it will cooperate, they are useful for specifying the other organizations with which there may be conflict. Goals appear to constitute claims to domains and, through consensus, determine the resources which are allocated to those domains. A stated goal may be regarded conceptually as a first claim or option on resources allocated to the delineated area. Should another organization be found already performing the same functions, the first organization may be given the option to redirect its resources to new functions, if these are deemed related to its goals, and even to acquire additional resources for this purpose. If the organization does not initiate new functions which are deemed necessary, the competing organization may initiate them and thereby lay claim to resources allocated to the domain. As claims to future resources, then, the formally stated goals of one organization may provide the basis for subsequent interorganizational conflict. Such was the case in the conflict between the Specific Disease Society and the General Disease Agency described by White. The GDA's conflict with the SDS was based on its perception that the SDS was threatening resources which the GDA claimed by virtue of its stated goals (White, 1968:289–304).

A problem in investigating this area is that even in the organizational world, conflict behavior is likely to be based on perceptions, and not necessarily on reality. As happened with the SDS and the GDA, the encroach-

---

[1]We are indebted to Erik Van Hove for this formulation.

ment on domain was perceived as constituting a threat to future resources, although an empirical investigation revealed that the actual on-going functions of the organizations would not be impaired or interfere with each other.

Empirically, the resolution of domain conflict among health organizations is, in most cases, not cooperation in the form of exchange of resources but cooperation in the recognition of mutually exclusive domains. These delineations are usually arbitrary. They are based upon such criteria as clients' age, geography, income (usually indigency), disease nosology, or specific services, for the purpose of eliminating or reducing competition for resources (and the uncertainty regarding the future procurement of these resources), rather than for the purpose of promoting system integration.

Exchange Networks

Another approach to explaining interdependence has been somewhat successful. The approach involves the imposition of rational integrative schemes or rational exchange networks on the activities of autonomous organizations. These networks are somewhat like overlays of rational flow systems that may be imposed on the collectivity of existing organizations. One then predicts interdependence on the basis of the conformity of organizational functions to those of the purportedly rational scheme. We have found it useful to classify organizational functions or activities in terms of their relationships to the stage or processes of disease intervention and rehabilitation. Since there is a logical flow of patients from one function to another, e.g., screening to treatment, organizational interchange flows in that direction.

The (structured) pattern of the flow of resources is also influenced by the particular disease in question. For example, in tuberculosis one might expect cases to flow from organizations with screening functions to special clinics and sanitaria where cases are treated. Alcoholics may be expected to be referred from hospitals to half-way houses. But such flow networks depend on the prevailing *technology* and professional *consensus* regarding the handling of cases. Alcoholics now ideally enter hospitals, then half-way houses or other facilities, and are followed up by supportive services. The discovery of a substance that could be injected to eliminate inebriation or the deleterious effects of alcohol could change this pattern. Similarly, professional ideology or belief concerning the nature of a health problem could radically modify ideal management of the problem and consequently the relationships among organizations with functions thought pertinent to solving the given health problem. With increasingly rapid developments in the medical field, delineation of present "rational" patterns of exchange is possible to a degree, but the prediction of future patterns is almost impossible.

The Basis of Exchange: Primitive Barter

To a limited extent, rational networks of exchange are realized among organizations. A major question is how to promote or encourage a greater realization of these ideal networks. The present pattern of exchange may to a large degree be attributed to the existing "complementarity"[2] of functions of different organizations. Although we may determine some of the bases of complementarity between the functions of two organizations, it is precisely because the needs of both the two participating parties must be fulfilled by a single exchange (i.e., that it must be beneficial to both) that an integrated and rational system of exchange does not evolve. There are many cases where a transfer of resources from one organization to another may be desirable from the vantage point of coordinated system but may be beneficial to only one party.

This discrepancy between the needs of the total system where resources flow according to an overall rational and integrative schema, and the motivation for exchange that obtains in the current system may be illustrated by comparing formal barter with what we shall term "primitive barter." In normal barter situations, one party may seek goods which have no immediate value to him but which may be useful at a later time or which may be used to obtain other goods. Among health organizations, we believe such transactions rarely occur. In primitive barter, as it obtains among health organizations, the needs of both parties must usually be met simultaneously without benefit of intervention of a middleman or of a common currency. (One variation of the "simultaneous" requirement is when one party may be promised repayment of goods or services at a subsequent point in time.)

The Philanthropic Orientation and Accountability

Two major factors tend to foster the condition of primitive barter. The philanthropic, nonprofit orientation of the organizations has at least two important effects. First, the organizations seldom expend funds to purchase the resources of other nonprofit organizations. The organizations spend to the limit of relatively fixed budgets, and they restrict their funds to expenditures for their own resources and services. There is the tacit assumption that the resources of other health organizations should be obtained through altruistic cooperation, since those organizations are also nonprofit and philanthropic. Money is therefore not used to any

---

[2]The term *complementarity* was employed by William M. Evan, "The Organization-Set: Toward a Theory of Interorganizational Relations," in James P. Thompson (ed.), *Organizational Design*. Pittsburgh: University of Pittsburgh Press, 1966.

significant degree to facilitate the flow of resources among nonprofit organizations.

The philanthropic orientation has a second important effect. Instead of being evaluated by the universalistic criterion of profit, as are organizations in the economic sector, each autonomous organization is accountable to its own distinctive major source of legitimation (usually its source or sources of direct monetary support) in terms of idiosyncratic criteria—usually that specific kinds of services are rendered to particular types of persons.

Organizational functions and activities seem to be more closely related to the organization's criteria of accountability than to its formally stated goals. This accountability in some cases may even effectively narrow the functions of the organization so that it no longer fulfills its stated goals. One example is vocational rehabilitation organizations where the "best" strategy for achieving the score for which one is accountable is to select the less serious cases and to employ them in the most readily available jobs. In some family planning programs, also, contraceptives may be dispensed; but the "non-use" or "drop-out" rate is ignored. In short, the criteria of accountability influence the specific needs to be fulfilled by the barter system and thereby affect the character of interorganizational exchange. The philanthropic orientation, then, has multiple interrelated effects: It discourages the use of money in interorganizational exchange; it influences the functions of the organization; and it determines the needs for particular resources in barter situations.

The Search for System Integration

In the health field, there has been a long search for a means of integrating the system. The various attempts that we have described, those based upon altruism and those controlling funding—either on the community or the national level—have not yet induced organizational conformity to any specific set of priorities. We shall now consider why these attempts have failed in terms of the characteristics of the nonprofit health system.

Most attempts to integrate health system services have focused on the rationale of fulfilling community needs and ensuring that sets of "necessary" services exist within areas to meet patients' needs, particularly those patients requiring multiple or comprehensive health services. Despite these attempts to integrate health services, there has been a constant process of fission in health services like the splintering of religious sects in the face of ecumenism. New organizations are constantly appearing. Often these are splinter organizations formed to initiate functions not carried out by parent organizations.

If one looks for clues to this dilemma of the struggle for integration in the face of constant fission of services, one sees that the constraints of organizations prevent much more integration than exists at present. Each organization, within the constraints of its accountability criteria, tends to coordinate its efforts with other organizations on the basis of primitive barter. Obviously, organizations could change their functions to make them more congruent with one another. Organizational functions do change; but they usually change as a result of technological innovation and rarely in order to become complementary to the functions of other organizations so that services to patients or clients are improved. Motivation to change for this purpose is virtually nonexistent, and its development is inhibited by the constraints of organizational accountability. Occasionally, a committee or a funding organization may perceive or discover a "need" for coordination and make recommendations for, or fund, a special referral operation. But lag times and lack of effective sanctions frequently prevent such efforts from achieving success.

We may gain some insights into the interrelationships of nonprofit organizations by comparing them with their profit-making counterparts. Although competition exists in the economic sector, parts of the profit-making system are relatively well integrated. In contrast to the health system organizations, production organizations that operate in market situations are subject to pressures that tend to integrate their efforts. In the market situation in which they operate, the problems of allocating resources to effect coordination of efforts and complementarity of functions are "solved" by price. If we consider the production of a single complex product, such as an automobile or an airplane, we see that the efforts of autonomous organizations are brought together by mechanisms that encourage "necessary" goods and services and discourage the "unnecessary." Purchasing and subcontracting are two such integrative mechanisms.

Thus, an automobile manufacturer can procure, or have produced to his specifications, metals or other materials and parts which permit him to fabricate automobiles. The production of distributors, batteries, and other parts depend on specific chains or series of coordinated processes. Furthermore, it is important to note that the final assembler does not mastermind the coordination of all of these activities. Integration of the system is achieved through the linkage of specific dyads of organizations in terms of reciprocal needs and demands. Even though the system is pluralistic, reasonable integration is achieved. A vital point is that in this process individual organizations adjust or modify their functions to conform to the requirements of others. The resulting complementarity of the functions of dyads of organizations produces system integration.

By contrast, in the health system, each organization attempts to "rationalize" its environment and to maximize its own criteria of accountability. Each organization sets its own goals, functions, and "accountability scores" independently, and the search for integration, to the extent it exists, is in terms of prevailing complementarity. In the market situation, the organizational function is a response to the need for congruence and organizations are rewarded for producing congruence. In the health system, organizational functions are determined by a range of factors other than the need for system integration.[3]

The Patient: Cost or Benefit?

In the health system, the patient or client constitutes an organizational resource and may be regarded conceptually as a necessary raw material. He is also the *raison d'être* of the system. Yet, certain patients with particular characteristics are not always resources for given organizations. When needed for the organization, he is a "benefit"; when not needed for the organization, he may be regarded as a "cost." Also, unlike other resources of the health system or the resources of organizations operating in market situations, he may be sent to a given organization, i.e., "referred," whether or not the organization desires him. Indeed, referral failures are probably a major basis for dissatisfaction with the present degree of health system integration. Since many organizations rely on referrals as a major source of patients, referral failure is a common occurrence and is regarded as a serious problem.

A consideration of the factors related to the referral process and to the rejection of referred patients should provide us with a further understanding of this problem. From the viewpoint of the initiating or referring organization, patients are sent for several reasons. First, the more common one is to procure valued services for these patients from legitimate organizations who may be seeking such patients; second, is to "dump" patients who are or have become "costs," and on whom the organization no longer desires to expend resources. The dumping relieves the organization of responsibility for the patient whereas simple discharge, not giving him an alternative, would not do this. A third type of referral might be called "casual." A patient may solicit services from an organization which does not offer them and be sent on. If, in this case, the referring organization has informa-

---

[3]The problem that confronts the health system also confronts hospitals. In a factory, activities are organized around the problems of producing a salable product and this provides a unifying principle for the organization. In a hospital, decisions about the "product" are made by many parts of the organization. The hospital administrator then faces the problem of producing complementarity of goods and services to support many unrelated "products." The solution to this situation might be to develop specialized hospitals which would be limited to handling specific syndromes or somatic systems. The specialists might then be able to reach decisions that further orderly development and integration of the organization.

tion on what other organizations do, the patient may gain entry into the health system. If it has little or no information on appropriate organizations, the patient may not gain entry.

From the point of view of the rejecting organization, patients are not accepted (1.) if they are surplus; (2.) if they do not accord with accountability criteria; (3.) for lack of payment when payment for service is involved. It might be predicted that where surplus patients exist relative to a given organization, the organization will act to maximize fulfillment of its accountability criteria. This may result in "creaming" the most desirable patients from those available (Miller and Robey, 1970 : 169). From a given organization's point of view, a waiting list may function to process surplus patients either in a random manner or to "cream." From the organizational point of view, it should be noted, waiting lists are probably desirable. They demonstrate a "need" for services, they provide a continuous supply of patients, and they may permit careful screening and selection.

It would seem, then, that the patient is a benefit only under rather limited conditions. In given cases, the specific conditions are expressed in interorganizational agreements on referrals. These agreements usually stipulate the conditions under which a patient will be accepted. It is interesting to note that agreements on other resources usually stipulate the conditions under which these resources will be sent. In the former case, organizational responsibility for fulfilling the conditions rests with the initiating organization; in the latter case, with the recipient organization.

Where no agreements exist, a frequent cause of referral failure is that the goals of the organization are mistaken for its functions. An organization, as we have said, may claim a domain but give low priority to given services in that domain. The Easter Seal organization is a case in point. Although it included cerebral palsied individuals within its aegis and strongly defended its claim to them, it gave them low priority and allocated few resources to them. Teele and Levine (1967 : 103–26) describe similar situations. They describe how the child guidance agency claimed delinquency problems as part of its domain, but tended not to accept those cases not amenable to psychiatric technology. It was not disposed to reallocate resources to the special problems they presented.

The above discussion considers whether the patient is a benefit or a cost to the organization. The conditions pertain to organizations in which the criterion for accountability is not money. The strategy in these organizations is to maximize their goals within given budgets. The procuring of larger budgets in fact depends on maximally fulfilling their accountability criteria. In organizations where payment for service is involved, the accountability criteria and the well-being and growth of the organization are more directly related to money and profit. It should be noted that the use of money in the health system (in the form of third-party payments) does not

produce the conditions of the market situation which encourage complementarity of functions or exchange of resources with money used as a
medium of exchange. The third-party payments help to solve the cost or
patient payment problem and to that degree they do contribute to system
integration; but, as we shall see, only within the limits imposed by the
primitive barter situation.

A Hypothesis on System Integration

If we examine the customary attempts to bring about health system
integration, we discover that they have operated within the constraints of
primitive barter. We shall classify these attempts which we have considered
previously as councils of peers, "outsiders" with sanctions, and "consumers"
with sanctions. To be sure, each modus has effected or would effect changes.
Unfortunately, this does not or would not provide a basis for maximizing
total system integration.

The literature is replete with evidence of the shortcomings of these
approaches. The council of peers merely facilitates communication and
does not otherwise affect the relationships of the organizations with one
another (Mott, 1968). The outsiders with sanctions are of two major types.
One, represented by community councils, ideally reviews community
needs in relation to organizational functions and rationally allocates
resources among them. However, the infinity of community needs, lack
of consensus on priorities, and the actors' parochial commitments to one
another (and to organizations on the boards of which they may serve),
limit the effectiveness of such collectivities in modifying the functions of
the recipient organizations.[4] Another type of outsider with sanctions is
categorical federal funding which attempts to effect complementarity by
inducing recipient organizations to modify their functions. In part effective,
it does little in itself to integrate the functions of the various organizations
and indeed leads to fission in the system. Regional medical programs,
which we are now studying, fall between these two types, a combination

---

[4]The hypothesis that overlapping board memberships in health organizations
produces system integration has never been substantiated. Our studies show no relationship to interorganizational exchange. The evidence is, to the contrary, that most
organizational leadership, i.e., determination of the disposition of resources, comes
from administrators. In general, the boards respond to information and interpretation
supplied by them. Overlapping boards probably do function to mediate the interorganizational conflicts—by defining mutually exclusive domains—and in "collusion"
to obtain resources from outside sources by supplying evidence of interorganizational
cooperation. There is reason to believe that the functions of overlapping boards in the
economic sector, because of the conditions we have enumerated, can and do have an
integrating effect.

of the existing interorganizational commitments and a recognition of respective domains, on the one hand, and outside manipulation of organizational functions, on the other. Underlying these approaches is an assumption that centralized direction or "masterminding" can stimulate necessary (from a given point of view) organizational functions and futhermore result in their integration. Anyone familiar with the cavalier manner in which organizations utilize categorical funds is familiar with a major weakness in this approach. It is interesting that the Soviet Union attempted to integrate its system of production through masterminding a comprehensive plan. The problems of system integration that resulted are similar in many respects to those encountered in our attempts to mastermind integration of the health system.

The third approach, consumers with sanctions, has special problems, some of which were raised in response to an innovative proposal by Warren (1970). Consumers were to be provided with chits to be given to the organization whose services they utilized. A fundamental problem with the scheme is that organizations, not consumers, determine the flow of patients through their referrals. Once a patient enters the health system, he has little control over where he is referred.

Another variation of consumers with sanctions is the OEO neighborhood health centers which have consumers represented on their boards. In such cases, it might be assumed that patient "needs" would be responded to in referral patterns, perhaps even with the neighborhood centers providing reimbursement to other organizations for rendering these services. In these cases, the accountability criteria of the clinics could include encouraging comprehensive services by involving other organizations. Unfortunately, evidence is accumulating that a primary interest of consumer board members is to use the organizations as a source of employment for the community rather than interest in integrating the system in terms of patient need.

In light of this discussion of attempts to integrate the system, we see that only the Warren proposal attempts to incorporate any features of the market situation. Our consideration of the market situation and of the existing primitive barter situation suggests a modification that might prove effective. The effects of the philanthropic orientation and accountability criteria, i.e., the inflexibility of functions and resulting lack of complementarity with other organizations, must be overcome. One solution would be to provide money to facilitate referrals when the goals of only one organization would be fulfilled by a transaction, in effect, to transform the existing primitive barter situation into a more flexible exchange situation.

Organizations would be provided with funds which could be used *only* for the goods and services of other nonprofit health organizations (perhaps only other local health organizations). Ideally, then, organizations would be motivated to refer patients or to purchase services which would satisfy their patients' needs, on the one hand, and would be motivated to accept patients who might not precisely fit their prevailing accountability criteria, on the other. Should there be an abundant demand for services of a marginal type, the given organization, or some other, would be motivated to modify its functions to make them complementary to the referring organizations. This might entail some degree of goal displacement, but it is likely that most organizations could modify their present functions, currently limited by accountability criteria, within the scope of existing goals. The awareness produced by this process also might result in modification of accountability criteria.

This proposal is in effect a hypothesis based on assumptions regarding the conditions governing exchange relationships between nonprofit organizations. At present, many nonprofit organizations already have relationships with profit-making organizations. In general, the latter appear to have greater complementarity of functions with the nonprofit organizations than do nonprofit organizations among themselves.

REFERENCES

Evan, William M.   "The Organization-Set: Toward a Theory of Interorganizational
1966   Relations." In James P. Thompson (ed.), *Organizational Design*. Pittsburgh:
        University of Pittsburgh Press.
Homans, George.   "Social Behavior as Exchange." *American Journal of Sociology*,
1958   63:596–606.
Lefton, Mark, and W. R. Rosengren.   "Organization and Clients: Lateral and
1966   Longitudinal Dimensions." *American Sociological Review*, 31:802–10.
Levine, Sol, and Paul E. White.   "Exchange as a Conceptual Framework for the
1961   Study of Interorganizational Relationships." *Administrative Science
        Quarterly*, 5:583–601.
Litwak, Eugene, and L. F. Hylton.   "Interorganizational Analysis: A Hypothesis
1962   on Coordinating Agencies." *Administrative Science Quarterly*, 6:129.
Mauss, Marcel.   *The Gift*. Glencoe, Ill.: The Free Press.
1955
Miller, S. M., and Pamela A. Robey.   *The Future of Inequality*: 169. New York:
1970   Basic Books, Inc.
Mott, Basil J. F.   *Anatomy of a Coordinating Council: Implications for Planning*.
1968   Pittsburgh: University of Pittsburgh Press.
Teele, James, and Sol Levine.   "The Acceptance of Emotionally Disturbed Children
1967   by Psychiatric Agencies." In Stanton Wheeler (ed.), *Controlling Delinquents*:
        103–26. New York: John Wiley.
Warren, Roland.   "Alternative Strategies of Inter-Agency Planning." In *Inter-
1970   Organization Research in Health: Conference Proceedings*. Washington,
        D.C.: Department of Health, Education, and Welfare.
White, Paul E.   "Myth and Reality in Interorganizational Relationships." *American
1968   Journal of Public Health*, 58:289–304.

15

Interorganizational Exchange: A Note on the Scarcity Hypothesis

RAYMOND J. ADAMEK, BEBE F. LAVIN

INTRODUCTION

Utilizing exchange theory as a framework for the study of interorganizational relations, Levine and White (1961) suggested that scarcity of needed elements within health and welfare systems is an underlying cause of exchange among organizations. Data gathered on 300 health and welfare agencies were used to test the hypothesis that there is a direct, positive relationship between scarcity at the organizational level and exchange. Results indicated that agencies enjoying a relative abundance of elements were most likely to engage in exchange. While scarcity at the systems level may provide a motive for exchange, it appears that organizations most willing to act upon this motive are those relatively rich in essential elements. Exchange theory is employed to explain this finding.

BACKGROUND

Whether a result of the natural development of organizational theory or a response to changes in the "real world" of organizations (Terreberry, 1968), or both, sociological interest in interorganizational relations has increased considerably in the past fifteen years (Aiken and Hage, 1968). Within this area of concern, a number of studies have focused on the variables affecting interorganizational cooperation, particularly among health and welfare agencies. For example, Form and Nosow (1958) found that organizations with similar internal structures were more likely to cooperate with one another in times of disaster than those with dissimilar structures. Reviewing the literature on interorganizational relations and applying Merton's

---

The authors wish to thank Edward O. Laumann and Paul E. White for their critiques of an earlier version of this paper, and the Ohio Governor's Council on Vocational Rehabilitation for making the data available.

(1957) concept of role set, Evan (1966) maintained that interorganizational cooperation is fostered by complementarity of functions, the ability of a given organization to invoke sanctions against the members of its set for not cooperating, a high degree of competition between a given organization and the members of the output organizations in its set, and a shortage of input resources. Lefton and Rosengren (1966) have suggested that the extent and breadth of an organization's concern with its clients affects its propensity to cooperate with others. Some support for their hypothesis has been found by the present authors, and by Eichhorn and Wysong (1968). The latter studied relations among organizations and physicians involved in tuberculosis control in a metropolitan region and found domain consensus, resource allocation, bureaucratic constraints, and organizational leadership to be additional variables affecting cooperation. Aiken and Hage (1968) suggested that intraorganizational staff diversity leads to innovative programs which demand additional resources for their support. This demand motivates organizations to participate in joint programs in order to secure needed resources.

The work of Levine and White (1961, 1963) and their colleagues (Levine, White, and Paul, 1963; White, Levine, and Vlasak, Chapter 14) is one of the most comprehensive theoretical approaches to interorganizational relations. Utilizing Mauss's (1955) notion of exchange as a conceptual framework for the study of such relations, they point out that an organization must possess or control three main elements to achieve its goals: clients, a work staff, and nonhuman resources, such as equipment, specialized knowledge, and funds. Focusing on health and welfare organizations, they note that these elements are often in rather short supply. This scarcity, they suggest, is a spur to interorganizational exchange, which they define as, "any voluntary activity between two organizations which has consequences, actual or anticipated, for the realization of their respective goals or objectives" (1961 : 588).[1]

Three major factors are seen by Levine and White as influencing the extent to which organizations enter into exchange relations. The first is the relative availability of needed elements outside the local community of organizations. Utilizing the federated-corporate distinction developed by Sills (1957), they note that corporate agencies have less local autonomy than federated agencies, and that corporate agencies are more likely to receive needed elements from their parent organizations—thus decreasing the need for exchange at the local level. In addition, the parent organization may intentionally discourage its affiliates from seeking cooperative ties

---

[1]This definition is broad enough to encompass "positive" exchanges, such as cooperation, and "negative" exchanges, such as competition or conflict. Levine and White, however, focused primarily upon positive exchange, as do we.

locally in order to insure its own goal attainment and maintain control over the affiliates. The second major factor influencing exchange is "the objectives of the organization and the particular functions to which it allocates the elements it controls" (1961 : 583). Thus, organizations with different goals, or those whose primary functions differ, both need and possess different amounts and types of elements. Organizational goals and functions may also determine whether an organization deals directly or indirectly with its clients, the prestige it enjoys in the community, and its leadership potential, all of which influence its propensity to engage in exchange. The third major factor influencing exchange is the extent to which domain consensus exists among a group of organizations. Where agencies have staked out identical or similar domains, competition for needed elements rather than cooperation is likely. Further, organizations are unlikely to enter into exchange relationships with those whose claims to a given domain are viewed as illegitimate.

Levine and White thus consider scarcity of elements (clients, staff, and various nonhuman resources) a major cause of interorganizational exchange. They state:

> ... were all the essential elements in infinite supply there would be little need for organizational interaction and for subscription to cooperation as an ideal. Under actual conditions of scarcity, however, interorganizational exchanges are essential to goal attainment (1961:587).[2]

While we generally agree that scarcity motivates organizations to enter into exchange relations, as do Evan (1966) and Aiken and Hage (1968), we feel the findings reported below indicate a qualifying note should be added to this hypothesis.

PROCEDURE

Levine and White's work focuses on scarcity at the level of health and welfare *systems*. We attempted to determine whether their analysis could be applied at the *organizational* level, operationalizing the concept of scarcity as a shortage of needed elements experienced by particular agencies. The basic question then became: Given an interorganizational system in which scarcity exists, which agencies are most likely to engage in exchange

---

[2]Although Levine and White stress the role scarcity plays in fostering cooperation, implicitly, at least, they recognize that scarcity may also lead to competition and conflict, a fact well documented in the literature of economics. Their consideration of organizational autonomy, goals and functions, and domain consensus may be viewed as an attempt to specify the conditions under which cooperation, rather than competition, conflict, or simply a lack of cooperation, is likely to occur.

to alleviate shortages of needed elements? Following Levine and White's analysis, we hypothesized that there would be a positive relationship between the degree of scarcity of clients, staff, and nonhuman resources experienced by organizations and the extent to which they engage in exchange with other organizations.

Sample

A secondary analysis of data gathered from 321 health and welfare agencies located in 60 Ohio communities enabled us to test this hypothesis. A questionnaire (developed by Greenleigh Associates of New York for the Ohio Governor's Council on Vocational Rehabilitation) was used in a survey of five of seven health and welfare regions in the state during the latter half of 1967. Regions I and II, comprised of an 18–county band across northern Ohio, with Toledo and Cleveland as their urban centers, chose to develop their own survey instrument; hence, no data from these regions are included in this paper.

The five committees in each region sought to obtain information from all agencies which in any way were or should have been interested in the health and welfare of disabled persons, with the term "disabled" being broadly interpreted. Overall, a return rate of approximately 56 percent was achieved, ranging from a low of 45 percent to a high of 69 percent for the five regions. The organizations responding and their numbers were social service agencies (30), hospitals (31) and extended care facilities (16), mental health clinics (20), public welfare departments (40), public (25) and private (69) health agencies, educational agencies (22), sheltered workshops (21), correctional institutions (17), antipoverty agencies (12), vocational rehabilitation centers (5), vocational training centers (4), employment services (3), recreational facilities (4), and research agencies (2). In 62 percent of the cases the chief executive of the agency supplied the information requested, while in 30 percent the staff member responsible for rehabilitation or working with the disabled did so. In the remaining cases, some other person, most often a board member, supplied the information.

Although this sample cannot be categorized as either random or definitely representative, it does include a broad range of organizational types from diverse locations within the state of Ohio.

Primary Variable Measures

Extent of agency exchange, the dependent variable, was measured by a four-item Guttman scale.[3] This scale was formed by four structured

---

[3] Utilizing the Cornell Technique, we obtained a coefficient of reproducibility of .94 and a minimal marginal reproducibility of .68. No item had more than 10 percent

responses to the question, "How do you assist handicapped people to achieve rehabilitation services not provided by your agency?"[4] The responses were:

1. Inform client of available community resources.
2. Make appointment for client with another agency.
3. Sharing of records with another agency.
4. Case conferences with another agency.

Client scarcity was measured by the presence or absence of a waiting list, it being assumed that agencies with such lists experienced less client scarcity than those without such lists. The size of the total client population served during the year, and the number of disabled persons currently receiving services provided two other rather crude measures of client scarcity.[5]

---

scale errors or more than 80 percent positive responses. Twenty-one agencies did not respond to these items, thus reducing our sample to 300. Those who did respond were classified on the basis of scale types as high, medium, or low on exchange. As is evident from the items, those indicating they engaged in all four activities were considered high on exchange, those engaged in the first two or three were considered medium, and those who indicated they did none of these things, or only informed clients of available resources, were considered low on exchange.

[4]The wording of this question presented a problem in interpreting our results. Nowhere on the questionnaire were the concepts "handicapped people" or "rehabilitation services" defined. This meant that each respondent could define these concepts for himself—some perhaps interpreting them in a broad sense and responding to include all clients who applied for agency services, and others interpreting them in a narrow sense, responding so as to include only some smaller subsample of clients. Hence, there was a possibility that the extent of exchange measured reflected only different respondent definitions of these key terms. We attempted to correct this difficulty in each cross-tabulation of the dependent and independent variables for the agencies by controlling responses to the question, "Is rehabilitation a primary purpose of your agency?" Those replying affirmatively (N = 130) were considered to be utilizing a broad definition of the terms, and/or as responding relative to their total client population. Those replying negatively (N = 180) were considered to be utilizing a narrow definition, and/or as responding relative to a smaller subsample of the client population. These controls did not alter the results reported below.

[5]Since this was a secondary analysis, we could not always measure the variables as we would have liked to measure them. For example, some measure of client population relative to agency capacity to handle clients would have been preferable to those used to measure client scarcity, but none was available. In an effort to compensate for these difficulties, we utilized multiple measures where possible, recognizing of course that three poor measures do not necessarily equal one good one.

Several critics have questioned whether an excess of clients constitutes additional

Staff scarcity was measured by comparing the number of staff positions actually occupied to the number budgeted for the organization in each of four staff categories: administrators, professionals, semiprofessionals, and service personnel.[6] The proportion of positions filled in each category for each agency was computed. Agencies were then categorized as high, medium, or low on staff scarcity relative to all other agencies for each staff category.

Scarcity of nonhuman resources was measured by total agency operating expenditures per client for the preceding fiscal year, and by total agency expenditures for rehabilitation services per disabled client for the preceding fiscal year. A final measure of scarcity of nonhuman resources was provided by considering the range of services an agency offered.[7] Each agency was asked to indicate which of 28 different services were available at that agency. The number of services actually provided by an agency was divided by the 28 services considered possible, and each agency was ranked relative to all others as high, medium, or low on range of services provided.

---

resources for an agency, or drains upon other resources, and have therefore questioned whether or not it is advantageous to have a waiting list. White, Levine, and Vlasak (Chapter 14) argue that such lists are desirable, since "they demonstrate a 'need' for services, they provide a continuous supply of patients, and they may permit careful screening and selection." The latter, a "creaming" process, increases the chances that an agency's success rate will be enhanced, which, given scarcity, is important in seeking continued community support.

A related objection which has been raised is that when an agency has an excess of clients, it may be motivated to "dump" those not retained in the creaming process by referring them to other agencies, thus increasing its exchange rate. Since our measure of exchange focused upon the extent or degree of exchange rather than upon frequency, however, it is relatively insensitive to client dumping.

[6]The occupations within each category are as follows: Administrators: agency director, other administrative and supervisory personnel; Professionals: research staff, physicians, psychiatrists, psychologists; Semiprofessionals: nurses, occupational therapists, physical therapists, speech therapists, teachers, vocational counselors, rehabilitation counselors, employment counselors, social workers, technical staff; Service Personnel: aids, clerical staff, service staff. The rather conservative definition of professionals was employed because the original survey instrument did not provide data on professional training, and we had no way to ascertain how many of those reported as nurses, therapists, counselors, etc. actually had professional degrees.

[7]We considered range of services a nonhuman resource because it implies specialized knowledge (e.g., counseling of various types, medical and psychiatric evaluation) and equipment (e.g., audiological testing devices, prosthetic appliances). Since staff are needed to apply this knowledge and utilize this equipment, one might argue that range of services also provides a measure of staff scarcity.

RESULTS

Tables 1 through 3 provide the findings relative to client scarcity. Whether scarcity is measured by the presence or absence of a waiting list, by total number of clients served in the past fiscal year, or by the number of disabled clients presently being served, the results indicate a positive association between exchange and a *lack of scarcity*. That is, contrary to our hypothesis, the results indicate that the more clients an agency has, the more likely it is to be high on exchange. Gamma values indicate a low to moderate degree of association, ranging between .20 and .35. Table 2 suggests that middle-sized agencies (1001–2000 clients) engage in the greatest extent of exchange, and both Tables 2 and 3 suggest that the smallest agencies are least likely to engage in exchange to any great extent.

Table 1
EXTENT OF EXCHANGE BY CLIENT SCARCITY (WAITING LIST)

	Waiting List	
Exchange	Present	Absent
High	63%	48%
Medium	25	35
Low	12	17
Total %	100	100
(Agency N)	(101)	(180)
Gamma = .26		

Table 2
EXTENT OF EXCHANGE BY PREVIOUS YEAR'S TOTAL CASE LOAD

	Total Case Load					
Exchange	Over 5000	2001–5000	1001–2000	501–1000	101–500	1–100
High	55%	61%	79%	56%	51%	32%
Medium	28	27	12	38	33	36
Low	17	12	9	6	15	32
Total %	100	100	100	100	99	100
(Agency N)	(65)	(33)	(34)	(34)	(72)	(47)
Gamma = .20						

Table 3
EXTENT OF EXCHANGE BY PRESENT DISABLED CASE LOAD

	Present Disabled Case Load				
Exchange	*Over* 1000	301– 1000	101– 300	51– 100	1– 50
High	64%	65%	53%	46%	32%
Medium	27	27	42	38	42
Low	9	8	5	16	26
Total %	100	100	100	100	100
(Agency N)	(22)	(37)	(38)	(37)	(66)
Gamma = .35					

When an effort was made to determine whether scarcity of staff was related to interorganizational exchange, no appreciable relationships were found for any of the four staff categories. Gamma exceeded .10 in only one of four instances, the service personnel cross-tabulation. Thus, staff scarcity appears unrelated to exchange. Our data may not have permitted an adequate test of this hypothesis, however. Most agencies reported that budgeted positions had been filled, so that there were few agencies high or medium on staff scarcity. For example, even after collapsing these two categories for administrators, we were contrasting 189 low-scarcity agencies with 33 others. The results, therefore, may not be statistically reliable. Further, the finding that most budgeted positions had been filled does not necessarily indicate that all of the agencies had all of the staff they needed. Assuming an adequate budget to begin with, an agency could have all staff slots filled and still experience staff scarcity. Our measure of staff scarcity, therefore, may not have provided a fair test of the hypothesis. In view of this, staff scarcity was not utilized in further analyses.

Tables 4 and 5 indicate our findings regarding the relationship between extent of exchange and scarcity of nonhuman resources as measured by agency expenditures per client. The results show a positive association between exchange and a lack of scarcity in both instances. Gamma values of .24 and .42 indicate a low to moderate degree of association. Again, the results are contrary to our hypothesis.

Finally, Table 6 indicates that those agencies offering the broadest range of services tend to be high on exchange, while those offering the fewest services tend to be low on exchange. Gamma (.39) indicates a moderate degree of association. These results are again contrary to the hypothesis that agencies which experience a scarcity of nonhuman resources are most likely to engage in exchange.

204

Table 4
EXTENT OF EXCHANGE BY TOTAL OPERATING EXPENDITURES
PER CLIENT

Exchange	Total Expenditures Per Client	
	Over $100	Under $100
High	58%	46%
Medium	28	33
Low	13	21
Total %	99	100
(Agency N)	(178)	(100)
Gamma = .24		

Table 5
EXTENT OF EXCHANGE BY TOTAL REHABILITATION
EXPENDITURES PER DISABLED CLIENT

Exchange	Expenditures Per Client	
	Over $100	Under $100
High	70%	45%
Medium	20	41
Low	9	14
Total %	99	100
(Agency N)	(78)	(113)
Gamma = .42		

Table 6
EXTENT OF EXCHANGE BY RANGE OF SERVICES PROVIDED

Exchange	Range of Services		
	High	Medium	Low
High	73%	51%	40%
Medium	22	32	34
Low	5	17	26
Total %	100	100	100
(Agency N)	(81)	(103)	(115)
Gamma = .39			

Control Variables

After the measures of scarcity were cross-tabulated with extent of exchange, eleven variables were employed, in turn, as controls to determine whether the relationships originally observed would be reversed or nullified. These variables were selected for at least one of the following reasons: (a.) data on them were available; (b.) theoretical considerations and the work of previous authors suggested they might be related to exchange; and (c.) cross-tabulation indicated they were associated with exchange to an appreciable degree. The variables were: autonomy from extra-local ties, agency type, function, direct vs. indirect client service, lateral-longitudinal orientation to client, auspices, community size, and staff structure (four measures). In addition to these eleven control variables, several of the measures of scarcity were utilized, in turn, as controls among themselves to determine whether their perceived relationships to exchange were independent of one another.

None of the eleven control variables discussed substantially altered the relationships presented above. That is, regardless of agency autonomy, type, function, direct/indirect service to clients, orientation to clients, auspices, proportion of administrators, professionals, semiprofessionals, or service personnel, and regardless of the size of the community in which the agency was located, there was generally a positive association between *lack of scarcity* (for the client load and nonhuman resources variables) and the extent of agency exchange. Of the 185 tables generated by employing the eleven control variables, positive gammas in excess of .10 were obtained in 153 (83 percent).[8] No discernible pattern was found among those tables in which gamma was either between .00 and .10, or negative. That is, no control variable accounted for a disproportionate number of tables in which the relationships between the primary variables were reversed or nullified.

When we utilized the measures of scarcity as controls among themselves, the results indicated that a relative abundance of clients, funds, and range of services contribute independently to exchange. That is, none of these measures as controls substantially or consistently reduced the relationships of the others with exchange. Of the 36 tables generated in this analysis, only five (14 percent) failed to yield a positive gamma over .10, and in 23 instances gamma exceeded .25. Combining agencies along two or three dimensions

---

[8]We considered a gamma at or below .10 to indicate essentially no relationship between two variables. This was a minimum figure, however, and most of the gammas obtained were considerably higher. For example, 123 of the tables yielded positive gammas in excess of .25. Negative gammas were obtained in only 15 tables, and in seven of these, small N's make the results statistically unreliable.

of scarcity and then cross-tabulating them with exchange also suggested that these dimensions are independently related to exchange. That is, the strength of association for the combined characteristics and exchange was generally higher than that between exchange and any *one* of the measures considered singly. Table 7 illustrates this point. Again, we see that the richer

Table 7
EXTENT OF EXCHANGE BY AGENCIES HAVING SELECTED
CHARACTERISTICS

Exchange	*Agencies Having*		
	Over 500 Clients *Over $100 Per Client* *High Range of Services*	*Mixed* *Characteristics**	*500 Clients or Less* *Under $100 Per Client* *Low Range of Services*
High	78%	54%	21%
Medium	19	32	26
Low	3	14	53
Total %	100	100	100
(Agency N)	(37)	(216)	(19)

Gamma = .58

*Those agencies with any of the other possible combinations of the three variables under consideration, e.g., agencies with over 500 clients, over $100 per client, and medium range of services, etc.

an agency is in essential elements, the more likely it is to be engaged in extensive exchange relationships.

SUMMARY AND DISCUSSION

Levine and White (1961) suggested the exchange model is useful for understanding interorganizational relations. This model implies the existence of a system in which elements needed by organizations are in short supply. To reach their goals, organizations exchange for needed elements. We attempted to extend this analysis to the organizational level, and hypothesized that organizations experiencing the greatest scarcity of needed elements would be most extensively engaged in exchange. Essentially, we found the opposite. Those organizations with the greatest abundance of elements were most likely to engage in exchange.[9] Litwak and Rothman

[9]We noted above, however, that agencies with intermediate-size case loads were most likely to exchange, rather than those with the largest case loads. Similarly, when we looked at the agencies' total operating expenditures in absolute figures (data not

(1970) report similar findings in a study of Detroit schools, as do Klonglan, et al. (1969), in a study of alcoholism-service agencies.

It should be emphasized that although the observed relationships did not reflect what we had hypothesized and expected, we do not consider our work as contradicting that of Levine and White, but rather as extending and specifying it. Thus, while we agree with Levine and White that scarcity at the systems level provides a motive for organizations to engage in exchange relationships, our data suggest that at the organizational level, those agencies most willing to *act upon* this motive are those relatively rich in clients and nonhuman resources. Exchange theory (Homans, 1958; Gouldner, 1960) helps to explain why we might expect this. If organization A enters into an exchange relationship with organization B, A may assume that B will also make some demands on it. Moreover, the norm of reciprocity implies that these exchanges should be mutually beneficial and roughly equivalent. If organization A is less well endowed than B in terms of clients and/or other resources, however, it may refrain from entering into a relationship in which it feels it cannot reciprocate. Further, the less well-endowed organization may see the cost of the exchange as too great relative to the reward it receives (more successfully attaining its objectives). In fact, the exchange relationship may be viewed as one wherein there is *no* reward. Like Blau's (1955) government workers who sought help from their more competent colleagues, referring clients to more favored agencies may be seen by the less favored agency as a reflection on its own effectiveness and worth, and as a threat to its continued support and very existence. Rather than being rewarding, exchange may seem to promise only further loss of prestige, encroachment by other agencies, and loss of community support.[10]

On the other hand, exchange theory would suggest that an organization with an abundance of clients, funds, and services to offer could best afford to enter into exchange relationships. It can better honor its obligations; and because of the wide range of services offered, it can expect to gain as

reported here), a similar "curvilinear" relationship appeared. We also noted that agencies with intermediate autonomy were highest on exchange, rather than those which were "completely" autonomous. Perhaps Levine and White (1961) were quite correct in stating that there would be no need to exchange were all needed elements in infinite supply, and the relationship between scarcity and exchange actually is curvilinear.

[10]Our data permit another interpretation of the finding that agencies experiencing a scarcity of nonhuman resources are low on exchange. Those low on exchange most often checked only the response on the exchange scale indicating that they informed a client of other agencies when they themselves could not provide a needed service. It may be that, compared with more well-endowed agencies, they are more willing to let such clients go in order to concentrate the resources they do have on clients they can assist more adequately.

many or more clients as it loses in these relationships. Furthermore, its ability and willingness to exchange will enhance its position and prestige[11] within the system, thus promising continued and perhaps increased community support.

Thus, in their relationships with one another, organizations appear to resemble individuals. Those who are relatively well endowed with various resources, who have the apparent support of others, and who might be considered as enjoying high status and self-esteem are more likely to be secure and feel free to engage in frequent interaction with their fellows, and to find such interaction rewarding. Those less well endowed, on the other hand, who lack support, and who may be considered as having low status and self-esteem, find social interaction unrewarding and even somewhat threatening.

The above explanation is offered as a tentative one in need of further testing. The precise nature of the causal links between scarcity, exchange, and relative abundance certainly have not been specified by our work. As one reviewer noted, our results may well have led us to the conclusion that those agencies most willing to act upon the scarcity motive (for whatever reason) were relatively rich in clients and other elements *because of* their exchange relationships.[12]

The fact that our results lend themselves to equally plausible but conflicting interpretations suggests that further research, with more exacting design and measurement, is necessary. While we consider our results quite suggestive, the shortcomings of secondary analysis are painfully apparent. We could not always measure the variables we were dealing with as we would have liked to measure them. Some variables felt to be important could not be measured at all, and we dealt with exchange in a somewhat restricted sense, even though it was in a way consonant with Levine and White's (1961) definition. We could not specify, for example, who was engaged in exchange with whom, for what purposes, and with what elements. Further, we were limited to considering "positive" or cooperative exchanges, and could not determine to what extent competition and conflict for needed elements characterized agency relations. These problems must be dealt with in future research.

---

[11] Levine and White's (1961) early study of 22 health agencies found that organizations high in prestige led in joint activities with other organizations.

[12] Turk's (1970, 1973) work demonstrates that the prior existence of an interorganizational exchange network is a better predictor of a city's ability to bring outside funds into the community than is the simple lack of and need for such resources, and that the existence of interorganizational networks is conducive to identifying needs which may be met through further interorganizational exchange.

REFERENCES

Aiken, Michael, and Jerald Hage. "Organizational Interdependence and Intra-
1968   organizational Structure." *American Sociological Review*, 33:912–30.

Blau, Peter M. *The Dynamics of Bureaucracy.* Chicago: University of Chicago
1955   Press.

Eichhorn, Robert L., and Jere A. Wysong. *Interagency Relations in the Provision
1968   of Health Services: Tuberculosis Control in a Metropolitan Region.* Lafayette,
        Indiana: Institute for the Study of Social Change, Department of Sociology,
        Purdue University.

Evan, William M. "The Organization-Set: Toward a Theory of Interorganizational
1966   Relations." In James D. Thompson (ed.), *Approaches to Organizational
        Design*: 173–91. Pittsburgh: University of Pittsburgh Press.

Form, William H., and Sigmund Nosow. *Community in Disaster.* New York: Harper
1958   and Row.

Gouldner, Alvin W. "The Norm of Reciprocity: A Preliminary Statement." *American
1960   Sociological Review*, 25:161–78.

Homans, George C. "Social Behavior as Exchange." *The American Journal of
1958   Sociology.* 62:597–606.

Klonglan, Gerald E., Don A. Dillman, Joel S. Wright, and George M. Beal. *Agency
1969   Interaction Patterns and Community Alcoholism Services.* Ames, Iowa:
        Department of Sociology and Anthropology, Iowa State University.

Lefton, Mark, and William R. Rosengren. "Organizations and Clients: Lateral
1966   and Longitudinal Dimensions." *American Sociological Review*, 31:802–11.

Levine, Sol, and Paul E. White. "Exchange as a Conceptual Framework for the
1961   Study of Interorganizational Relationships." *Administrative Science
        Quarterly*, 5:583–601.

————. "The Community of Health Organizations." In Howard E. Freeman,
1963   et al. (eds.), *Handbook of Medical Sociology*: 321–47. Englewood Cliffs,
        N.J.: Prentice-Hall.

Levine, Sol, Paul E. White, and Benjamin D. Paul. "Community Interorganizational
1963   Problems in Providing Medical Care and Social Services." *American Journal
        of Public Health*, 53:1183–95.

Litwak, Eugene, and Jack Rothman. "Towards the Theory and Practice of Coordina-
1970   tion between Formal Organizations." In William R. Rosengren and Mark
        Lefton (eds.), *Organizations and Clients:* 137–86. Columbus, Ohio: Charles
        E. Merrill.

Mauss, Marcel. *The Gift.* Glencoe, Ill.: The Free Press.
1955

Merton, Robert K. *Social Theory and Social Structure.* Glencoe, Ill.: The Free
1957   Press.

Sills, David L. *The Volunteers: Means and Ends in a National Organization.* Glencoe,
1957   Ill.: The Free Press.

Terreberry, Shirley. "The Evolution of Organizational Environments." *Adminis-
1968   trative Science Quarterly*, 12:590–613.

Turk, Herman. "Interorganizational Networks in Urban Society: Initial Perspectives
1970   and Comparative Research." *American Sociological Review*, 35:1–19.

————. "Comparative Urban Structure from an Interorganizational Perspective."
1973   *Administrative Science Quarterly*, 18:37–55.

16

A Strategy for Creating Interdependent Delivery Systems to Meet Complex Needs

The objective of this paper is to suggest a strategy for creating inter-dependence in an organizational network or delivery system. Previously, Aiken and I (1968) have been concerned with predicting how the internal properties of structure affect the development of joint programs—our measure of interdependence—in single organizational relationships or dyads. This paper differs from the earlier effort by moving from a focus on the organization to one on the network, from an interest in how internal properties affect interdependence to one in how external strategies create them, and from hypothesis-testing to one of hypothesis-generating. While these might seem as discontinuities, they parallel the development of the organizational literature in recent years. It has moved from inside the organization to outside and, in the process, discovered the need to generate new models that conceptualize or include the organizational environment (Azumi and Hage, 1972 : Chapter 1); thus we find the interest in organi-zational relationships and networks, an important part of the environment (for others, see pp. 33–39).

Concomitant with this intellectual evolution has been a parallel develop-ment in the recognition, especially by the federal government, of the com-plexity of many problems—mental retardation, water pollution, residential segregation—that appear to be beyond the grasp and ken of single organi-zations and communities (Rosengren, 1970 : 130; Starkweather, 1970 : 4). This present paper grows out of a concern for how one might create delivery systems for the mental retardate where it is clearly recognized (see President's Panel, 1962) that somehow a large number of organizations need to be brought together to provide what is called a continuum of care and a fixed point of referral within a coordinated delivery system.

Since we (Aiken, et al. 1972) became involved in the study of these five demonstration projects after most of them were finished, it was im-possible to do a rigorous study. Instead, we had to rely upon retrospective questions about salient events, minutes of meetings, and other dubious sources. In broad outline, however, there was considerable collaboration of testimony, enough to be sure that in general most of the strategies tried *partially* failed. The attempt to understand why and the desire to propose what would appear to be a more effective approach is the objective of this paper. It might be seen as one effort to provide some fill-in for the gap of studies about planned change in the community literature (Warren, 1971: 8–9).

Since the ideas grew out of research in a rather esoteric area (the study of mental retardation systems), some attention must be given to whether the proposed strategy has relevance beyond this immediate context. What is suggested is that it may be relevant wherever the objective is too big for one organization to handle. Increasingly, there is evidence that these kinds of large, complicated goals are being faced not only in the health and welfare area, where the problem of integrating services is a current theme, but in many other sectors of society. Some consideration of these other areas is given at the end of the paper. The strategy suggested, while developed in one specific area of health and welfare, hopefully has relevance to many other areas which might be called multiorganizational problems—problems that can be solved only with a network of organizations that are interdependent in certain ways.

The particular term interdependence (Litwak, 1970:147; Evan, 1966), which is defined below, is chosen quite deliberately. While the old ideas of integration and coordination would appear equally viable, they also carry with them some unfortunate associations of hierarchical control. Implied in interdependence is the notion of a confederation. In this sense, recent work on mergers as a form of interdependence would not be in line with what is intended by our meaning or theoretical definition. In fact, the strategy we suggest for bringing about interdependence does not perceive merger as a very viable approach, nor even a desirable one, even in the economy where it is common (for hypothesis about mergers in hospitals, see Starkweather, 1970).

The objective of this paper is to suggest a strategy for increasing the degree of interdependence in organizations so that it is more than the present exchange of clients and information, yet less than a merger or some system of hierarchical control among organizations. We are searching for a network that is more than a confederation and less than a federation, an approach that is somewhere between an elitist and pluralist structure. This does not mean a lack of concern with the problem of integrating and coordinating organizations. It simply places greater emphasis on a modus operandi that might bring these conditions about. Thus the choice of a label is quite deliberate and designed to build upon a concept that is already in the literature.

Definition of the Concept

What is an organizational network? It is all of the groups and organizations, as well as the consumers (who usually are not organized into either groups or organizations, one of the basic reasons why their interests remain unrepresented), associated with a particular production system designed to service some client or customer. Litwak (1969:13) has suggested that interdependence exists when organizations must take account of each other's action; this is a good working definition of the boundary of the network. Production system in this instance includes organizations and groups that provide inputs, such as funds, consumers, and staff, as well as organizations that provide services directly, or the throughput (Katz and Kahn, 1966). Likewise, it includes groups or organizations that attempt to plan or coordinate the services provided (for example, see Turk's recent work on coordinating councils, 1970 and 1973), as well as those that might try to represent the interests of the consumer. Thus, the concept of a network is broader than the unit-set (Evan, 1966), which takes a single focal organization, but, like the unit-set, includes the competitors as well as the integrators (Azumi, 1972:93). Our unit of analysis is an aggregate of organizations whose boundaries are defined relative to some input-throughput-output process.

If one examines the interorganizational literature, one finds that linkages between organizations are conceived of in a variety of ways: passage of information, transfers of clients or funds or the input-output exchange, and the sharing of facilities (Levine and White, 1961; Thompson, 1962; Litwak and Rothman 1970; Aiken and Hage, 1968); yet there are enormous differences between these. In fact, we have implied here a continuum of increasing interdependence. The choice of indicator leads to very different conceptions of just how interdependent certain organizational networks actually are.

Our own research reveals that most organizations have surprisingly high rates of interorganizational communication. In addition, there are various interorganizational committees or quasi-coordinating bodies (Aiken and Hage, 1972), so that this is not a useful or distinctive indicator. If one does want to rely upon the passage of information, then a key might be the transfer of communication about the treatment of clients and the development of a central record office. This is rare. Similarly, the work of Levine and White (1961) shows that there are many exchanges of clients and funds. It could not be otherwise since many treatment processes can be usefully conceptualized as sequential (Thompson, 1967), with different organizations specializing at different stages (Rosengren, 1970). Again, from my point of view, this represents fairly low interdependence. Indeed, in this kind of arrangement (see Figure 1) there would probably be few linkages since, in graphic terms, the network would look somewhat like a chain. For these reasons, I would suggest that the number of joint programs where there is a *sharing* of facilities, staff, and/or funds is a more critical measure. What is being assumed, and perhaps incorrectly, is that the multiple-problem client (such as the mental retardate) needs simultaneous treatment—interdependent technology in Thompson's terms (1967)—in a variety of joint efforts that are especially designed to take care of what might be called the special effects (interaction in statistical terms) of combining a recreation program with psychological treatment. In other words, joint programming as a definition for interdependence makes an implicit technological assumption that the production process requires joint efforts or teams that transcend organizational boundaries. This seems plausible wherever the client has a multitude of problems or where, as Lefton and Rosengren (1966) suggest, one must be concerned with both the latitude and the longitude of the client's career in the treatment process. If there are a number of joint programs (and the number involved in any particular program can vary from a minimum of several up to many more than there are organizations in the network), then we begin to approach the wheel configuration, as can be seen in Figure 1.

Therefore, the indicator that one chooses for measuring interdependence leads to very different conclusions regarding what needs to be done. On the

Figure 1
DIAGRAMS OF ORGANIZATIONAL NETWORKS*

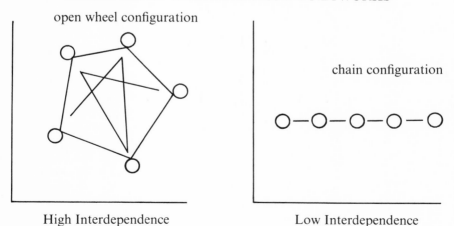

open wheel configuration

chain configuration

High Interdependence   Low Interdependence

*See Bavelas (1960) for the general inspiration.

basis of communication flows, exchanges of clients, and even the presence of coordinating councils, one can say that there is a considerable amount of coordination and integration in the Durkheimian (1933) sense of these terms. But this is strange to say because it is not in accord with the popular image about the fragmentation of services. While this image is perhaps overdrawn, it is also clear that there are a number of problems or needs not being met. A simple example might make this clear. The mental retardate has a large number of problems: he is the case par excellence of the multi-handicapped person. Typically, there are economic, emotional, and other needs along with a mental deficiency. The mental retardate (hereafter the MR) carries his disability for life and thus needs specialized services throughout the various stages of the life cycle. He must not only have specialized classrooms when young, but carefully designed work places, such as sheltered workshops, when older. He must have recreational facilities and health services at all ages, and even further specialized services when he is aged. Even simple things like sex and marriage become terribly complicated for the MR and necessitate special handling and consideration. During the 1960's there were many gaps in services for the MR, especially for those age 18 and older. The networks of organizations had low interdependence and were mainly aggregates that did not even transfer clients between them, let alone have joint programs. In jargon, the problem was conceptualized as the lack of a continuum of care and the lack of a fixed point of referral (President's Panel, 1962). But this means the same thing: not enough interdependence between organizations, and particularly not enough joint programming.

How does the concept of interdependent networks differ from integrated and coordinated networks? The concept of integration can mean just the passage of information or resources, such as clients and funds, as we have noted above. Thus interdependence, by focusing on the number of joint programs and calling attention to simultaneous handling of problems rather than sequential processing, is a more restricted form of task integrated networks and interdependent. Also, coordinated networks do not necessarily imply the presence of joint programs; coordination can be effected via a variety of mechanisms, such as coordinating councils or the passage of information. More importantly, the presence of joint programs suggests a whole new kind of coordination mechanism, one where the organizations do the coordinating together at various points or stages in the production process—what Seip (1973) means by autocoordination—rather than having some fixed hierarchical coordination system. It might be conceived of as a *new* form of coordination, but perhaps, despite this, a more effective one within the context of organizational networks.

The essential theoretical problem is how to go about creating an organizational network or delivery system, or, more specifically, a joint program as a form of interdependence. Elsewhere, Gouldner (1959b), Aiken and Hage (1968), and others have noted that organizations like to maintain their autonomy. There is, then, a natural tendency for organizations to avoid creating interdependencies except in relatively safe areas that are auxiliary to the main organizational objectives. For example, welfare agencies are likely to enter into joint programs in education and research. For this reason, the crucial question is to get the competitors together into some joint programs, a point that our previous work has largely ignored (Aiken and Hage, 1968). Another aspect of the problem, besides the strain towards autonomy, stems from the fact that the delivery system frequently must be created across political boundaries. The MR, especially the more severely handicapped, is rare, and one needs a minimum population base of about 250,000 before a network of organizations is efficient. Who will pay for the rehabilitation thus becomes a major issue and results in a major struggle for scarce resources.

Social and Rehabilitation Services (formerly Vocational Rehabilitation Administration) in Washington, D.C. became concerned with this problem (as have most health and welfare agencies in one way or another) and funded five demonstration projects, each of which was designed to set up a coordinated continuum of care (see Aiken, et al., 1972). The sponsor agency and method varied in each case; thus we have an opportunity, retrospectively, to study five strategies for creating interdependent organizational networks.

Classification of Strategies

The five demonstration projects occurred in San Francisco, Bridgeport, Milwaukee, Los Angeles, and Cleveland. In each instance, the sponsor agency was different: a social-work group, a parents of retardates group, a sheltered workshop, a joint powers agreement among public organizations, and a United Fund planning agency. Not unexpectedly, each sponsoring agency attempted to fill in gaps in services and achieve coordination among organizations in different ways. But the choice of means and ends was by and large not haphazard, even though all were influenced by the President's Panel (1962) and, of course, the desires of the federal funding agency. The classification of these strategies is important if we are to understand why they partially failed.

Parsons (1959) once suggested that there were four levels of sociological analysis: group-technical, management or organizational, institutional or board, and, of course, the societal. Each of these sponsoring agents can be seen as functioning on one of the first three levels, as is suggested in Figure 2. These can be conceptualized as points of intervention into an organizational network. How should one try to influence the development of more joint

Figure 2
CLASSIFICATION OF NETWORK STRATEGIES BY POINT OF INTERVENTION, MEANS, AND ENDS

Projects	Point of Intervention	Means	Ends
Cleveland	Institutional-Community	Old Elite and Planning	Coordination
Los Angeles	Institutional-Community	New Elite and Planning	Coordination
Milwaukee	Organizational	Management Committee	Development of New Service
Bridgeport	Group-Technical	Poorly Defined	Socio-Emotional Ends
San Francisco	Group-Technical	Poorly Defined	Socio-Emotional Ends

programs between organizations? By starting with a group, as in San Francisco? Or a board, as in Cleveland? From the perspective of the client, as in Bridgeport? Or from the perspective of the system, as in Los Angeles? As can be easily imagined, these can and do represent various ideological positions about what is wrong and what needs to be done about it.

Each demonstration project had, or through the process of time developed, a strategy or an approach. This strategy can be conceived of in terms of both the goals that they chose to emphasize and the means for achieving those goals. All projects, with the possible exception of Bridgeport, started with the same relatively lofty goals of creating a continuum of care in a coordinated delivery system. As they met failure, they displaced their goals (Selznik, 1949) in particular directions which reflected the positional bias of their intervention point. *In other words, the directions of change were not random and instead say a great deal about how the world is perceived at particular points of intervention.*

Thus, while all were ostensibly concerned with both coordination and the development of new services, those agencies operating at the group-technical level became primarily concerned with group integration—and indeed experienced a great deal of internal conflict. The agency on the organizational level finally began to emphasize the development of services and those on the institutional level became concerned with coordination. This is to be expected and illustrates *how* the classification of strategies allows us to understand the direction in which goals are displaced, an important problem in its own right (Selznik, 1949).

There is, of course, more to a strategy than just its ends. Another component is the methodology. Here it is somewhat difficult to classify the means to these ends with just a few words. And, in fact, the demonstration projects varied considerably in their sophistication and ability to articulate how their objectives might be achieved. In general, those sponsoring agencies operating on the institutional level were most clear about their means. Their methodology might be called the mobilization of elites and planning. Cleveland and Los Angeles differed greatly in their definition of who were the key elites, a point of some interest in considering the success of their strategies. The project on the organizational level had, at least in its first phase, an approach that might be called the management committee strategy. The sponsoring agencies on the group-technical level did not have an articulate methodology as such, and as a consequence, their demonstration projects proceeded in a more haphazard way.

It is, of course, not hard to understand the connections between the point of intervention and the choice of strategy. Individuals at the institutional level see the world controlled by elites and therefore define their basic strategy as one of mobilizing those elites. Traditional community organization methods have placed a great emphasis on this strategy, and it has been a particularly dominant perspective in welfare. What is important to observe is that whether one has a traditional or a modern conception of who are the elites, it is an important theoretical problem and has buried within it implied differences in tactics. (Of course, there is another and newer approach, the organization of the clients, an approach represented by Bridgeport.) Not unexpectedly, individuals who prefer this strategy also tend to focus on institutional problems and share elite values, specifically the concern for reducing duplication of services and creating more efficient coordination. Another essential and typical method is planning. This is seen as a means to this end, although it frequently becomes an end in itself as failure to achieve coordination occurs.

Heads of organizations tend to be more concerned with the development of new services rather than the elimination of duplicative services because this is a pathway to justify the use of more scarce resources. Each program is a mandate, a legitimization for more funds and staff. Not unexpectedly, their approach to developing interdependence is via a management committee of executive directors or key assistants relative to the problem at hand, a device that is used internally and then projected on the external network as well. Many of the interorganizational committees that we studied in Milwaukee, and one suspects many of the councils in Turk's work (1970, 1973), really function like management committees concerned with the passage of information rather than joint decision making per se.

It would be atypical to expect groups to have well thought-out strategies. In part, they lack permanence and thus do not have articulated approaches. Their structural position does not afford a clear vantage point, especially of a delivery system. Both groups were voluntary associations, one of professionals and the other of parents. They moved ahead spasmodically and down a pathway of considerable conflict over both ends and means. In part, this is inherent in groups that attempt to function as organizations; there is an inherent dilemma between emphasizing the socio-emotional needs and achieving specific tasks (Parsons, 1956a, 1956b). Thus, problems of internal integration removed any possibility of being concerned about external interdependence. And as groups, what they did accomplish tended to occur in an ad hoc way, resulting in less incremental gain. While there was no sustained effort in any one direction, this was partly because there was lack of clear strategy.

These strategies and demonstration projects can be categorized on more than these few dimensions. One dimension, in retrospect, is the relative emphasis on the public vs. private welfare. Each sponsoring agency tended to work with one or the other kind of agency with consequences for the development of a completely coordinated delivery system. Milwaukee, Bridgeport, and Cleveland concentrated more on the private, while the two California projects had a public focus. (Some of this is also a simple historical statement about the relative development of the two sectors, which can be predicted by age of city.) Another dimension is whether or not the parents' groups are involved in the project. Again, there were considerable differences along the continuum from Bridgeport, where the parents' groups were dominant, to Cleveland and Milwaukee, where they were part of the boards, to Los Angeles and San Francisco, where involvement was more tangential. The organizational dilemma is to have the representatives of the consumer both near and far. These two dimensions—relative emphasis on the public vs. private welfare and closeness of the relationship with parents of the clients—cut across these three levels and their strategies. But they are part of the explanation of why these various projects and their strategies did not succeed.

FIVE BRIEF HISTORIES

San Francisco

This demonstration grant was sponsored by a group, a professional association that included most of the professionals involved in mental retardation. They did not have a concrete plan as to how to bring about changes in the delivery system, although their objectives were to create a continuum of care and a coordinated system. The board of the association continuously supervised the executive director and, not unexpectedly, there were five executive directors in five years. Along with this turnover, there was considerable structural change within the staff; some twelve positions were created during the five years, many of which existed only for a short time. Seven of these were in existence for less than two years. Here, too, there was considerable turnover, with the twelve positions being held by nineteen people. Two of the five positions with the longest duration had yearly turnovers in membership; thus, neither the structure nor the staff were stable. The causes of this are not hard to find. When the board is composed of professionals within the same profession as the staff, conflict is inevitable. The board members consider themselves as experts—and they are—and the normal insulation of knowledge does not operate.

During the course of the grant, debates and disagreements occurred regarding the goals and methods of the council. The major conflict occurred between those who wanted action and those who wanted planning. Again, part of this stemmed from the nature of the sponsoring agency, a voluntary professional association. Some desired it to remain this group and others wanted it to become an interest group. These conflicts, of course, are another factor in the turnover of staff. Some of these conflicts also represent disagreements as to which level the group should function on, the institutional or the organizational.

The council tried to develop several services, but in most cases these efforts failed. They were effective in doing some planning and in disseminating professional information. They also lobbied for various changes, but these generally were not effective in obtaining new legislation. The exception to this was a special bill in California where a number of other groups, organizations, and boards also claimed credit. At the end of the demonstration grant period, the council was absorbed by the San Franscisco Comprehensive Health Planning Council.

Bridgeport

A parents' group entitled the Friends and Parents of Retarded Children had been successful in building a large center for retarded children. It then discovered that it was too large a financial burden to operate; however, it was able to convince the state of Connecticut to take over the operation of the center. This particular group also had been quite active in lobbying for legislation and, as a consequence, the state was one of the more progressive and advanced in terms of the benefits provided to MRs. Most of the members were parents of retarded children, and the board members of the association had been quite stable over a ten-year period—a cohesive group.

The demonstration grant was funded before the center was absorbed by the state, so that part of the funds in the first year were used to operate this facility. Another part of the funds was used to hire a program director. He, in turn, added services and hired a number of professionals once the state took over the facility as a regional center.

Within a short period, conflict between professionals and parents developed. The parents felt that the professionals did not show enough emotional concern, and the professionals felt that the parents would not allow for higher quality care. The parents did not want services expanded to include more MRs or transfers from other client groups. In this instance, the board was completely controlled by clients and they fired the program director. Half the professional staff quit during this conflict. Several other executive directors were tried, but no one could survive more than one year. Finally, the parents breathed a sigh of relief when the federal grant was finished. They decided they did not want more money or more professionals working for them!

Milwaukee

A sheltered workshop entitled Jewish Vocational Service received a grant to establish a structured community services delivery system via joint programming. In certain respects, this agency was a coalition of organizations being actively involved with a few other agencies, one of them a parents' group. This particular community had been characterized by a great deal of interagency conflict, especially in the area of rehabilitation. This was particularly the case with the Jewish Vocational Service.

The project set up a committee of executive directors and key program people and this management committee seldom agreed to do cooperative programming among its members. An attempt to set up a fixed point of referral with a central record office was unsuccessful, largely due to opposition from the school system. The project was able to develop a number of joint programs in recreation.

After three years, little had been accomplished and we set this forth in our first project report. At this point, Jewish Vocational Service decided to shift strategies and develop a coalition of organizations called the A.I.D. project. Despite the great conflict that had existed previously, all the relevant public and private agencies agreed to band together and make a joint grant application for joint programming, including a fixed point of referral. Although Social and Rehabilation Services had for some time advocated joint coordinated efforts, it did not know how to respond and delayed funding for a whole year. It finally agreed to fund, but only under the provision that the grant be administered via a single agency; the county public welfare department was taken as the most benign and agreeable fixed point.

Although not well funded, this coalition of organizations is still in operation today. Thus, it has survived the first test: the capacity to keep competitors together in some interdependencies. There is, however, not too much joint programming in a strict sense. But there are many more client referrals.

Los Angeles

This project started with an extremely well thought-out plan for creating coordination among organizations. Their concept was to create a joint powers agreement among the major public agencies at the city, county, and state levels. Thus a board of organizations was created rather than a coalition, as in Milwaukee. The participants provided funds for the staff attached to the board.

This staff did do some new programming, but, in general, not much coordination was accomplished per se. The board members represented the interests of their organizations, hence they did not eliminate duplicative services. They did attempt, in particular areas, to expand the services that were available. The staff attached to the board was also instrumental in getting some legislation passed, specifically state funds for regional centers. They also did a great deal of planning, some of which was implemented.

What was especially interesting about this particular project was the conception of who were the elites. In their view, these were the heads of the various large public organizations with their budgets in the hundreds of millions of dollars, as well as the key professionals in particular sectors relative to the problem of mental retardation. The private sector was ignored and this proved to be the undoing of the project.

When the regional center was created, the contract was given to a large private hospital which had pioneered in the problems of mental retardation. The board thus discovered itself frozen out of a major source of revenue and removed from any supervisory control over client referrals. Not unexpectedly, the single hospital tended to spend most of the money internally, although technically it was to distribute funds.

The new legislation creating the regional centers also created community boards. Thus it spelled the final demise of the joint powers agreement, which proved to be too inflexible to admit changes in its contract.

Cleveland

The essential strategy of the traditional community organization is to pursuade the elites, influentials in the community, to participate in various committees and boards. Plans are then given to the elites, and once enough awareness of problems is created, the stimulus is withdrawn and the organizational network continues to grow in interdependence.

In general, few programs or plans were implemented. In part, this stemmed from the state creating several boards. Here, the emphasis on the private sector and a lack of a permanent structure meant that the creation of boards in the community completely bypassed the Welfare Council and its demonstration project. It must be remembered that this is consistent with the strategy of a temporary stimulus. But it is also clear that no coordinated delivery system was established. In the final analysis, this must remain an important criterion of a strategy whether it is an objective or not.

Although these are extremely brief discussions of the five projects (one should really read the project report and various documents attached to it), it is interesting to note that those demonstration projects which most closely bordered between one level or another of analysis also acted the most like the two levels. Thus we see Bridgeport, which did have a service organization, moving toward the development of new programs, that is relative to San Francisco. Likewise, Los Angeles, which was a board of organizations, did more implementing than did Cleveland. What is of particular interest here is that all agencies *tried* to implement services, but they varied considerably in their efforts.

Another point well worth observing is that the lack of public agencies involved in Cleveland and the lack of private agency involvement in Los Angeles in various ways hampered the transition from a demonstration project to a continuing effort at coordination and planning. And yet the second phase of the Milwaukee project would suggest that it is possible for the two kinds of organizations to live together in some cooperative interdependency and, indeed, that this may be the best way of obtaining legitimacy from a larger environment.

Finally, the parent group was too involved in Bridgeport and too little involved in San Francisco, where lack of its support became crucial at times. Milwaukee, where a parent group was part of the J. V. S. coalition, appears to strike a correct balance between nearness and farness—involved but not dominating the coalition.

THE PROPOSED STRATEGY

One might become discouraged except that each of these projects had certain strengths as well as weaknesses. Insofar as we can specify these, then, there is the possibility of designing an optimal strategy. Based on these findings, I would recommend the following:

1. Coalitions of organizations with joint programs and central record keeping, and not single organizations, should be funded when the consumer has multiple problems and must be treated both laterally and longitudinally, to use Lefton and Rosengren's (1966) terms for it. If one accepts the idea that there is a strain toward specialization in organizations, then one does need a delivery system of organizations to handle the multiproblem client. This proposal really suggests that a coalition of organizations be created, as was done in the second phase of the Milwaukee demonstration project and in part in the Los Angeles project. What should be understood is that there is joint funding for joint programs, thus the organizations are encouraged to operate as a team. So long as the funding does not go to a single organization,

We have also assumed that the client needs are best served if handled simultaneously in joint programs, in some open-wheel fashion, rather than piecemeal in some sequential or chain-line fashion. If these assumptions are not fulfilled, then there is less of a functional necessity for the creation of a supracorporate identity.

There is a certain desire created to cooperate whenever there is a clear technological imperative or functional necessity for this (Lefton, 1971). One might call this a domain consensus (Levine and White, 1961; Aldrich, 1973). But this force is not strong enough to overcome the inherent strain towards autonomy, and especially given the conflict between competitors. Thus, one needs to provide a sustained basis for entering into an exchange, one that recognizes the autonomy needs of organizations. By suggesting the creation of stable and relatively permanent coalitions (and thus departing from typical coalition theory) to meet new and complex problems, one creates new channels of funding that leave undisturbed corporate identities and traditional funding avenues. Something is added rather than subtracted or rearranged, the usual reason for the reluctance to enter into mergers or centralized arrangements of organizations.

Operationally, organizational coalitions work in the following way. Sheltered workshops develop specialized services for the MR in conjunction with the school system, to take an example. Both the schools and sheltered workshops still provide their traditional programs. Thus they are asked to develop new programs for new clients *jointly* so that the complexities of the new technology are recognized. It is in this sense that something is added rather than subtracted. Both the sheltered workshop and the school system keep their separate services intact and unfettered. *This means that the organization's investment and thus risk is kept to a minimum since only some of its programs or services are involved in a new delivery system.*

A hidden benefit is the gain in power. Coalitions of organizations can fight far more effectively, as the industrial-military complex (most people lose sight of the fact that this is really a relatively small group of very large organizations) has so aptly demonstrated. An organizational coalition represents a large number of potential voters. It also has many contacts with key influentials in the community, the state, and the nation. Thus, there is an exponential growth in its capacity to mobilize power for the needed key votes.

The possibility of autocoordination as opposed to central planning may in itself be a major inducement for participation. Through this comes not only the possibility to contribute more to the joint decision making (Tuite, Chisholm, and Radnor, 1972) involved in an on-going way, but also the method to set checks on the power of other organizations. If one organization attempts to dominate, the others quickly unite to prevent this. This is one of the major features that distinguishes the coalitional funding as opposed to a fixed point, as occurred in each of the demonstration projects and as also occurred in the alternatives discussed above. Perhaps organizations lose some autonomy, but they gain much more power vis-a-vis the larger environment. By power we mean the capacity to make decisions. This includes not only having more funds about which to decide, but being able to free oneself from various kinds of controls that may interfere with the objectives of the larger collectivity, the coalition of organizations.

The major inducement, however, remains the fact that this would represent a new source of funding that leaves previous sources undisturbed. Nor should one assume that the funding comes first, for it did not in Milwaukee. Indeed, here we have a particularly compelling case of arguing for the efficacy of the coalition because it was formed in the light of considerable conflict between some of the organizations and before there was any guarantee of funding.

What would be some of the costs involved? An obvious one is that there would be some conflict in the organizational coalition. It is perhaps surprising to say that the coalition funding would provide a basis of cooperation and yet also conflict. But this is inevitable. Competitors working together means some strains. However, recent research (Hall and Clark, Chapter 9) suggests that there is more conflict in cooperative relationships than had been previously realized. Earlier work done on joint programming (Aiken and Hage, 1968) also indicated that internal coordination problems are created by the interorganizational relationships. There is also some surrender of autonomy, but as I have tried to suggest, the gains in power to control the external environment would appear to more than offset the autonomy losses.

Therefore, in sum it would appear that *this proposal maximizes organizational benefits and minimizes organizational costs.* It is a proposal that has meaning, however, only when there is a relatively clear functional necessity—the need to create a delivery system of organizations—and a technological imperative—the need to work co-jointly in providing services for the consumer.

2. *Since there is a supracorporate identity, there must be a supracorporate board to protect the public interest; its membership should be one-third elites, one-third professionals relevant to the multiple-problem client, and one-third individuals representing the interests of the consumer.* This might be called the three estate model, and it is an attempt to both recognize various power groups in the larger community (from whom one needs support for resources), and avoid focusing on only one or the other interest group, as was the case in all of our demonstration projects. If one-half or more of the board members represent the clients, the professional-client conflict will become too great. If there are only one or two representatives of clients, they will not talk and represent the interests of their group, as

has been demonstrated in other experiments. There is a certain reluctance upon the part of everyone to admit that elites exist and especially to state that their interests should be represented. From a power perspective, this denial seems unwise. Elites can block resource gains and thus they should be part of the original conception. But there are other considerations besides pragmatic ones. Each of these interest groups also represents values that should be represented on any supracorporate board. Elites, as already suggested, emphasize efficiency and a concern about reduction of costs. Professionals are most concerned about quality care and the representatives of the consumers are more concerned about the social-emotional needs of the consumer. Bridgeport is a striking example of where the latter consideration can override quality care. The parents were unwilling to accept any money because it would mean professionalism, and this they did not want!

Hopefully, a dialectic can be created if there are about five to ten members representing each of these interests. Each interest group needs a check on its power, but it also needs a forum to present its viewpoint. Denying the existence of the power structure is no more realistic than denying the abuse of clients by professionals, nor any more credible than denying there is a lack of expertise on the part of most people, be they elites or representatives of consumers. We need to create dialectics between these perspectives.

Recent legislation has been moving in this direction but so far has failed in two respects:

1. There is still an unwillingness to recognize the reality of elites.
2. There is still an unwillingness to give the boards an effective sanction and thus something to do.

In this proposal, I am suggesting we can solve these two difficulties simultaneously. If each power group is represented, then they will support it; perhaps not with enthusiasm, but they will support it reluctantly. If elites, professionals, and consumer representatives support the proposal, then legislators are more likely to provide the sanction and thus membership becomes meaningful. Presently, community boards with one-half or more members representing consumers do not have a political compromise that seems unnecessary. If the three main interest groups are represented, then it seems likely that more political support for the proposal can be obtained.

As we have already noted, governments are presently reluctant to fund coalitions of organizations. They think in terms of fixed responsibility and this, so far, means only one thing to them: either a single organization or a single board. Thus the board provides an essential legitimizing function for a coalition of organizations.

Implicit in this idea is that organizations would not only have their own corporate board, but as many coalitional boards as they participate in. For those who worry about a proliferation of institutional structures, I might comment that the present problem for most communities today, from my own personal view, is that there is not enough participation in a permanent way by various interest groups rather than too many institutional structures. We need to create more of these to bring more interest groups into the decision-making process, and especially at what Parsons (1959) calls the institutional-community level. In fact, my own concern is that our present power structure does not allow for the utilization of enough people. The creation of supracorporate boards along the lines I am suggesting is an attempt to broaden the basis of political participation.

The purposes of the board are exactly those of any corporate board: to make policies about interorganizational relationships, transfers and exchanges, joint programming, and the like, and to protect the interests of the larger community regarding the allocation of funds. The boards would not do planning nor have a coordinating responsibility per se. This would be left to the coalition of organizations to work out on their own. Again, I am assuming that multiple-problem clients provide a clear functional necessity or rationale for the existence of coalitional boards, just as corporate goals provide a legitimacy for organizations.

This is the theory as to how boards operate, but they seldom do. Instead, their purpose is really to provide a way for organizations to fight the larger environment and gain resources from it. They are the bases upon which the organization builds political support. Thus the supracorporate board will primarily spend its time trying to get more money, staff, prestige, etc., for the delivery system. This does not bother me since it is what boards usually do anyway, especially in the health and welfare area.

But if the board does not protect the interests of the community, who will? In part, the presence of consumer representatives means that gross abuses by professionals and gross unmet needs will probably be corrected. But consumer representatives do not provide the kind of fine organizational control that one needs. The problem of evaluation has been much talked about, especially relative to various community boards. I just don't think that this is realistic. Boards lack detailed information about quality service and are unlikely to get it. Heads of organizations always report that they provide quality service and it is hard to prove otherwise. The professionals on the board would protect the interests of their colleagues in this respect. How, then, can we realistically protect the interests of the community, especially as a delivery system becomes a very powerful coalition?

3. *Paradoxically, by creating an organizational coalition, we are also increasing the amount of organizational control via the mechanisms of joint programming and autocoordination over what would occur in some hierarchical board arrangement.* Joint programming means high visibility of what is

occurring and thus the presence of a great deal of control, especially because the visibility is before experts who are in the best position to judge the quality of work. Organizational members do worry about what other organizations think of their work, so to create visibility is a major step in the control process. Autocoordination allows for development of more sophisticated kinds of control that represent combinations of the best features of various programs.

The creation of an open-wheel organizational network, a high interdependence, means that the volumes of communication about new procedures, new standards, and new techniques will be considerably augmented. This in itself should provide a major means of control, as I have argued elsewhere (Hage, 1974). This is because the real problem in controlling organizational behavior, besides creating visibility, is to keep organizations abreast of current technological developments. A coalition of organizations would appear to be the best structural arrangement for this.

Explicity, this scheme is arguing for the formation of relatively permanent coalitions supervised by relatively stable interest groups. In other words, it is *not* a model of shifting coalitions of interest groups, although it does represent a frank recognition of their importance. It is an attempt to also argue that inherent in every delivery system are three major interest groups, each of which must be represented if there is to be effective action on all fronts.

How generalizable is this proposal? Melcher and Adamek (1971) have correctly observed that most of the work on interorganizational relationships has been done in the health and welfare field and this is a major problem. The fragmentation of services and the multiple-problem client are easily seen in this area. But I think the proposed idea of organizational coalitions when there is interdependence to begin with, and tri-party interest group formation, has applicability beyond this area. There are multiple-faceted problems that require the resources of more than one organization in most sectors of society.

Let us take the economy and business organizations as a case in point. Certain problems are so large and complex they cannot be handled by a single organization. The development of a pollution-free gasoline is best handled by a consortium of organizations, with a board to protect public interests. The building of ships and planes would seem to be another area where there is a need for a variety of technologies and thus a delivery system of organizations. Traditionally, the defense department has directed orders for military equipment to a single firm that then controls all the subsidiary contracts. Consortiums of organizations would change very much the nature of the military-industrial complex by bringing in competitors in cooperative relationships as well as the smaller contractors. Coalitional funding reduces organizational risk and moves away from the feast-famine arrangement, which creates all the desperation and temptation for corruption that presently exists. It would presumably reduce the amount of public lobbying at the same time. In one sense the military-industrial complex would be made larger and thus seem more powerful——a paradox, but one that seems true. But organizational coalitions, especially when competitors are involved, have their own checks and balances, as I have argued above.

The establishment of supracorporate boards would also result in more protection of the public interest than occurs. The Pentagon might not be happy with this proposal, but again, the need for a delivery system would appear to justify the necessity for a supracorporate board. Certainly this would be the best way of solving the fiscal responsibility problem which, in this case, is very critical.

In the political area, there are a large number of problems that cover the jurisdiction of more than one political entity in our urban communities. Coalition, rather than either annexation, the counterpart of merger, or pluralism, appears to offer a nice compromise in the suburban-urban dilemmas. Pollution and environmental control, transportation, zoning, tax rates, and a host of other problems might be solved much more effectively if a coalition of community governments were created. Certainly urban planning does not make sense without at least this extent of interdependence.

In the educational area, we find some beginnings toward the idea of organizational coalitions, but so far mostly for the purposes of lobbying. In many cities, pooling hospital and college resources can make strong medical schools where presently none exist (we need to build one new medical school a year for the next twenty years). The same can be said for graduate welfare and education schools, although the need here seems much less. In general, there appear to be many areas where coalitions of organizations might operate effectively to handle complex needs.

If one strikes a balance between organizational needs for autonomy and coordination needs for the solution of complex problems, then the proposal of a coalition of organizations arranged in some delivery system makes sense. Organizations lose some autonomy, but gain much more power to get resources from their environment. Coalitional funding leaves undisturbed the traditional sources and corporate indentities of the organization and adds new sources and supracorporate identities.

The basis of the organizational coalition is first, a functional necessity, a complex problem that can only be solved by a delivery system of organizations, and second, a technological imperative of the problems requiring joint programming or technological interdependence. These two bases will not bring competitors together. One needs more than this. The proposal appears to maximize gains and minimize losses when compared with the two typical proposals, the creation of new organizations or merger and the creation of a central board with dictatorial powers. For a variety of reasons, these latter choices are not viable.

The creation of a supracorporate board, composed in equal parts of the three main interest groups relative to any delivery system, increases the probability that this proposal might be adopted. But beyond this pragmatic consideration is the desire to bring together three values that normally conflict and yet are desirable to have represented: efficiency, quality care, and consumer social-emotional needs. Hopefully, by frankly recognizing these three interests and having them represented, an interesting dialectic between them can occur.

The major source of control over the organizations cannot come from the board but instead must occur via the mechanisms of joint programming and autocoordination. By increasing visibility of the treatment, as well as increasing communication relative to that treatment, one is providing a much more finely tuned evaluation system than is possible via board control.

In sum, the proposal is a middle way between elite control and a pluralist system. A funded coalition of organizations is more than a confederation and yet not quite a federation, since there is no central authority. Interest groups are represented on the board and yet the proposal is different from normal interest group and coalitional theory. It advocates the creation of relative permanent coalitions that involve incompatible interests and competitors. While seemingly utopian, the evidence from our research indicates that it might just be what we need.

REFERENCES

Aiken, Michael, et al. "The Coordination of Services for the Mentally Retarded:
1972   A Comparison of Five Community Efforts." Madison, Wisc.: Department of Sociology, University of Wisconsin at Madison (mimeographed project report).

Aiken, Michael, and Jerald Hage. "Organizational Structure and Interorganizational
1968   Dynamics." *American Sociological Review*, 30:912–30.

————. "Organizational Permeability, Boundary Spanners and Organizational
1972   Structures." Paper presented at the American Sociological Association meetings, New Orleans, Louisiana.

Aldrich, Howard. "An Organizational-Environment Perspective on Cooperation
1973   and Conflict between Organizations in the Manpower Training System." In Anant R. Negandhi (ed.), *Conflict and Power in Complex Organizations: An Inter-Institutional Perspective*. Kent, Ohio: The Comparative Administration Research Institute, College of Business Administration, Kent State University.

Azumi, Koya. "Environmental Needs, Resources, and Agents." In Koya Azumi
1972   and Jerald Hage (eds.), *Organizational Systems: A Text-Reader in the Sociology of Organizations*. Lexington, Mass.: D. C. Heath.

Azumi, Koya, and Jerald Hage. *Organizational Systems: A Text-Reader in the*
1972 *Sociology of Organizations.* Lexington, Mass.: D. C. Heath.

Bavelas, Alex. "Communication Patterns in Task-Oriented Groups." In Dorwin
1960 Cartwright and Alvin Zander (eds.), *Group Dynamics*: 669–82. Evanston,
Ill.: Row, Peterson.

Cohen, Arthur. "Changing Small-Group Communication Networks." *Adminis-*
1962 *trative Science Quarterly*, 6:443–62.

Durkheim, Emile. *Division of Labor in Society* (trans. by George Simpson). New
1933 York: Macmillan.

Evan, William M. "The Organization-Set: Toward a Theory of Interorganizational
1966 Relations. In James Thompson (ed.), *Approaches to Organizational Design.*
Pittsburgh: University of Pittsburgh Press.

Gouldner, Alvin. "Organizational Analysis." In Robert K. Merton, Leonard Vroom,
1959a and Leonard Cottrell (eds.), *Sociology Today*: 400–28. New York: Basic
Books.

————. "Reciprocity and Autonomy in Functional Theory." In Llewellyn Gross
1959b (ed.), *Symposium on Sociological Theory.* Evanston, Ill.: Row, Peterson.

Hage, Jerald. "An Axiomatic Theory of Organizations." *Administrative Science*
1965 *Quarterly*, 10: 289–320.

————. *A Cybernetic Theory of Organizational Control.* New York: Wiley-Inter-
1974 science.

Katz, Daniel, and Robert Kahn. *The Social Psychology of Organizations.* New
1966 York: Wiley and Sons.

Lefton, Mark. "Client Characteristics and Structural Outcomes: Toward the Speci-
1971 fication of Linkages." In William Rosengren and Mark Lefton (eds.),
Organization and Clients: Essays in the Sociology of Science: 17–36.
Columbus, Ohio: Merrill.

————. "Client Characteristics and Organizational Functioning: Interorganiza-
1973 tional Focus." In Anant R. Negandhi (ed.), *Modern Organizational Theory*:
160–73. Kent, Ohio: Kent State University Press.

Lefton, Mark, and William Rosengren. "Organizations and Clients: Lateral and
1966 Longitudinal Dimensions." *American Sociological Review*, 31:802–10.

Levine, Sol, and Paul White. "Exchange as a Conceptual Framework for the Study
1961 of Interorganizational Relations." *Administrative Science Quarterly*, 5:
583–601.

Litwak, Eugene. "Towards the Theory and Practice of Coordination between
1969 Formal Organizations." Ann Arbor, Mich.: School of Social Work, University of Michigan (mimeographed report).

Litwak, Eugene, and Jack Rothman. "Towards the Theory and Practice of Coordina-
1970 tion between Formal Organizations." In William Rosengren and Mark
Lefton (eds.), *Organizations and Clients: Essays in the Sociology of Science*:
137–86. Columbus, Ohio: Merrill.

Melcher, Arlyn, and Raymond Adamek. "Interorganizational Models: A Critical
1971 Evaluation." In Anant R. Negandhi (ed.), *Organizational Theory in an
Interorganizational Perspective.* Kent, Ohio: Comparative Administration
Research Institute, College of Business Administration, Kent State University.

Merton, Robert K., Leonard Vroom, and Leonard Cottrell (eds.) *Sociology Today.*

1959   New York: Basic Books.

Mott, Basil.   "Coordination and Inter-Organizational Relations in Health." In
1970   Paul White and George Vlasak (eds.), *Interorganizational Research in Health:*
        Conference Proceedings. Washington, D.C.: United States Department of
        Health, Education, and Welfare, Public Health Services, National Center
        for Health Services Research and Development.

Negandhi, Anant R. (ed.)   *Organizational Theory in an Interorganizational Perspective.*
1971   Kent, Ohio: Comparative Administration Research Institute, College of
        Business Administration, Kent State University.

————— (ed.) *Conflict and Power in Complex Organizations: An Inter-Institutional*
1972   *Perspective.* Kent, Ohio: Comparative Administration Research Institute,
        College of Business Administration, Kent State University.

Parsons, Talcott.   "General Theory in Sociology." In Robert K. Merton, Leonard
1959   Vroom, and Leonard Cottrell (eds.), *Sociology Today:* Chapt. 1. New York:
        Basic Books.

—————.   "Suggestions for Sociological Approach to the Theory of Organizations—
1956a   I." *Administrative Science Quarterly*, 1:63–85.

—————.   "Suggestions for Sociological Approach to the Theory of Organizations—
1956b   II." *Administrative Science Quarterly*, 1:225–39.

President's Panel on Mental Retardation.   *National Action to Combat Mental Retarda-*
1962   *tion.* Washington, D.C.: United States Department of Health, Education
        and Welfare.

Reid, William.   "Interorganizational Cooperation: A Review and Critique of Current
1970   Theory." In Paul White and George Vlasak (eds.), *Interorganizational*
        Research in Health: Conference Proceedings: Chapt. 7. Washington, D.C.:
        U.S. Department of Health, Education, and Welfare, Public Health Services,
        National Center for Health Services Research and Development.

Rosengren, William.   "The Careers of Clients and Organizations." In William
1970   Rosengren and Mark Lefton (eds.), *Organizations and Clients: Essays in the*
        Sociology of Science: 117–36. Columbus, Ohio: Merrill.

Rosengren, William, and Mark Lefton (eds.)   *Organizations and Clients: Essays in*
1970   *the Sociology of Science.* Columbus, Ohio: Merrill.

Seip, Conrad.   Personal communications.
1973

Selznik, Philip.   *T.V.A. and the Grass Roots: A Study in the Sociology of Formal*
1949   *Organizations.* Berkeley, Calif.: University of California.

Starkweather, Davis.   "Health Facility Merger and Integration: A Typology and
1970   Some Hypotheses." In Paul White and George Vlasak (eds.), *Interorganiza-*
        tional Research in Health: Conference Proceedings: Chapt. 2. Washington,
        D.C.: United States Department of Health, Education and Welfare, Public
        Health Services, National Center for Health Services Research and Develop-
        ment.

Stinchcombe, Arthur.   "Social Structure and Organizations." In James March (ed.),
1965   *Handbook of Organizations*: 142–93. Chicago: Rand-McNally.

Thompson, James D.   "Organizations and Output Transactions." *American Journal*
1962   *of Sociology*, 68:309–24.

————. *Organizations in Action.* New York: McGraw-Hill.
1967

Tuite, Matthew, Roger Chisholm, and Michael Radnor (eds.) *Interorganizational*
1972   *Decision Making.* Chicago: Aldine Publishing Company.

Turk, Herman.   "Interorganizational Networks in Urban Society: Initial Perspectives
1970   and Comparative Research." *American Sociological Review*, 35:1–19.

————. "Comparative Urban Structure from an Interorganizational Perspective."
1973   *Administrative Science Quarterly*, 18:37–55.

Warren, Roland.   "Alternative Strategies of Inter-Agency Planning." In Paul White
1970   and George Vlasak (eds.), *Interorganizational Research in Health: Conference
        Proceedings*: Chapt. 10. Washington, D.C.: United States Department of
        Health, Education, and Welfare, Public Health Services, National Center for
        Health Services Research and Development.

————. *Truth, Love, and Social Change, and Other Essays on Community Change.*
1971   Chicago: Rand-McNally.

White, Paul, and George Vlasak (eds.)   *Interorganizational Research in Health:*
1970   *Conference Proceedings.* Washington, D.C.: United States Department of
        Health, Education, and Welfare, Public Health Services, National Center
        for Health Services Research and Development.

White, Paul, Sol Levine, and George Vlasak.   "Exchange as a Conceptual Framework
1973   for Understanding Interorganizational Relationships: Applications to Non-
        profit Organizations." In Anant R. Negandhi (ed.), *Modern Organizational
        Theory*: 174–88. Kent, Ohio: Kent State University Press.

17

Conceptualization at the Societal Level: A Critical Appraisal

Editor's Note

This chapter provides the critical evaluation of papers by Professors Hage, Warren, et al., and White, Levine, and Vlasak. Commentators are Professors Raymond Adamek (Kent State University), Arlyn Melcher (Kent State University), Malcolm MacNair (North Carolina University), Richard Osborn (Southern Illinois University), and Michael Ferrari (Bowling Green University).

Comments on Professor Hage's paper were taken from recorded transcripts of the discussion session where conference participants raised questions. This discussion material was arranged in question form by Professors Arlyn Melcher and Anant Negandhi.

All of the authors in this section were invited to respond to the critical comments. Their responses follow the critical remarks.

Comments on Hage's Paper

QUESTION:

In your paper there are some basic concepts like "Resolution of Conflict," "Interdependency of Organizations," "Coalition Formation," "Prestige," "Coordinated Delivery System," "Coalition Theories," etc. Could you provide some further insights as to how these various concepts are defined and utilized in your study?

RESPONSE:

As soon as you get a coalition of organizations together, they are pretty much competitors. Of course, you immediately build that in. I did mention in my paper that one of the inevitable reasons why organizations are analyzed in a cost-benefit analysis is because there will be conflict. What you are really trying to do is provide enough inducement so that the organizations will be willing to tolerate that conflict. Now, my personal position is that conflict is a very useful dialectic. What one really strives to do is to keep opposing parties talking to each other and interacting, particularly in the context of working together. One can do this precisely because one assumes each organization has its strengths and weaknesses; but that awareness can only come about as the result of the dialectic.

Each organization must maintain its own identity. It presumably has its own mandate and legitimate relations. But what really happens with a coalition is that these organizations acknowledge that, in addition to their own individual mandates, there is a supramandate of very complex problems. On the other hand, I am not trying to argue in favor of creating a supra-bureaucracy. That would raise the question of whether these organizations were able to manage their own affairs and imply that they must, instead, manage their affairs through management committees and executive boards, etc. This really isn't acceptable either.

Now, one thing I really did not get a chance to explore very much is interdependence as a variable. At one end, the definition used by most people is that you take into account the individual organization and what it does for the individuals. At the other end, at least based on some of the more recent research, you might talk about the usual bureaucracies. What I am arguing about is this question of continuance and whether the organization is stable. You might argue for a variety of reasons that interdependence per se may not lead to satisfactory solutions. For one thing, each organization has its own mandate and, for the supramandate, only part of the organization is involved. The organizations, on the other hand, are not all doing the same thing. They are involved in some production process, like starting schools, starting workshops, etc. Some are even welfare agencies. This is a very important reason why all of us working with different types of organizations cannot use the same concepts in our research. I think that a coalition is likely to remain stable so long as something continues. Now, *will* something continue? Once there is recognition that complex problems must be solved, be it the legislature, the community, business organizations, or whatever, and that these problems must be resolved whether or not there is opposition, a coalition becomes feasible.

Now, I can see the possibility of setting up a framework where there is a dialectic between the different technologies and strategies when you are working for a common purpose. You can create a collective conscience that will lead, for example, to quality care. This needs to be tested; but at least that is a good reason to form a coalition—or one of the possible reasons.

Another reason for this dialectic is having different interest groups on the executive board. This answers the power problem, that is the power needed to mobilize the larger community, to bring pressure to bear on legislature, etc. It is also useful because each of those interest groups has a value it wants to emphasize, the value that leads to proficiency. This is the positive side of saying, "we want to keep taxes down, but this is worthwhile." I think the professionals are going to be more concerned with quality care, and the consumers are going to be concerned with the ease and benefits of these services. With a coalition, all of these factions are represented.

A really good example regarding the advantages of the coalition took place in Milwaukee. In some respects, this is the source of many of my ideas. Several agencies were involved, and one quite small agency happened to be the Easter Seal organization. Milwaukee happened to be a particularly interesting case because there was an intense conflict among several of these agencies. In fact, the Easter Seal group had been involved with another agency, which will go nameless, and they broke away from that agency. Yet despite that fact, the same leaders who were involved in the conflict, and who had just spent several years arguing with each other, were still willing to sit down in a committee, along with leaders from other public and private organizations, and say, "let's see if we can get some funding for this mental-retardate delivery system."

Now, why would they be willing to do this? I think one of the dynamics is that the small guy realized that he could not endure in a one-to-one relationship (i.e., the other person representing the agency he had previously had conflict with) unless there were other agencies that might well take his side. And indeed, that is the system of checks and balances that might lead us into a coalition. The small guy is paradoxically protected so long as there are several big guys. You see, all coalition theories have postulated that there is one big guy and a couple of small guys. That is one of its intellectual problems. The real truth of the matter is that frequently there is more than one big guy, so what you must do is get *them* together.

QUESTION:

Is the coordination mechanism you discuss in your paper a unitary concept, or is it a pattern of similar and conflicting different mechanisms?

RESPONSE:

There are a multiplicity of mechanisms; however, most of these can be categorized into two major ones. I think there are really two major ways in which coordination is achieved. One is through specialization and feedback communication, which my paper discusses. The second is dependent upon the kind of organization and the kind of mechanism available.

For example, you have certain rewards and punishments, and I think most of the integrative mechanisms that are talked about in organization theory can be classified as one or the other. Despite the variety of these mechanisms, their use is determined largely by the political climate in a given situation within the organization, as well as by the professionals involved. This is particularly so from the community and society context.

I am inclined to think that the first strategy, the communication perspective, is by far the better coordination mechanism. First of all, the idea of communication as a coordination mechanism seems quite logical based on the implicit assumption that the major problem involved in coordination is that situations are always changing too fast. This means an almost continuous flow of information is required from a coordinating point of view. On the other hand, from the control point of view, logic dictates that perhaps the right method is not to argue culpability. That is largely a reward and punishment sanction behavior model whereby you seek someone who can do the right thing, or at least some of the right things, and reward them Perhaps one could argue here that the problem is simply improper socialization. To a large extent, society is moving away from punishments and rewards as coordinating mechanisms. The movement seems to be more toward some concept of rehabilitation, which may in a sense be a form of implicit acceptance. In fact, there is even a trend away from using sanctions to control student behavior in universities. Instead of saying there is another system whereby we can provide control and coordination simultaneously, the trend seems to be toward coordination through communication.

QUESTION:

Are you talking about a manipulative socialization process for designing communication and coordination networks? Is this ethical?

RESPONSE:

The implicit reasoning used in sociology is to think of socialization in terms of norms and values. Now those things are involved, but what my analysis suggests is that the bigger core of socialization is just learning sheer facts and the tools and techniques to handle them. A frequent problem, and this is especially true at the professional level, is how to keep the information flowing from professional conferences and journals, how to keep professionals abreast of what is going on. Many professional abuses that everyone talks about are really that the professional is ten, fifteen, even twenty years behind the times. People do not become aware of a particular study until someone else points out that there is a side effect, as with drugs. Perhaps the professionals are not aware that there are artificial aids that can be used in the classroom, or elsewhere, to build what may be in effect some sort of communication network. What I am really arguing is that we have to shift our models. It is no longer acceptable to simply see people socialized when young, then get their Ph.D.'s, then that's the end of it. I have my Ph.D., and one of the major reasons I obtained it was because it put me into a position where I was better connected with various communication networks. Is this unethical?

QUESTION:

What is your aim in using such concepts as social control, normative control, information control, etc.? Are you interested in exploring the effectiveness of the medical system in the United States, or exploring some sort of interrelationships between independent and dependent variables?

RESPONSE:

What you are talking about is the problem of what causes particular kinds of systems to be the way they are today. Alright, I might agree that one looks over the particular variables in order to understand the causes. However, I was talking about something else. I was really saying that if you change the system, in what direction do you change it in order to get the most effective means of coordination and control?

QUESTION:

You talk about organizational strategy. From your frame of reference, is this concept a control mechanism, or a means to an end, or an end in itself?

RESPONSE:

First, let me say that my use of strategy does not come out of political science or policy literature. It is the result of my major interest, the problem of change, from both a theoretical and practical perspective. I use the word "change" in a loose sense at present; however, I am not particularly committed to defending my use of the word. I am quite willing to accept suggestions on the definition of change.

I will say this regarding the three aspects you mentioned. The means used and the ends obtained, I have found, are a useful way of categorizing not only approaches or strategies, but in general terms one can apply them widely. My emphasis is more on trying to derive some sort of scheme that will allow me to look at a variety of situations. Whenever you use this schema, it can be a means at one time or an end at another, and so on. I just feel there is no satisfactory solution to that problem except to look at the participants and classify their means and aims. With this approach, perhaps I can—as an objective observer—alter their course when it appears their ends are really different than they state.

In answer to your question, then, I have no clearly defined definition of change; but I have a strategy.

QUESTION:

It seems that you are using such terms as "strategy," "interdepencency," "goals," and "objectives" interchangeably. Are you?

RESPONSE:

I am not sure of the point you are making. Are you saying that if other people had looked at these particular case histories they might have coined the terminology differently? Well, this is a possibility but I doubt it. Many of these terms were already being used because of the nature of the grant proposal and the manner in which it had to be written for the federal government. This forces you into some kind of language.

You really have to say here that we are going to create interdependent systems, or maybe coordinate a particular system, and then fill in the gaps. Would this make everyone happy?

QUESTION:

What determines an organization coalition? Under what conditions are coalitions formed? Is it generally for more resources or to achieve greater effectiveness?

RESPONSE:

A point was made in this discussion about the higher educational board. Well, this board was not created as a result of voluntary actions brought forth by each of the institutions in the state. This was really a representative of the legislature created by the legislature to provide the function of control rather than increase resources. In many cases, these higher boards have done very little, if anything, to increase resources. In some cases, they have even eliminated the discretionary measures that were long-standing devices used by the various institutions to obtain increased resources. I guess this argument is less persuasive under conditions where you have ample resources. The probability of a voluntary coalition is much greater when organizations know there is more money available through this device.

Comments on Warren and his Colleagues' Paper

PROBLEMS OF ADDITIVITY AND OPERATIONALIZATION
OF VARIABLES—*Arlyn J. Melcher and Raymond J. Adamek*

Some of the problems of additivity in the area are illustrated in this paper. In an earlier article, Warren (1967) provided two useful analytical frameworks. He offered a typology for describing the relationships that exist among different types of organizations ranging from organized to unorganized (or what he calls unitary to social choice). This typology was in terms of commonality of goals, formal mechanisms for coordination, methods and the extent to which decisions are ratified by the unit organizations, and formal provisions for the division of labor. He also presented a set of factors that influence the relations among organizations, including the extent to which data banks provide a common data base, the procedures established to obtain feedback on the effects of policies and programs, the extent of overlapping membership existing in governing boards, the degree of provision for interaction among personnel, and the type of arrangements for participation in planning and resolving conflict. These appear to be useful starting points in describing the type of organization and evaluating the factors influencing relationships.

In the study of community decision organizations in nine cities, Warren and his colleagues treat organizations ranging from the board of education to urban renewal authorities as identical in character. They may be; but in light of the typology presented earlier, it is unlikely that they are. The independent variables explored in these nine cities were leadership style, input-output constituency configurations, organizational decision-making context, ratio of planning activities to program activities, manner of handling internal contradictions in Model Cities programs (an element that appears to apply to only one of the CDOs), and arena participation. It may be that these factors are the same ones developed in the 1967 article under different labels, but this is unlikely. It appears that the authors shifted focus, presumably on the basis of some pragmatic rather than theoretical considerations.

We are not provided here with information on the way independent variables are operationalized, but any researcher who has concerned himself with measurement recognizes the complexities involved in dealing with these variables even on a semirigorous basis. The dependent variables offer similar problems since attention is focused on coordination, innovation, and responsiveness among the CDOs. This is not to say it would be more useful to focus on narrower variables, but simply that it is difficult to evaluate the work without carefully considering the definition of each variable and the manner in which such variables are operationalized.

The methods of collecting data raise some additional questions. Carrying over the idea of a critical incident to interorganizational relations, the authors take as a basic unit of analysis "action episodes": the more or less semiautonomous activities related to organizational goals which have a definite beginning and end. Without some analytical framework to guide the selection of these incidents, it is extremely difficult to obtain any meaningful generalizations. If some critical dimensions of interorganizational relations were specified and systematically explored, such as White, Levine, and Vlasak's breakdown in exchange, these episodes would likely be more revealing. One could, for example, systematically examine the giving and receiving of clients, material, labor, or other services. The trading relationship could be studied among different organizations and possibly some meaningful generalizations derived. But in the absence of such a classification system, it is difficult to see how a pattern of episodes is additive.

In the large-scale study, where Warren and his colleagues look at half a dozen different organizations in nine different cities, and where there are serious problems of conceptualization and measurement of variables, one would expect the major thrust to be evaluating and building an adequate conceptual framework and model. Instead, we find the emphasis is on testing hypotheses. Warren takes a cautious note in discussing research design, suggesting that the hypotheses should be viewed only as guidelines to direct attention toward particular relationships. Yet, in discussing the research results, he largely throws caution to the wind and emphasizes which hypotheses are accepted or rejected. At best, hypothesis testing is a tenuous process, even under highly controlled conditions; given the state of knowledge in the area, it seems neither appropriate nor useful to pursue this direction in this type of study. The authors have a great deal of material and a good basis for evaluating variables for their usefulness, definitions, and measurement; yet it is apparent that pressures for specific findings, perhaps required by funding agencies, have caused this thrust.

REFERENCE

Warren, Roland. "The Interorganizational Field as a Focus for Investigation."
1967   *Administrative Science Quarterly*, 12:396–419.

LIMITED FOCUS-LIMITED UTILITY—*Malcolm MacNair*

Warren, in illustrating his research findings, views interorganizational relations as a chess game where the participants are individually motivated to win and are governed collectively by the rules of the game. The rules of the game, he stresses, include and are analogous to common social values (good sportsmanship, for instance) that the players share by being members of the same and larger society which imputes value to playing chess. These shared values are the glue of the relationship, the explanation of cooperative behavior, and, perhaps, the basis for conflict resolutions.[1] Warren's shared values, given emphasis as a limiting case, constitute a common conscience model. White, Levine, and Vlasak, in similar analogy, represent a market (liberal pluralist) model, stressing individual organizational statuses or interests and conflict resolution by all that the market will brutally bear.

One other model implied by Warren's analogy (as far as he went with it) is that of the command mechanism itself—the formal rules defining the game, the statuses of the players, the role of the referee (championship chess!) or some third dominant entity—which is much like Weber's bureaucracy. There can be no conflict in bureaucracy; but, should it arise, it is in theory quickly resolved by the imperative from higher authority or interpretation of the rule.

These are appropriate models for a chess game as a game of mixed motives of constant sum outcome. The fourth model, I propose, encompasses a more real reality. It is a mixed motive nonconstant sum game in which the two chess players not only are governed by the authority of the rules of the game, common conscience, and individual motives to win, but also by the purposes of the collective entity they constitute. In the instance of the chess game, both strive individually to win. They also strive together to have a good game. This—although by the formal rules of chess there can be only one "winner"—is a nonconstant sum situation. Both, in view of the collective purpose which they could identify if asked what they were doing as a group, have *more* after the game than either had before, and both have more than if the game had not been played at all.[2] This is an instrumental model. Collective purpose and its continual interpretation, mutually recognized interdependencies, and interactive processes among the elements of the collective make up the mechanisms for conflict resolution and change.

The command model assumes that every superior is able to give integrated and rationally consistent comands. This assumes that each superior has knowledge of the specializations within the span of his control, and that status rewards and punishments are necessary and effective in achieving coordination. Trends toward specializations and division of component parts have outrun command as a technique. It is increasingly less able and less acceptable as a social mechanism to resolve conflict. As to achieving directed change, the strain upon command directs and channels the interorganizational enterprise away from ends to an emphasis upon means.

[1] For greater elaboration of the effect of shared values from Warren's perspective, see: Roland Warren, "Toward a Non-Utopian Normative Model of the Community," *American Sociological Review* 35 (1970), especially 221–22.

[2] Perhaps tennis or football are more appropriate analogies, particularly in stressing the interdependence created by the particular collective purpose of having a good game.

Legitimacy and authority are stressed instead; the rewards and punishments invoked kill the generation of ideas. Initiative declines and sensitivity to change in the environment is diminished. As a model, it is appropriate to simple environments where both ends and means can be viewed as relatively certain—the converse of the environmental situations of Model Cities, health planning, urban renewal, large business enterprises (such as the relationship between Lockheed and Rolls Royce), or other complex enterprises.

It is encouraging that Warren has obtained empirical results implying that there is a reality to the desirability of pursuing the interorganization as a unit.[3] Research so far has usually explained how interorganizational enterprise comes to failure. We need instead research directed to how to achieve success for interorganizational endeavors. This task will draw, I assume, greater attention, and test the notion of a collective purpose in the instrumental model. Perhaps the variables in this future research may include some of Kaplan's requirements for a developmental organization. This seems logical and desirable. Many of those variables are, it seems to me, preconditions for the requisite freedom for ideas.

REFERENCE

Warren, Roland.   "Toward a Non-Utopian Normative Model of the Community."
    1970   *American Sociological Review.* 35:221–22.

INTERORGANIZATION MODEL-DEFINITION AND
CONCEPTUAL PROBLEMS—*Richard N. Osborn*

While Warren's major contribution appears to be in the treatment of the interorganizational field as a unit of analysis, there is some question as to his definition of the field and its operational usage in the research project. Additionally, the nature of Warren's research design severely limits the scope of his empirical findings. From a theoretical view, the interorganizational field may be defined as an interacting set of organizations sharing some common set of goals. It seems clear that the elements constituting the set would be a major factor in operationally defining a particular field. Although the set of CDOs for a particular community would appear to meet these simple criteria, the units selected by Warren may not.

---

[3]Warren's results, along with the work of Litwak, are perhaps the only findings in the literature based upon a comparative design. His proposals seem to consist of a combination of the common conscience and market models. This would seem to be impossible if implemented, or, if not that, productive of none of the advantages of either model and multiplicative of their disadvantages.

1. salient characteristics of the parties to the exchange (organizational affiliation, goals, functions, prestige, size, staff and client characteristics);

2. the entities exchanged (organizational elements, such as clients, staff, and nonhuman resources or information on the availability of these elements and norms regarding exchange);

3. the nature of the agreement underlying exchange (formal and explicit, or informal and implicit);

4. the direction of the exchange (unilateral, reciprocal, or joint); and

5. the relative abundance of resources within the system.

The authors suggest that every organization must have access to three classes of elements to accomplish its goals: clients, a work staff, and nonhuman resources, such as equipment, money, and information. These elements are often in short supply, prompting organizations to enter into exchange relationships as a means of alleviating their scarcity. The amount of exchange which takes place within any system of organizations is determined primarily by the presence and nature of the organizations' extrasystem ties, their objectives and functions, and the amount of domain consensus which exists among members of the system. While some parts of this conceptual scheme have been developed more than others, it is nonetheless comprehensive, and their present paper refines it further still.

Adamek and Lavin (Chapter 15) have come across several problems and findings that suggest criticisms of the model and the need for elaboration and refinement. Some confusion is generated because White, Levine, and Vlasak define exchange broadly but deal only with a limited aspect of it. Exchange is defined as "any voluntary activity between organizations which has consequences, actual or anticipated, for the realization of their goals and objectives." While this definition is broad enough to encompass such social processes as competition and conflict, the authors appear to limit their application of the term to positive or cooperative interactions, and to an exchange of *elements* (clients, staff, nonhuman resources). This leads them to conclude that "domain consensus is a prerequisite to exchange." However, a lack of domain consensus may lead to competition or conflict(a fact which they note but do not consider an example of exchange), and even to the exchange of elements for the purpose of doing harm to another organization. In dealing with competitors making illegitimate domain claims, organizations may send them difficult clients, or even staff members whose hidden purpose is to "get the goods on" the competitor. While the authors are certainly free to focus on cooperative exchange in their analyses, we think more would be gained by incorporating negative exchange processes such as competition and conflict directly into their schema, rather than treating them outside the exchange framework as they do now. Whyte's (1969 : 147–70) discussion of various types of exchange (or transactions as he calls them) is helpful here.

Further, we question the utility of discussing unidirectional or unilateral exchange, which seems a contradiction in terms. Perhaps if the notion of exchange were expanded beyond an exchange of elements, the need for this concept would dissipate. Even though organization A sends B clients, and B never sends any elements in return, B may still respond with a sense of obligation, gratitude, or ill will for them. Given the exchange framework, it is difficult to think of one organization remaining totally inert while another is engaged in an activity which has consequences for the former's goals. White, Levine, and Vlasak suggest that health organizations are motivated to act only if immediately tangible and directly usable rewards are available in an exchange situation, which they term "primitive barter." However, other types of welfare organizations (some of which typically do buy services for their clients) also are motivated to exchange in "normal barter" situations if they can gain prestige, good will, or promise of support from fellow agencies in the future. These variables are more difficult to measure than the flow of elements but constitute valuable resources nonetheless.

Beyond problems of definition, Adamek and Lavin's empirical work focused upon the role scarcity plays in generating exchange relationships. White, Levine, and Vlasak stated if:

> . . .all the essential elements [were] in infinite supply there would be little need for organizational interaction and for subscription to cooperation as an ideal. Under actual conditions of scarcity, however, interorganizational exchanges are essential to goal attainment.

From this statement the following hypothesis was developed: There will be a direct relationship between the degree of scarcity of clients, staff, and nonhuman resources experienced by organizations and the extent to which they enter into exchange relationships with other organizations. This hypothesis was partially tested with data on 300 health and welfare agencies in the state of Ohio. Although several measurement problems were encountered and no adequate test of staff scarcity was applied, the results suggest that those organizations with the greatest abundance of elements are most likely to engage in cooperative exchange relationships. Litwak and Rothman (1970 : 137–86) report a similar finding in a recent study of Detroit schools.

We agree with White and his colleagues that, as a property of the interorganizational system, scarcity provides a motive for organizations to enter into exchange relationships. In addition, however, these data suggest that, as a property of individual agencies, scarcity is likely to inhibit action based on this motive. Exchange theory, as developed by Homans (1958 : 597–606) and Gouldner (1960 : 161–78), helps to explain why. If organization A enters into an exchange relationship with organization B, A may assume that B will also make some demands on it. Moreover, the norm of reciprocity implies that these exchanges should be mutually beneficial and roughly equivalent. If organization A is less well endowed than B in terms of clients and/or other resources, however, it may refrain from entering into a relationship where it cannot reciprocate. Further, the less well-endowed organization may see the cost of the exchange as too great and the exchange may, in fact, be viewed as one wherein there is *no* reward. Like Blau's (1955) government workers who sought help from their more competent colleagues, a less favored agency may view referring clients to more favored agencies as a poor reflection on its own effectiveness and worth, and as a threat to its continued support and existence. Rather than being rewarding, exchange may suggest further loss of prestige, encroachment by other agencies, and loss of community support.

On the other hand, exchange theory suggests that an organization with an abundance of clients, funds, and services can best afford to enter into exchange relationships. It can better honor its obligations and, because of the wide range of services offered, expect to gain as many or more clients as it loses in these relationships. Furthermore, its ability and willingness to exchange enhances its position and prestige within the system, thus promising continued and perhaps increased community support.

In their relationships with one another, organizations appear to resemble individuals. Those who are relatively well endowed with various resources, have the apparent support of others, and enjoy high status and self-esteem are more likely to feel secure enough to interact with their fellows and find such interaction rewarding. Those less well endowed, on the other hand, who lack support and have low status and self-esteem, find social interaction unrewarding and even threatening.

The White-Levine-Vlasak proposal to better integrate the health organization system probably would be effective, therefore, if communities could supply existing agencies with abundant resources and insure their continued support. In such a case, organizations would have relatively little to lose by changing or experimenting with new goals or functions. Under conditions of scarcity, however (which would still create the problem of how much money should be allocated to particular agencies initially), conflicts over domain consensus and strategies meant to insure agency survival in spite of the adequacy of response to patients' needs, are still likely to occur. This pattern does exist to some extent among other types of organizations. Production organizations in the market situation do not always respond to the needs of other organizations and the general public, but give priority to activities that enhance organizational survival and growth.

REFERENCES

Blau, P. M. *The Dynamics of Bureaucracy*. Chicago: The University of Chicago
1955   Press.
Gouldner, A. W. "The Norm of Reciprocity: A Preliminary Statement." *American*
1960   *Sociological Review*, 25:161–78.
Homans. G. C. "Social Behavior as Exchange." *American Journal of Sociology*,
1958   62:597–606.
Litwak, E., and J. Rothman. "Towards the Theory and Practice of Coordination
1970   Between Formal Organizations." In W. R. Rosengren and M. Lefton (eds.),
          Organizations and Clients: 137–86. Columbus, O.: Charles E. Merril Co.
Whyte, W. F. *Organizational Behavior*. Homewood, Ill.: Richard D. Irwin, Inc.
1969

DEFINITION AND CONCEPTUALIZATION
PROBLEMS—*Michael R. Ferrari*

In using the critical concept of *exchange*, White, Levine, and Vlasak emphasize the transfer or flow of resources from one organization to another, rather than positive, cooperative relationships per se. The basic questions become: Why are resources transferred from one organization to another? In what ways do organizations respond to their clients? And, based on such orientations, what are the resultant effects on organizational structures, processes, and external relationships?

There may be fundamental differences between profit-oriented and nonprofit-oriented organizations with respect to their:

1. conceptual and operational measures of effectiveness, goals, and reasons for being;

2. articulation of the importance and dynamics of client relationships; and

3. mechanisms for handling authority and legitimacy.

It seems the proposition that the intraorganization theorist and the interorganization theorist, while both concerned with organizational structure and function, may be operating at different levels of abstraction. While there appeared to be some utility, insights, and complementarity between intra and interorganization models, each is focusing on different kinds of questions. Moreover, there seemed to be a high degree of uncertainty on the part of intraorganization participants as to how valuable the current development of the interorganization approach (and its apparent marriage to nonprofit organizations) is to the intraorganization theorist. It was evident that this uncertainty also stemmed from a realization that the interorganization theorists seemed to be concentrating more on building static, descriptive models (conceptually in contrast to the models), while the intraorganization theorists now appear more oriented toward building and testing dynamic, predictive models, with higher rigor in their conceptualization.

RESPONSES FROM PROFESSORS WHITE, LEVINE, AND VLASAK

Several of the problems raised in the critical evaluation have been resolved or at least given attention in the revision of our paper that appears in this publication. However, there remain several issues that require comment.

The definition of terms has not been quite so infrequent as noted. Several of the papers in this volume are elaborations of previously described frameworks, and restatement of core definitions would amount to repetition. Rather than respond to generic criticisms of a loosely constituted field, however, we should like to focus on several important issues, the clarification of which should further the understanding of the phenomena we are studying.

The question of what constitutes "part of an organization" is, if posed in isolation, a spurious question. A legalistic or formalistic definition that includes or excludes clients, students, or patients is not useful to either the theorist or the researcher. The question is rather, "what are the relationships of various types of phenomena to the dependent variable one is studying?" Our primary task is to explain the relationships of variables to one another and, in this endeavor, open-system approaches have more promise of giving answers than do general definitions that include or exclude variables regardless of the problem being studied.

The problem then is one of specifying relationships among variables and not of defining what is and what is not part of an organization. Concern about "parts" is reverting to the conception of the organization as an organism. Indeed, even in the study of living organisms the distinction between "inside and outside" phenomena has been relinquished, e.g., in the study of such problems as specific diseases.

The second issue concerns the concept of scarcity. Our original paradigm stated that, "the scarcity of elements impels the organization to restrict its activities to limited specific functions. The fulfillment of these limited functions, in turn, requires access to certain kinds of elements, which an organization "seeks to obtain by entering into exchanges with other organizations" (Levine and White, 1961 : 587). Furthermore, "the interdependence of the parts of the exchange system is contingent upon three related factors: (1.) the accessibility of each organization to necessary elements from sources outside the health system; (2.) the objectives of the organization and particular functions to which it allocates the elements it controls; and (3.) the degree to which domain consensus exists among the various organizations" (p. 589). The paradigm employs the concept of scarcity only in the general sense that organizations cannot procure all the resources to accomplish their goals. They are therefore impelled to exchange with one another.

Adamek focuses on what might be called "temporary scarcity." What happens when an organization is committed to allocating resources to specific functions but experiences temporary shortages of those resources *from its normal source of supply?* In other words, this implies that the organization's exchanges with other organizations, its usual sources, have decreased. We would posit that temporary shortages are "normal" in the system and that only when a chronic shortage is evident, or in a crisis, would the organization formally readjust to the situation by seeking new sources in the community, pirating of personnel, or restricting its domain. Furthermore, such temporary shortages produce lacunae in the organization and should decrease its efficiency, its output, and consequently its exchange with other local organizations.

Finally, we should like to discuss our use of the term "unilateral exchange." We have defined this as follows: "Where elements flow from one organization to another and no elements are given in return" (Levine and White, 1961 :600). Regardless of the term employed, it is useful to distinguish situations in which resources flow only from A to B from other situations. The conditions under which this type of exchange occurs are empirically and conceptually different from situations in which resources are exchanged reciprocally (whether simultaneously or over time) or pooled in joint endeavors.

REFERENCE

Levine, Sol, and Paul E. White.   "Exchange as a Framework for the Study of Inter-
1961   organizational Relationships." *Administrative Science Quarterly*, 5:587–600.

18

Interorganization Theory: A Step Beyond the Present

ANANT R. NEGANDHI

The purpose of this volume was to examine the conceptual schemes and research findings of major studies in interorganizational relationships. In the preceding chapters, we examined a total of nine studies in this area. Two additional papers were included in the first section of this volume to provide a critical review of the literature. Attempts were also made to critically evaluate both the conceptual schemes and the research findings discussed in each of the presentations. To this end, a number of scholars were invited to offer their evaluations of a particular schema or specific research finding. In many ways, then, enough has been said about what we know, what we think we know, and what we do not know about interorganization interaction processes, relationships, and interdependencies, and their implications on the structure, behavior patterns, and effectiveness of social units interacting with each other in given social systems.

In the course of these discussions and analyses, specific biases and preoccupations, as well as the intense concerns of various researchers, have been brought into focus. However, it should be clearly stated at this point that our efforts were guided by one and only one motive: to increase our understanding of the functioning of complex organizations. In this light, we believe that all of the authors and commentators in this volume have made sizeable contributions toward advancing knowledge in this field. The criticisms, and at times even unkind attacks on their efforts were therefore not intended to belittle or diminish their contributions to interorganization theory. As the sophisticated reader will recognize, the concepts and methodological developments in this field are still very much in the preliminary stages; hence, the critical evaluation of these efforts is sine qua non for developing comprehensive theories.

The purpose of this final chapter is to identify some additional issues and problems encountered in examining and researching interorganizational relationships. Unlike Chapters 5, 8, 12, and 17, these observations are not offered as criticisms of any specific conceptual scheme or study included in this volume or reported elsewhere. The comments here are directed toward larger issues, many of which the individual researchers may have encountered but have been unable to address because of immediate concerns and preoccupations. These comments will cover the following areas:

1. basic assumptions of interorganization theory;

2. the relevance of independent and dependent variables utilized in current interorganization studies;

3. a theoretical perspective and approach, the systems framework;

4. a concept of boundaries.

Basic Assumption: A Modus Operandi

As mentioned in Chapter 1, one of the differentiating attributes of interorganizational analysis is its assumption concerning conflict. As Litwak and Hylton (1962) have argued:

> ... conflict between organizations is taken as given in interorganizational analysis, which starts out with the assumption that there is a situation of partial conflict and investigates for forms of social interaction designed for interaction under such conditions. From this point of view, the elimination of conflict is a deviant instance and likely to lead to the disruption of interorganizational relations (i.e., organizational mergers and the like)" (p. 397).

These authors further point out that unless the researcher is sensitized about this basic assumption of conflict, "he might concentrate on showing that value conflicts lead to organizational breakdown without appreciating that interorganizational relations permit and encourage conflict without destruction of the overall societal relations" (p. 397).

In a sense, Litwak and Hylton are saying that to preserve interorganizational relationships, one must deal simultaneously with both conflict between organizations and the autonomy of their existence. "If the interorganizational character is to be retained, there must be some procedures for preserving autonomy and conflict" (p. 413).

Although a majority of the scholars working in the interorganizational field recognize and accept this basic assumption concerning conflict, very few studies have explicitly dealt with this issue. Hage (Chapter 16), for example, stresses the importance of preserving a balance between the autonomy of an individual organization and the creation of elite control over interacting organizations. In so doing, he seems to recognize both the inevitability of conflict between organizations and the need for coordination in creating effective delivery systems. As he proposes: "If one strikes a balance between organizational needs for autonomy and coordination needs for the solution of complex problems, then the proposal of a coalition of organizations arranged in some delivery system makes sense." Hage further advocates that a coalition "is a middle way between elite control and a pluralist system ... (it) is more than a confederation and yet not a federation. ... It advocates the creation of relatively permanent coalitions that involve *incompatible interests and competitors*" (emphasis added).

Among others, Aldrich (Chapter 4) also recognizes the limited focus on conflict in interorganizational studies. He states that, "conflict between organizations has received less attention, and most of it has been at the theoretical rather than the empirical level."

This lack of concern may be due in part to the training and orientation of scholars presently undertaking interorganizational studies. By and large, many of these researchers began their studies in intraorganizational settings where the tradition has been to stress the importance of stable and harmonious relationships between different units and/or groups of people (Mayo 1946).

The basic premise here is that conflict is harmful and dysfunctional in achieving organizational objectives, and should therefore be avoided. Conversely, it follows that cooperation and harmony among different subsystems and/or individuals and groups are useful for the effective functioning of organizations. The origin of this basic assumption can perhaps be traced to the thoughts of Marx and Engels (1906) at the societal level, and to Follet (1918) and Mayo (1946) at the organizational level.

To a large extent, this orientation or "*hang-up*" on intraorganization theory has stubbornly remained with us. Tuite, Chisholm, and Radnor (1972), for example, state:

> ... One objective of a theory of optimal interorganizational decision making is to move from conditions of mixed conflict-cooperation to conditions of pure cooperation. ... A viable theory of interorganizational decision making would allow for reduction of the conflict of interest. ... organizational structures must include factors which motivate boundary personnel to engage in mutual problem solving rather than bargaining behavior (pp. 3–4).

Relevance of Dependent Variables

This fixation on establishing harmony and cooperative relationships between different social units, although *desirable* in its own right, has affected the modes of our conceptual schemes and research designs. As revealed throughout this volume, current interorganizational models and conceptual schemes are designed to seek cooperative relationships rather than to examine the dynamics of conflict and the creative use of this device in establishing effective interdependence among social units.

To begin with, many of the *inter*organizational studies undertaken to date are in reality *intra*organizational studies, as pointed out by Van de Ven and his colleagues (Chapter 2). Consequently, the nature and type of dependent variables have changed very little. Most of the dependent variables under study today concern some aspect of organization structure and/or they are harmony-related variables, such as interpersonal relationships, employee morale, the nature of coordination, responsiveness, etc.

If we accept the existence of conflict between and among organizations as a given reality, then it seems obvious that both the dependent and the independent variables in interorganization studies ought to reflect this basic assumption. Not only the nature of conflict, but also the power structure and the bargaining strength and strategies of different organizations may become more relevant variables in this perspective.

Such a change in focus would enable us to test several of Thompson's (1967 : 32–141) seminal ideas and propositions in an interorganizational perspective. A number of these are listed below. While this list is by no means exhaustive, it certainly illustrates examples of unexplored areas awaiting our attention.

1. UNDER NORMS OF RATIONALITY, ORGANIZATIONS SEEK TO MINIMIZE THE POWER OF TASK-ENVIRON-MENT ELEMENTS OVER THEM BY MAINTAINING ALTERNATIVES (p. 32).

2. ORGANIZATIONS SUBJECT TO RATIONALITY NORMS AND COMPETING FOR SUPPORT SEEK PRESTIGE (p. 33).

3. WHEN SUPPORT CAPACITY IS CONCENTRATED IN ONE OR A FEW ELEMENTS OF THE TASK ENVIRON-MENT, ORGANIZATIONS UNDER NORMS OF RATIONALITY SEEK POWER RELATIVE TO THOSE ON WHOM THEY ARE DEPENDENT (p. 34).

4. WHEN SUPPORT CAPACITY IS CONCENTRATED *AND BALANCED AGAINST CONCENTRATED DEMANDS* THE ORGANIZATIONS INVOLVED WILL ATTEMPT TO HANDLE THEIR DEPENDENCE THROUGH CONTRACT-ING (p. 36).

5. WHEN SUPPORT CAPACITY IS CONCENTRATED *BUT DEMAND DISPERSED*, THE WEAKER ORGANIZATION WILL ATTEMPT TO HANDLE ITS DEPENDENCE THROUGH COOPTING (p. 36).

6. WHEN SUPPORT CAPACITY IS CONCENTRATED AND BALANCED AGAINST CONCENTRATED DEMANDS, BUT THE POWER ACHIEVED THROUGH CONTRACTING IS INADEQUATE, THE ORGANIZATIONS INVOLVED WILL ATTEMPT TO COALESCE (p. 36).

7. THE MORE SECTORS IN WHICH THE ORGANIZATION SUBJECT TO RATIONALITY NORMS IS CONSTRAINED, THE MORE POWER THE ORGANIZATION WILL SEEK OVER REMAINING SECTORS OF ITS TASK ENVIRONMENT (p. 36).

8. THE ORGANIZATION FACING MANY CONSTRAINTS AND UNABLE TO ACHIEVE POWER IN OTHER SECTORS OF ITS TASK ENVIRONMENT WILL SEEK TO ENLARGE THE TASK ENVIRONMENT (p. 37).

9. INDUCEMENTS/CONTRIBUTIONS CONTRACTS AT CONTINGENT BOUNDARIES OF THE ORGANIZATION ARE DETERMINED BY (A.) THE POWER OF A TASK-ENVIRONMENT ELEMENT AND (B.) THE INDIVIDUAL'S ABILITY TO HANDLE THE ORGANIZATION'S DEPENDENCE ON THAT ELEMENT (p. 111).

10. TO THE EXTENT THAT THE ORGANIZATION GAINS POWER OVER TASK-ENVIRONMENT ELEMENTS, IT REDUCES ITS DEPENDENCE ON THE BOUNDARY-SPANNING JOBS WHICH DEAL WITH THOSE ELEMENTS (p. 112).

11. TO INCREASE THEIR POWER IN ORGANIZATIONS, INDIVIDUALS IN HIGHLY DISCRETIONARY JOBS MAY FORM COALITIONS WITH ESSENTIAL ELEMENTS OF THE TASK ENVIRONMENT (p. 126).

12. THE MORE SOURCES OF UNCERTAINTY OR CONTINGENCY FOR THE ORGANIZATION, THE MORE BASES THERE ARE FOR POWER AND THE LARGER

THE NUMBER OF POLITICAL POSITIONS IN THE
ORGANIZATION (p. 129).

13. THE MORE DYNAMIC THE TECHNOLOGY AND TASK
ENVIRONMENT, THE MORE RAPID THE POLITICAL
PROCESSES IN THE ORGANIZATION AND THE MORE
FREQUENT THE CHANGES IN ORGANIZATIONAL
GOALS (p. 129).

14. WHEN ORGANIZATIONS COMMIT FUTURE CONTROL
OVER RESOURCES IN EXCHANGE FOR PRESENT
SOLUTIONS TO CONTINGENCIES, THEY CREATE
LIMITATIONS ON THEIR ABILITIES TO ADAPT
TO FUTURE CHANGE OF TECHNOLOGIES OR TASK
ENVIRONMENTS (p. 130).

15. POTENTIAL FOR CONFLICT WITHIN THE DOMI-
NANT COALITION INCREASES WITH INTERDEPEN-
DENCE OF THE MEMBERS (AND THE AREAS THEY
REPRESENT OR CONTROL) (p. 138).

16. POTENTIAL FOR CONFLICT WITHIN THE DOMI-
NANT COALITION INCREASES AS EXTERNAL FORCES
REQUIRE INTERNAL COMPROMISE ON OUTCOME
PREFERENCES (p. 138).

17. THE ORGANIZATION WITH DISPERSED BASES OF
POWER IS IMMOBILIZED UNLESS THERE EXISTS AN
EFFECTIVE INNER CIRCLE (p. 141).

Effectiveness Measures

Another limitation of the present focus in interorganization studies
lies in our inability to raise further questions, such as "structure for what?"
"Coordination for what?" Although many of the current studies implicitly
assume organizational effectiveness as eventual dependent variables,
systematic attempts have not been made thus far to establish linkage between
the so-called intervening variables and effectiveness measures. As a result,
both the concepts and criteria of organizational effectiveness have remained
largely underdeveloped even though some scholars have made a very
worthwhile beginning (Price, 1968; Ghorpade, 1971; Negandhi, 1974).[1]

---

[1]This is equally applicable to intraorganizational studies. See, A. R. Negandhi (ed.),
Modern Organizational Theory (Kent, Ohio: Kent State University Press, 1973),
p. 400.

The Systems Approach

As was noted in Chapter 1, interorganization theory derives its intellectual and conceptual base from systems theory. References and the utilization of various general systems concepts, such as open-system, holism, input-throughput-output, systems boundaries, steady state, dynamic equilibrium, feedback mechanism, internal elaboration, multiple goal-seeking, etc., abound in many interorganization studies.

A close examination of this work, however, will reveal that many of the systems concepts are utilized in *name only*. For example, one of the main attributes of a system is the interdependence of subsystems within a given system. This itself implies and forces one to think in terms of *multiple causation* rather than in single causal terms. Yet our traditional mechanistic approach, which stresses determining the causal link between two variables, still dominates our way of thinking as well as our research approaches. While the patterns of relationships and the interdependence of various subsystems are explicitly recognized by some scholars (Warren, Rose, and Burgunder, 1974), very few interorganization studies have utilized multivariate models and analyses which, in fact, are needed to examine such patterns of relationships. In other words, the following remarks of Kast and Rosenzweig (1972) concerning "contingency theory" seem equally applicable to present-day interorganization studies. They state:

> ... It is not enough to suggest that a "contingency view" based on systems concepts of organizations and their management is more appropriate than the simplistic "principles approach." If organization theory is to advance and make contributions to managerial practice, it must define more explicitly certain patterns of relationships between organizational variables (p. 460).

Concept of Boundaries

One of the main assumptions underlying the study of organization-environment interactions (which, as we discussed in Chapter 1, is the first stage of interorganizational analysis) is that the boundary between the organization and its environment be clearly delineated and thus easily identified. Many of the conceptual schemes presented here and published elsewhere begin with this very assumption. And yet our knowledge about the concept of boundaries is hopelessly limited. What is "inside" and what lies "outside" the given organization is at best arbitrary. In other words, as Starbuck (1973) has stated:

> ... At present virtually all organizational research implicitly or explicitly assumes organizations can be sharply distinguished from their environments. A given person or phenomenon is inside or outside or relevant or irrelevant.

This practice is analogous to trying to develop a physics of gases on the basis of dichotomy like breathable-unbreathable, which scrambles together and ignores fine gradations in temperature, pressure and chemical composition. The dichotomy makes such strong monotonicity assumptions and discards so much information that is nearly valueless and its acceptability as measurement standard blocks systematic observations of temperature, pressure, and composition. Such simple and useful relations as Boyle's and Avogadro's laws may indefinitely remain undiscovered (pp. 20–21).

The concept of boundary lines itself assumes that organizations are subsets of society. In contrast to this prevailing view, as Starbuck (1973) has argued provocatively, organizations can be conceived as simply hills in a geography of human activities and "social groups and networks would appear as mounds and ridges on the organizational hills, and societies and economies would appear as islands and continents" (p. 19). He further argues that "since there are many activity dimensions, one must choose whether to map altitudes, climates, population densities or transport networks—and the shapes of organization hills will shift as functions of the dimensions mapped" (p. 20).

The above discussion thus brings us to a very uneasy situation. On the one hand, the concept of boundaries is essential for examining inter-organizational relationships; while on the other hand, our knowledge "gaps" in understanding this concept are so vast that little progress is made in designing conceptual schemes for exploring organization-environment interactions and interorganizational relationships.

It is hoped that this volume, with its varied contributions from renowned scholars in the interorganization field, will provide some stimulus for other researchers to undertake further studies in this vital area. For better or for worse, the world has become increasingly interdependent. Accordingly, interorganization theorists, with an explicit focus on the interdependence of various social units, can play an important role in achieving effective interdependence among various communities in our shrinking world.

REFERENCES

Follet, Mary Parker. *The New State: The Group Organization, The Solution of*
1918   *Popular Government.* London: Longmans, Green, and Company.
Ghorpade, J. (ed.) *Assessment of Organizational Effectiveness.* Pacific Palisades,
1971   Calif.: Goodyear Publishing Company, Inc.
Kast, Fremont E., and James E. Rosenzweig. "General Systems Theory: Applications
1972   for Organization and Management." *Academy of Management Journal,*
        15:463.
Litwak, Eugene, and Lydia F. Hylton. "Interorganizational Analysis: A Hypothesis
1962   on Co-ordinating Agencies." *Administrative Science Quarterly,* 6:395–420.

Marx, Karl, and Frederick Engels. *Manifesto of the Communist Party.* Chicago:
1906   Kerr.
Mayo, Elton. *The Human Problems of an Industrial Civilization.* Boston: Harvard
1946   University Press.
Negandhi, Anant R. *Organization Theory in an Open System.* New York: Dunellen.
1974
————. (ed.) *Modern Organizational Theory.* Kent, Ohio: Kent State University
1973   Press.
Price, James L. *Organizational Effectiveness: An Inventory of Propositions.*
1968   Homewood, Ill.: Richard D. Irwin, Inc.
Starbuck, William M. "Organizations and Environments." *Preprint Series No. 10*:
1973   20–21. Berlin: International Institute of Management. Reprinted in M. D.
        Dunnett (ed.), *Handbook of Industrial and Organizational Psychology.*
        Chicago: Rand-McNally, 1974.
Thompson, James D. *Organizations in Action*: 32–141. New York: McGraw-
1967   Hill.
Tuite, Matthew, Roger Chisholm, and Michael Radnor (eds.) *Interorganizational*
1972   *Decision Making.* Chicago: Aldine Publishing Company.
Warren, Roland L., Stephen M. Rose, and Ann F. Burgunder. *The Structure of*
1974   *Urban Reform.* Lexington, Mass.: D.C. Heath and Company.

Additional Reading in Interorganization Theory

Adrian, C. R., and C. Press. "Decision Costs in Coalition Formulation." *American*
1968   *Political Science Review*, 62:556–63.

Aiken, M., and J. Hage. "Organizational Interdependence and Intraorganizational
1968   Structure." *American Sociological Review*, 33:912–30.

————. "Organizational Alienation: A Comparative Analysis." *American Socio-*
1966   *logical Review*, 13:497–507.

Alford, R. B. "Research Note: Problems of Data Measurement in Interorganiza-
1974   tional Studies of Hospitals and Clinics." *Administrative Science Quarterly*,
         19:485–92.

Alinsky, S. D. "The War on Poverty—Political Pornography." *Journal of Social*
1965   *Issues*, 21:41–47.

Anderson, R. C. "A Sociometric Approach to the Analysis of Interorganizational
1969   Relationships." *Technical Bulletin B-60*. East Lansing, Mich.: Institute for
         Community Development and Service, Michigan State University.

Arnold, M. F. "Basic Concepts and Crucial Issues in Health Planning." *American*
1969   *Journal of Public Health*, 59:1686–97.

Arnold, M. F., and D. L. Hink. "Agency Problems in Planning for Community
1968   Health Needs." *Medical Care*, 6:454–66.

Assael, H. "Constructive Role of Interorganizational Conflict." *Administrative*
1969   *Science Quarterly*, 14:573–82.

Baker, F. "An Open-System Approach to the Study of Mental Hospitals in Transi-
1969   tion." *Community Mental Health Journal*, 5:403–12.

Baker, F., and H. C. Schulberg. "Community Health Caregiving Systems: Integra-
1968   tion of Interorganizational Networks." Presented at the Symposium, Systems
         and Medical Care. Cambridge, Mass.: Harvard University Faculty Club.

Bales, R. F., and E. F. Borgotta. *Small Groups: Studies in Social Interaction*. New
1955   York: A. A. Knopf.

Balke, W. M., K. R. Hammond, and G. D. Meyer. "An Alternate Approach
1973   to Labor Management Negotiations." *Administrative Science Quarterly*,
         18:311–27.

Barnett, H. G. *Innovation*. New York: McGraw-Hill.
1953

Baty, G. B., W. M. Evan, and T. W. Rothemel. "Personnel Flows as Interorganiza-
1971   tional Relations." *Administrative Science Quarterly*, 16:430–43.

Beal, G. M., et al. "Systems Linkages Among Women's Organizations." *Rural*
 1967 *Sociology Report 42.* Ames, Iowa: Department of Sociology and Anthro-
       pology, Iowa State University.
Belknap, I., and J. Steinle. *The Community and Its Hospital.* Syracuse, N. Y.: Syracuse
 1963 University.
Bellin, L. E. "Discussion of William J. Reid's Paper, 'Interorganizational Coopera-
 1970 tion: A Review and Critique of Current Theory.'" In P. E. White and G. J.
       Vlasak (eds.), *Inter-Organizational Research in Health: Conference Proceed-
       ings*: 84–101. Washington, D.C.: National Center for Health Services
       Research and Development.
Bennis, W. G., K. D. Benne, and R. Chin (eds.) *The Planning of Change.* New York:
 1961 Holt, Rinehart and Winston.
Bennis, W., and P. Slater. *The Temporary Society.* New York: Harper and Row.
 1968
Bertalanffy, L. von. "General Systems Theory." *Yearbook of Society for General
 1966 Systems Research*, 1:1–10.
Bertrand, A. L. "The Stress-Strain Element of Social Systems: A Micro Theory of
 1963 Conflict and Change." *Social Forces*, 42:1–9.
Blau, P. M. *Exchange and Power in Social Life.* New York: John Wiley and Sons.
 1964
————. *The Dynamics of Bureaucracy.* Chicago: University of Chicago Press.
 1955
Blau, P. M., and R. W. Scott. *Formal Organizations*: 42. San Francisco: Chandler.
 1962
Boddewyn, J. "The Environment of Business." *Mississippi Valley Journal of Business
 1966 and Economics*, 2:1–7.
Boulding, K. E. "Organization and Conflict." *Journal of Conflict Resolution*, 1:
 1957 122–34.
Briggs, J. L., and S. Levine. "Control Over Local Affiliates by National Health
 1961 Organizations." Paper presented at the annual meeting of the American
       Sociological Association, St. Louis, Missouri.
Brown, M., N. Pinney, and W. Saslow. *Innovation in New Communities.* MIT Report
 1972 No. 23. Cambridge, Mass.: The MIT Press.
Buckley, W. (ed.) *Modern Systems Research for the Behavioral Scientist.* Chicago:
 1968 Aldine Publishing Company.
Burns, T., and G. M. Stalker. *The Management of Innovation.* London: Tavistock
 1961 Publications.
Byrne, D., and J. Buehler. "A Note on the Influence of Propinquity upon Acquain-
 1955 tanceships." *Journal of Abnormal and Social Psychology*, 51:147–48.
Child, J. "Organization Structure, Environment and Performance: The Role of
 1972 Strategic Choice." *Sociology*, 6:1–22.
Chin, R., and G. M. O'Brien. "General Inter-System Theory: The Model and a
 1970 Case of Practitioner Application." In A. Sheldon, et al. (eds.), *Systems
       and Medical Care.* Cambridge, Mass.: MIT Press.
Clark, B. R. "Interorganizational Patterns in Education." *Administrative Science
 1965 Quarterly*, 10:224–37.

Cohen, A. M., E. L. Robinson, and J. L. Edwards. "Experiments in Organizational
1969   Embeddedness." *Administrative Science Quarterly*, 14:200–21.
Cohen, A. R. *Attitude Change and Social Influences.* New York: Basic Books.
1964
Coleman, J. S. "Foundations for a Theory of Collective Decisions." *American*
1966   *Journal of Sociology*, 71:615–27.
————. "Collective Decisions." *Social Inquiry*, 34:166–81.
1964
Corwin, R. G. "Patterns of Organizational Conflict." *Administrative Science*
1969   *Quarterly*, 14:507–20.
Davis, J. W., Jr., and K. M. Dolbeare. *Little Groups of Neighbors.* Chicago: Markham
1968   Publishing Co.
DeVise, P. "Methods and Concepts of an Interdisciplinary Regional Hospital Study."
1968   *Health Services Research*, 3:166–73.
Dill, W. R. "Environment as an Influence on Managerial Autonomy." *Administrative*
1958   *Science Quarterly*, 2:409–43.
Dillman, D. A., and P. Yarborough. "Leadership Linkages Among Natural Group-
1967   ings of Structurally Linked Women's Voluntary Organizations in a Local
         Community." Paper presented at the Rural Sociological Society Meeting,
         San Francisco, California.
Dunaye, T. "Community Planning Impact on Areawide Systems of Health Facilities
1970   and Services." Ph.D. dissertation. University of California at Los Angeles.
Eberly, C. G., and D. C. Smith. "Preface to 'The Teacher Student Relation.'" *Ad-*
1970   *ministrative Science Quarterly*, 15:135.
Eichhorn, R. L., and J. A. Wysong. *Interagency Relations in the Provision of Health*
1968   *Services: Tuberculosis Control in a Metropolitan Region.* Monograph 2.
         Lafayette, Incl.: Institute for the Study of Social Change, Purdue University.
Elling, R. H. "The Shifting Power Structure in Health." *Milbank Memorial Fund*
1968   *Quarterly*, 46:119–43.
Elling, R. H., and S. Halebsky. "Organizational Differentiation and Support: A
1961   Conceptual Framework." *Administrative Science Quarterly*, 6:185–209.
Emery, F. E., and E. L. Trist. "The Causal Texture of Organizational Environment."
1965   *Human Relations*, 18:21–32.
Epstein, E. M. *The Corporation in American Politics.* Englewood Cliffs, N.J.: Prentice-
1969   Hall.
Etzioni, Amitai. *A Comparative Analysis of Complex Organizations.* New York:
1961   The Free Press.
Etzioni, A., and W. R. Taber. "Scope, Pervasiveness, and Tension Management in
1963   Complex Organizations." *Social Research*, 30:220–38.
Evan, W. M. "Superior-Subordinate Conflict in Research Organizations." *Adminis-*
1965a   *trative Science Quarterly*, 10:52–64.
————. "Toward a Theory of Interorganizational Relations." *Management*
1965b   *Science*, 11:B217–30.
Farmer, R. N., and B. M. Richman. *Comparative Management and Economic Pro-*
1965   *gress.* Homewood, Ill.: Richard D. Irwin, Inc.
Fisher, L. "Politics of Impounded Funds." *Administrative Science Quarterly*, 15:
1970   361–77.

Follet, M. P. "Teacher-Student Relations." *Administrative Science Quarterly*, 15:
1970   137–48.

Form, W., and S. Nosow. *Community in Disaster*. New York: Harper and Row.
1958

Fraser, D. C. "The Relations of an Environmental Variable to Performance in a
1953   Prolonged Visual Task." *Quarterly Journal of Experimental Psychology*,
         5:31–32.

Friedlander, F., and H. Pickle. "Components of Effectiveness in Small Organiza-
1968   tions." *Administrative Science Quarterly*, 13:289–304.

Friedson, E. *Professional Dominance: The Social Structure of Medical Care*. New
1970   York: Atherton.

——— (ed.)   *The Hospital in Modern Society*. Glencoe, Ill.: The Free Press.
1963

Friesema, H. P. "Interjurisdictional Agreements in Metropolitan Areas." *Adminis-
1970   trative Science Quarterly*, 15:242–52.

Gamson, W. A. "Rancorous Conflict in Community Politics." *American Sociological
1966   Review*, 31:71–80.

Gawthrop, L. C. *Administrative Politics and Social Change*. New York: Martin's
1971   Press.

Georgopoulos, B. S. "The General Hospital as an Organization: A Social-Psycho-
1969   logical Viewpoint." *The University of Michigan Medical Center Journal*,
         35:94–97.

———. "The Hospital System and Nursing: Some Basic Problems and Issues."
1966   *Nursing Forum*, 5:8–35.

Georgopoulos, B. S., and F. C. Mann. *The Community General Hospital*. New York:
1962   Macmillan.

Georgopoulos, B. S., and A. Matejko. "The American General Hospital as a Complex
1967   Social System." *Health Services Research*, 2:76–112.

Georgopoulos, B. S., and G. F. Wieland. *Nationwide Study of Coordination and
1964   Patient Care in Voluntary Hospitals*. Ann Arbor, Mich.: Institute for Social
         Research, University of Michigan.

Gersuny, C. "Sheltered Workshops and Differential Client Characteristics. Un-
1968   published Ph.D. dissertation. Case Western University, Cleveland, Ohio.

Glueck, W. F. "Organization Change in Business and Government." *Academy of
1969   Management Journal*, 12:439–50.

Goerke, L. S. "The Relationship of Health Agencies and Planning Agencies."
1964   *American Journal of Public Health*, 54:713–20.

Goldman, R. M. "A Theory of Conflict Processes and Organizational Offices."
1966   *Journal of Conflict Resolution*, 10:328–43.

Golembiewski, R. T., and S. B. Carrigan. "Planned Change in Organization Style
1970   Based on the Laboratory Approach." *Administrative Science Quarterly*,
         15:79–93.

Gonzalez, R. F., and C. McMillan, Jr. "The Universality of American Management
1961   Philosophy." *Academy of Management Journal*, 4:33–41.

Gordon, D. W., and N. Babchuck. "A Typology of Voluntary Associations."
1959   *American Sociological Review*, 24:22–29.

Goss, M. E. W.   "Influence and Authority Among Physicians in an Outpatient Clinic."
1961   *American Sociological Review*, 26:39–51.

Gouldner, A. W.   "The Norm of Reciprocity: A Preliminary Statement." *American*
1960   *Sociological Review*, 25:161–78.

————.   *Patterns of Industrial Bureaucracy*. Glencoe, Ill.: The Free Press.
1954

Gross, B. M.   "The Coming General Systems Model of Social Systems." *Human*
1967   *Relations*, 20:357–74.

————.   "What Are Your Organization's Objectives: A General-Systems Approach
1965   to Planning." *Human Relations*, 18:195–216.

Grusky, O.   "Role Conflict in Organization: A Study of Prison Camp Officials."
1959   *Administrative Science Quarterly*, 3:452–72.

Hage, J., and M. Aiken.   "Relationship of Centralization to Other Structural Proper-
1967   ties." *Administrative Science Quarterly*, 12:72–92.

Hall, R. H.   "Some Organizational Considerations in the Professional-Organizational
1967   Relationships." *Administrative Science Quarterly*, 12:461–78.

Hanson, R. C.   "The Systematic Linkage Hypothesis and Role Consensus Patterns
1962   in Hospital-Community Relations." *American Sociological Review*, 27:
         304–13.

Hare, P. A., and R. G. Bales.   "Seating Position and Small Group Interaction."
1963   *Sociometry*, 26:480–86.

Hassinger, E.   "Social Relations Between Centralized and Local Social Systems."
1961   *Rural Sociology*, 26:354–64.

Haurek, E. W., and J. P. Clark.   "Variants of Integration of Social Control Agencies."
1967   *Social Problems*, 15:46–60.

Heskett, J. L., and R. H. Ballou.   "Logistical Planning in Inter-Organizational
1966   Systems." In M. P. Hottenstein and R. W. Millman (eds.), *Research Toward
         the Development of Management Thought*: 124–36. San Francisco: Academy
         of Management.

Hinings, C. R., D. J. Hickson, J. M. Pennings, and R. E. Schneck.   "Structural
1974   Conditions of Interorganizational Power." *Administrative Science Quarterly*,
         19: 22–44.

Homans, G. C.   *Social Behavior*. New York: Harcourt, Brace, and World.
1961

————.   "Social Behavior as Exchange." *American Journal of Sociology*, 63:
1958   597–606.

Horowitz, I. L.   "Consensus, Conflict, and Cooperation: A Sociological Inventory."
1962   *Social Forces*, 41: 177–88.

Jaques, E.   *The Changing Culture of a Factory*. London: Tavistock Publishing, Ltd.
1951

Kaplan, B. H.   *Blue Ridge: An Appalachian Community in Transition*. Morgantown,
1971   W. Va.: Center for Appalachian Studies, University of West Virginia.

Katz, D., and R. L. Kahn.   *The Social Psychology of Organizations*. New York:
1966   John Wiley and Sons.

Klein, D. C.   "The Community and Mental Health: An Attempt at a Conceptual
1965   Framework." *Community Mental Health Journal*, 1: 301–08.

Klonglan, G. E., et al.   *Agency Interaction Patterns and Community Alcoholism*
1969   *Services*. Sociology Report 73. Ames, Iowa: Iowa State University.

Landsberger, H. A. "The Horizontal Dimension in Bureaucracy." *Administrative*
1961   *Science Quarterly*, 6: 299–332.
Lawrence, P. R., and J. W. Lorsch. *Organization and Environment*. Homewood,
1969   Ill.: Richard D. Irwin, Inc.
———. "Differentiation and Integration in Complex Organizations." *Administra-*
1967   *tive Science Quarterly*, 12:1–47.
Lefton, M. "Client Characteristics and Structural Outcomes." In W. Rosengren
1970   and M. Lefton (eds.), *Organizations and Clients*: 17–36. Columbus, Ohio:
        Charles E. Merrill.
Lefton, M., and W. R. Rosengren. "Organizations and Clients: Lateral and Longi-
1966   tudinal Dimensions." *American Sociological Review*, 31: 802–10.
Levey, S. "Must There Be Conflict in an Organization." *Hospitals*, 37: 53–57.
1963
Levine, S., and P. E. White. "Exchange as a Conceptual Framework for the Study
1961   of Interorganizational Relationships." *Administrative Science Quarterly*,
        5: 583–601.
Levine, S., P. E. White, and B. D. Paul. "Community Interorganizational Problems
1963   in Providing Medical Care and Social Services." *American Journal of Public
        Health*, 53:1183–95.
Lewis, C. E. "Discussion of Basil J. F. Mott's Paper, 'Coordination and Inter-
1970   Organizational Relations in Health.'" In P. E. White and G. J. Vlasak (eds.),
        *Inter-Organizational Research in Health: Conference Proceedings:*70–77.
        Washington, D.C.: National Center for Health Services Research and
        Development.
Lippitt, R., J. Watson, and B. Westly. *Planned Change*. New York: Harcourt, Brace.
1950
Litterer, J. A. "Conflict in Organization: A Re-Examination." *Academy of Manage-
1966   ment Journal*, 9: 178–86.
Litwak, E. "Models of Bureaucracy Which Permit Conflict." *American Journal of
1961   Sociology*, 67: 177–84.
Litwak, E., and L. F. Hylton. "Interorganizational Analysis: A Hypothesis on Co-
1962   ordinating Agencies." *Administrative Science Quarterly*, 6: 395–420.
Litwak, E., and H. F. Meyer. "A Balanced Theory of Coordination Between Bureau-
1966   cratic Organizations and Community Primary Groups." *Administrative
        Science Quarterly*, 2:31–58.
Litwak, E., et al. *Towards the Multi-Factor Theory and Practice of Linkages Between
1970   Formal Organizations*. Washington, D.C.:Department of Health, Education,
        and Welfare.
Maiolo, J. R. "From Social Movement to Complex Organizations: Some Conse-
1969   quences of Interorganizational Competition for Control." Paper presented
        at the annual meeting of the American Sociological Association. San Fran-
        cisco, California.
Maniha, J., and C. Perrow. "The Reluctant Organization and the Aggressive En-
1965   vironment." *Administrative Science Quarterly*, 10:238–57.
McCaulay, S. "Non-Contractual Relations in Business: A Preliminary Study."
1963   *American Sociological Review*, 28:55–67.

McNeil, K., and J. D. Thompson. "The Regeneration of Social Organizations."
1971   *American Sociological Review*, 36:624–37.

Miller, D. "Industry and Community Power Structure: Comparative Study of an
1958   American and English City." *American Sociological Review*, 23:9–15.

Miller, E. J., and A. K. Rice. *Systems of Organization*. London: Tavistock Publica-
1967   tions.

Miller, J. G. "Living Systems: Basic Concepts." *Behavioral Science*, 10:193–237.
1965

————. "Toward a General Theory for the Behavioral Sciences." *American*
1955   *Psychologist*, 10:513–31.

Miller, L. Kieth, and R. L. Hamblin. "Interdependence, Differential Rewarding, and
1963   Productivity." *American Sociological Review*, 28:768–78.

Miller, R. E. *Innovation, Organization and Environment*. Sherbrooke, France:
1971   Institut de Recherche et de Perfectionnement en Administration.

Miller, W. B. "Inter-Institutional Conflict as a Major Impediment to Delinquency
1958   Prevention." *Human Organizations*, 17:20–23.

Morgan, J. S. *Business Faces the Urban Crisis*. Houston: Gulf.
1969

Morris, R. "Basic Factors in Planning for the Coordination of Health Services."
1963   *American Journal of Public Health*, 53:462–72.

Mott, B. J. F. "Coordination and Inter-Organizational Relations in Health." In
1970   P. E. White and G. J. Vlasak (eds.), *Inter-Organizational Research in Health:
        Conference Proceedings*:55–69. Washington, D.C.: National Center for
        Health Services Research and Development.

————. *Anatomy of a Coordinating Council: Implications for Planning*. Pittsburgh:
1968   University of Pittsburgh Press.

Negandhi, A. R. *Organization Theory in an Open System*. New York: Dunellen.
1974

Negandhi, A. R., and B. D. Estafen. "A Research Model to Determine the Appli-
1965   cability of American Management Know-How in Differing Cultures and/or
        Environments." *Academy of Management Journal*, 8:319–23.

Newton, J. Wayne. "Cooptation Among Community Decision Organizations."
1970   Mimeographed report. Waltham, Mass.: Brandeis University.

Olshansky, B. "Planned Change in Interorganizational Relationships." Ph.D.
1961   dissertation. Brandeis University, Waltham, Mass.

Olson, M., and R. Zeckhauser. "Collective Goods, Comparative Advantage and
1967   Alliance Efficiency." In R. N. McKean (ed.), *Issues in Defense Economics*.
        New York: National Bureau of Educational Research, Columbia University
        Press.

Parsons, T. "Suggestions for a Sociological Approach to the Theory of Organiza-
1956   tion." *Administrative Science Quarterly*, 1:63–85.

Perrow, C. *Organizational Analysis: A Sociological View*. Belmont, Calif.:
1970   Wadsworth.

————. "Reality Adjustment: A Young Organization Settles for a Humane Case."
1966   *Social Problems*, 14:69–79.

————. "Hospitals: Technology, Structure, and Goals." In J. March (ed.), *Hand-
1965   book of Organizations*. Chicago: Rand McNally.

————. "Organizational Prestige: Some Functions and Dysfunctions." *American*

1961   *Journal of Sociology*, 66:335–41.

Perrucci, R., and M. Pilisuk. "Leaders and Ruling Elites: The Interorganizational
1969   Bases of Community Power." Working Paper No. 28. Lafayette, Ind.:
        Institute for the Study of Social Change, Department of Sociology, Purdue
        University.

Pfeffer, J. "Size, Composition, and Function of Hospital Boards of Directors: A
1973   Study of Organization-Environment Linkage." *Administrative Science
        Quarterly*, 18:349–64.

Pondy, L. R. "Varieties of Organizational Conflict." *Administrative Science Quarter-
1969   ly*, 14:499–505.

————. "Organizational Conflict: Concepts and Models." *Administrative Science
1967   Quarterly*, 12:296–320.

————. "Budgeting and Intergroup Conflict in Organizations." *Pittsburgh Business
1964   Review*, 34:1–3.

Price, J. L. "The Impact of Departmentalization on Interoccupational Cooperation."
1968   *Human Organization*, 27:362–68.

————. *Organizational Effectiveness*. New York: Irwin Dorsey.
1967

Pruden, H. O. "Interorganizational Conflict, Linkage, and Exchange: A Study of
1969   Industrial Salesmen." *Academy of Management Journal*, 12:399–50.

Randall, Ronald. "Influence of Environmental Support and Policy Space on Organi-
1973   zational Behavior." *Administrative Science Quarterly*, 18:236–47.

Raynolds, P. A. "Developing Managerial Capabilities for Coping with Turbulent
1971   Environments." *Proceedings of the 31st Annual Meeting of the Academy of
        Management*: 86–91. Atlanta, Ga.: Academy of Management.

Reid, W. J. "Inter-Organizational Cooperation: A Review and Critique of Current
1970   Theory." In P. E. White and G. J. Vlasak (eds.), *Inter-Organizational Research
        in Health: Conference Proceedings*: 84–101. Washington, D.C.: National
        Center for Health Service Research and Development.

————. "Inter-Organizational Coordination in Social Welfare: A Theoretical
1969   Approach to Analysis and Intervention." In R. M. Kramer and H. Specht
        (eds.), *Readings in Community Organization Practice*: 188–200. Englewood
        Cliffs, N.J.: Prentice-Hall.

Rice, A. K. *Productivity and Social Organization: The Ahmedabad Experiment*.
1953   London: Tavistock Publications.

Richards, C. B., and H. Dobyns. "Topography and Culture: The Case of the Chang-
1957   ing Cage." *Human Organization*, 16:16–20.

Rico, L. "Organizational Conflict: A Framework for Reappraisal." *Industrial
1964   Management Review*, 6:67–80.

Roos, L. L., Jr., and N. P. Roos. "Administrative Change in a Modernizing Society."
1970   *Administrative Science Quarterly*, 15:69–78.

Rose, A. M. "Voluntary Associations Under Conditions of Competition and Con-
1955   flict." *Social Forces*, 34:159–63.

Rosengren, W. R. "The Careers of Clients and Organizations." In W. Rosengren
1970   and M. Lefton (eds.), *Organizations and Clients: Essays in the Sociology of
        Service*: 117–36. Columbus, Ohio: Charles Merrill Publishing Co.

————. "Organizational Age, Structure, and Orientations Toward Clients."

1968   *Social Forces*, 47:1–11.

Rosengren W. R., and M. Lefton.   *Organizations and Clients: Essays in the Sociology*
1970   *of Service*. Columbus, Ohio: Charles Merrill Publishing Co.
————.   *Hospitals and Patients*. New York: Atherton Press.
1968

Rubin, R. R., and A. L. Stinchcombe.   "Interorganizational Networks as Systems of
1967   Functional Interdependence." Presented at the annual meeting of the American Sociological Association, San Francisco, Calif.

Rushing, W.   "Differences in Profit and Nonprofit Organizations: A Study of Effective-
1974   ness and Efficiency in General Short-Stay Hospitals." *Administrative Science
Quarterly*, 19:474–84.

Saunders, J. V. D.   "Characteristics of Hospitals and of Hospital Administrators
1960   Associated with Hospital Community Relations in Mississippi." *Rural
Sociology*, 25:229–32.

Schelling, T.   *The Strategy of Conflict*. Cambridge, Mass.: Harvard University
1963   Press.

Scott, W. R.   "Some Implications of Organization Theory for Research on Health
1966   Services." *Milbank Memorial Fund Quarterly*, 44:35–64.
————.   "Reactions to Supervision in a Heteronomous Professional Organization."
1965   *Administrative Science Quarterly*, 10:65–81.

Scurrah, M. J., M. Shani, and C. Zipfel.   "Influence of Internal and External Change
1971   Agents in a Simulated Education Organization." *Administrative Science
Quarterly*, 16:113–20.

Segal, J.   "Correlates of Collaboration and Resistance Behavior Among U.S. Army's
1957   POW's in Korea." *Journal of Social Issues*, 13:31–40.

Selznick, P.   *T.V.A. and the Grass Roots*. Berkeley, Calif.: University of California
1949   Press.

Shaw, D. M.   "Size of Share in Task and Motivation in Work Groups." *Sociometry*,
1960   23:203–08.

Simpson, R. L.   "Vertical and Horizontal Communication in Formal Organizations."
1959   *Administrative Science Quarterly*, 4:188–96.

Simpson, R. L., and W. H. Gully.   "Goals, Environmental Pressures, and Organiza-
1962   tional Characteristics." *American Sociological Review*, 27:344–51.

Singer, J. D.   "The Level of Analysis Problem in International Relations." In K.
1961   Knorr and S. Verba (eds.), *The International System*. Princeton, N.J.:
Princeton University Press.

Smith, C. G.   "A Comparative Analysis of Some Conditions and Consequences of
1966   Intra-Organizational Conflict." *Administrative Science Quarterly*, 10:504–29.

Smith, C. G., and A. S. Tannenbaum.   "Organizational Control Structure." *Human
1963   Relations*, 16:299–316.

Smith, H. L.   "Two Lines of Authority: The Hospital's Dilemma." In E. G. Jaco
1958   (ed.), *Patients, Physicians and Illness*: 468–77. New York: The Free Press.

Sommer, R.   "Further Studies in Small Group Ecology." *Sociometry*, 27:337–48.
1965

Stanley, D. T., and C. L. Cooper.   *Managing Local Government Under Union Pressure*.
1972   Washington, D.C.: The Brookings Institution.

Starbuck, W. H.   "Organizations and Their Environments." In M. D. Dunnette (ed.),

1973   *Handbook of Industrial and Organizational Psychology*. Chicago: Rand
        McNally.
Starkweather, D. B.   "Health Facility Merger and Integration: A Typology and
1970   Some Hypotheses." In P. E. White and G. J. Vlasak (eds.), *Inter-Organiza-
        tional Research in Health: Conference Proceedings:4–44*. Washington,
        D.C.: National Center for Health Services Research and Development.
————   "Hospitals: As Viewed by Health Planners." In H. L. Blum (ed.), *Notes
1968   on Comprehensive Planning for Health*. Berkeley, Calif.: American Public
        Health Association and Comprehensive Health Planning Unit, University
        of California.
Starkweather, D. B., and A. I. Kisch.   "A Model of the Life Cycle Dynamics of Health
1971   Service Organizations." In M. Arnold, et al. (eds.), *Administering Health
        Systems*. New York: Atherton.
Stinchcombe, A. L.   "Bureaucratic and Craft Administration of Production."
1959   *Administrative Science Quarterly*, 4: 168–87.
Strauss, A., et al.   "The Hospital and Its Negotiated Order." In E. Friedson (ed.),
1963   *The Hospital in Modern Society*: 147–69. New York: The Free Press.
Strauss, G.   "Tactics of Lateral Relationships." *Administrative Science Quarterly*,
1962   7: 161–87.
Stringer, J.   "Operational Research for Multi-Organizations." *Operational Research
1967   Quarterly*, 18: 105–20.
Swinth, R. L.   "Organizational Planning: Goal Setting in Interdependent Systems."
1966   *Industrial Management Review*, 7: 57–70.
Terreberry, S.   "The Evolution of Organizational Environments." *Administrative
1968   Science Quarterly*, 12: 590–613.
Thomas, K. W., R. E. Walton, and J. M. Dutton.   "Determinants of Interdepartmental
1972   Conflict." In M. Tuite, R. Chisholm, and M. Radnor (eds.), *Inter-
        organizational Decision Making*. Chicago: Aldine Publishing Company.
Thompson, J. D.   "Thoughts on Inter-Organizational Relations: A Conclusion."
1970   In P. E. White and G. J. Vlasak (eds.), *Inter-Organizational Research in
        Health: Conference Proceedings:156–67*. Washington, D.C.: National
        Center for Health Research and Development.
————.   *Organizations in Action*. New York: McGraw-Hill.
1967
————.   "Organizations and Output Transactions." *American Journal of Sociology*,
1962   68: 309–24.
————.   "Organizational Management of Conflict." *Administrative Science Quar-
1960   terly*, 4: 389–409.
Thompson, J. D., and W. J. McEwen.   "Organizational Goals and Environment."
1961   In A. Etzioni (ed.), *Complex Organizations*. New York: Holt, Rinehart
        and Winston, Inc.
————.   "Organizational Goals and Environment: Goal-Setting as an Interaction
1958   Process." *American Sociological Review*, 23: 23–31.
Thompson, V. A.   "Hierarchy Specialization and Organizational Conflict." *Adminis-
1961   trative Science Quarterly*, 7: 22–49.
Tosi, H., R. Aldag, and R. Storey.   "On the Measurement of the Environment: An
1973   Assessment of the Lawrence and Lorsch Environmental Uncertainty Question-

naire." *Administrative Science Quarterly*, 18:27–36.

Trist, E. L., and F. E. Emery. "The Causal Texture of Organizational Environments."
1965   *Human Relations*, 18:21–32.

Tullock, G. "A Model of Social Interaction." In J. F. Herndon and J. L. Bernd
1971   (eds.), *Mathematical Applications in Political Science V*. Charlottesville,
          Va.: University Press of Virginia.

Turk, H. "Comparative Urban Structure from an Interorganizational Perspective."
1973   *Administrative Science Quarterly*, 18:37–55.

————. "Comparative Urban Structure from an Interorganizational Perspective."
1971   Paper presented at the Conference on Research on Interorganizational
          Relationships in Health, New York, New York.

————. "Interorganizational Networks in Urban Society: Initial Perspectives
1970   and Comparative Research." *American Sociological Review*, 35:1–19.

————. "Comparative Urban Studies in Interorganizational Relations." *Socio-
1969   logical Inquiry*, 39:108–10.

————. "The Establishment of Manpower Poverty Projects and Relations Between
1967   Them in Large American Cities." Report for the U.S. Department of Labor,
          Los Angeles, California.

Turk, H., and M. J. Lefcowitz. "Towards a Theory of Representation Between
1962   Groups." *Social Forces*, 40:337–41.

Udy, S. *Work in Traditional and Modern Society*. Englewood Cliffs, N.J.: Prentice-
1970   Hall.

————. "Technical and Institutional Factors in Production Organizations: A
1961   Preliminary Model." *American Journal of Sociology*, 67:247–60.

————. *The Organization of Work*. New Haven, Conn.: Human Relations Area
1959   Files.

Van Hove, E. "Collective Decision-Making in a Government Health Agency:
1971   The Regional Medical Program." Ph.D. dissertation, Johns Hopkins Univer-
          sity, Baltimore, Maryland.

Vlasak, G. J. *Interorganizational Study: An Analysis of Interaction Among Community
1963   Agencies*. Miami: University of Miami and Chronic Illness Project, Inc.

Vollmer, H. M., and D. Mills (eds.) *Professionalization*. Englewood Cliffs, N.J.:
1966   Prentice-Hall.

Walton, R. E. "Third Party Roles in Interdepartmental Conflict." *Industrial Relations*,
1967   7:29–43.

————. "Theory of Conflict in Lateral Organizational Relationships." In J. R.
1966   Lawrence (ed.), *Operational Research and the Social Sciences*. London:
          Tavistock Publications.

Walton, R. E., and T. P. Cafferty. "Organizational Context and Interdepartmental
1969   Conflict." *Administrative Science Quarterly*,14:522–42.

Walton, R. E., and J. M. Dutton. "The Management of Interdepartmental Conflict:
1969   A Model and Review." *Administrative Science Quarterly*, 14:73–84.

Walton, R. E., J. M. Dutton, and T. P. Cafferty. "Organizational Context and
1969   Interdepartmental Conflict." *Administrative Science Quarterly*, 14:522–42.

Warren, R. L. "Alternative Strategies of Inter-Agency Planning." In P. E. White
1970   and G. J. Vlasak (eds.), *Inter-Organizational Research in Health: Conference*

Proceedings: 114–28. Washington, D.C.: National Center for Health Services and Development.

———. "The Interaction of Community Decision Organizations: Some Basic
1967a Concepts and Needed Research." *The Social Service Review*, 41:261–70.

———. "The Interorganizational Field as a Focus of Investigation." *Administrative*
1967b *Science Quarterly*, 12:396–419.

Warren, Roland L., Stephen M. Rose, and Ann F. Burgunder. *The Structure of*
1974 *Urban Reform*. Lexington, Mass.: D.C. Health and Company.

White, H. "Managing Conflict in Sociometric Structure." *American Journal of*
1961 *Sociology*, 67:185–99.

White, L. A. *The Evolution of Culture*. New York: McGraw-Hill.
1959

White, P. E. "Myth and Reality in Interorganizational Behavior: A Study of Com-
1968 petition Between Two National Voluntary Health Agencies." *American
Journal of Public Health*, 58:289–304.

———. "Health Organizations in the Community." Ph.D. dissertation. Harvard
1964 University, Cambridge, Mass.

White, P. E., and E. Van Hove. "Study of the Strategies and Problems of the Regional
1961 Medical Programs in Developing Programs for Residents of Inner Cities."
Mimeographed report. Baltimore: Department of Behavioral Sciences,
School of Hygiene and Public Health, Johns Hopkins University.

Whyte, W. F. "Imitation or Innovation: Reflections on the Institutional Develop-
1968 ment of Peru." *Administrative Science Quarterly*, 13:370–85.

Wilson, R. N. "The Physician's Changing Hospital Role." In W. R. Scott and E. H.
1966 Volkart (eds.), *Medical Care*. New York: John Wiley.

Wren, D. A. "Interface and Interorganizational Coordination." *Academy of Manage-
1967 ment Journal*, 10:69–81.

Yuchtman, E., and S. E. Seashore. "A System Resource Approach to Organizational
1967 Effectiveness." *American Sociological Review*, 32:891–903.

Zald, M. N. "Power Balance and Staff Conflict in Correctional Institutions." *Ad-
1962 ministrative Science Quarterly*, 7:22–49.

Subject Index

Author Index

Interorganization theory